COURTING DISASTER

COURTING DISASTER

HOW THE SUPREME COURT IS
USURPING THE POWER
OF CONGRESS AND THE PEOPLE

PAT ROBERTSON

INTEGRITY®
PUBLISHERS
Nashville

Published by Integrity Publishers, a division of Integrity Media, Inc.,
5250 Virginia Way, Suite 110, Brentwood, TN 37027.

HELPING PEOPLE WORLDWIDE EXPERIENCE *the* MANIFEST PRESENCE *of* GOD.

Cover Design: Bill Chiaravalle
Interior: Inside Out Design & Typesetting

Library of Congress Cataloging-in-Publication Data

Robertson, Pat.
    Courting Disaster / Pat Robertson.
        p. cm.
        Includes bibliographical references and index.

    ISBN 1-59145-142-6
    1. Christianity and politics—United States—History. 2. Christianity and law.
    I. Title.
    BR115.P7R714   2004
    261.7′0973—dc22   2004016281

Printed in the United States of America
04 05 06 07 08 PHX 9 8 7 6 5 4 3 2 1

CONTENTS

CONTENTS

PART THREE: A PRESCRIPTION FOR CHANGE

ACKNOWLEDGMENTS

I want to express my deep gratitude to Dr. Jim Nelson Black for his invaluable work on this manuscript. Jim is a scholar of history and a brilliant researcher without whose patience and skill this book would not have been possible.

I would also like to thank Jay Sekulow, the general counsel of the American Center for Law and Justice, as well as Stuart Roth, senior counsel, and law clerks Erik Zimmerman, Jim Breckinridge, Nathan Bruner, Nate Cook, Spring Rowell, and Joy Weber for their incredible diligence in checking Supreme Court cases and for bringing their valuable insights to bear and providing the case citations on 167 Supreme Court cases cited in this manuscript.

This work has been a cooperative effort, which I hope brings it to the highest level of scholarship and insight into the workings of the Supreme Court and our federal judiciary.

The candid citizen must confess that if the policy of the government, upon vital questions, affecting the whole people, is to be irrevocably fixed by decisions of the Supreme Court . . . the people will have ceased to be their own rulers, having, to that extent, practically resigned their government into the hands of that eminent tribunal.

—ABRAHAM LINCOLN

PROLOGUE:
A PARABLE

Demetrius looked down at the crowd assembled in hushed reverence before him and his fellow priests presiding at the oracle of Apollo at Delphi. He allowed himself a brief smile of satisfaction.

At forty-four years of age, Demetrius had been elevated above his peers to become high priest. To hide his youth, he had shaved the top of his head and allowed his rapidly graying beard to flow down onto his chest. For days before the public audience, he carefully practiced his regal walk, majestic posture, and grave demeanor. Since his youth, Demetrius had, like Demosthenes, month after month practiced shouting above the roaring breakers at the shoreline near his village on the Aegean Sea. His once high-pitched voice was now resonant and at times made to sound deep like thunder. When he rose to speak, dressed in a black robe, Demetrius seemed to the awestruck crowd in the temple to be the very personification of one of the gods from Mount Olympus.

The temple at Delphi was the center of life throughout the amphictyony, which was the confederation of Greek states served by Demetrius and the others. They believed that Apollo, the powerful son of Zeus, had descended here to bring a marvelous gift. Apollo himself would visit the temple virgin, known as the Pythia, and give her the power to foretell the future. This middle-aged virgin would thereafter be able to grant to the faithful success in battle, bountiful crops, fruitful marriages, great achievement in sports, and the blessings of the gods.

Finally the day had come: today was the day to reveal to those who crowded into the temple the secrets of the oracle for the year ahead. This was no ordinary assembly. Foremost among them was Odrysae, the king of Thrace. His question to the oracle: should he launch his armies against Macedonia? Would they be victorious?

Philonius was there. He was the richest man in the confederacy, owning a fleet of one thousand trading vessels that plied the waters of the Aegean, seeking ever-increasing bounty. Philonius clasped his fleshy, ring-adorned fingers in supplication. What would the oracle reveal to him about the success of his business prospects for the coming year? Those in charge knew that success for Philonius meant success for the temple and its priests; for Philonius, with all of his obscene self-indulgence, was always generous to those who tended to the temple of Apollo.

In the crowd were merchants waiting for a signal to buy or sell, farmers hoping for word of a good harvest, and legislators who wanted a word from the oracle—whether to raise taxes or lower taxes, spend more or spend less, stiffen criminal penalties or reduce them. All looked up to the elevated platform, where nine priests in black robes were preparing to render the word of the oracle that could determine their destiny.

Demetrius was suddenly oblivious to the moment as his mind retraced the events of the preceding week. Behind the assembly hall was a stone grotto enclosing a pool of water. As light struck the colored stones surrounding the grotto and then reflected back into the pool of water, there was created a lovely, sparkling, iridescent setting that was intoxicatingly beautiful. The Pythia, the virgin priestess of Apollo's oracle, had walked to and fro in this overwhelmingly beautiful grotto for seven days prior to this gathering.

On the eighth day, Demetrius, the high priest, gathered leaves of special plants, placed them on a stone ledge in the grotto, and then set them ablaze. As the smoke rose to fill the grotto, the Pythia breathed the smoke deeply and fell into a trance. Her body writhed in uncontrolled contortions as she began to moan and shriek.

"Aeee! Aeee! Aeee!" she screamed. Then a torrent of words came from her lips. Demetrius and his fellow priests strained to hear every word.

"You will go—you will return not in battle—you will perish. Sun and rain. Burning heat and freezing cold. Wind and storm. Heaven above. Earth beneath. Waves on the water. Ships on the sea. Armies marching. The strong will overcome the weak. The lion and the bear. Life and death. Good and evil. The snake will strike. The rat will eat. Happiness and sorrow. Aeee! Aeee! Aeee!"

Then the Pythia collapsed and was silent.

Demetrius and the ashen-faced priests looked at each other in amazement. They had just heard babbling nonsense, but they were not selected to criticize, only to interpret. After several moments of silence, the most senior priest, Gaius, spoke softly. "It is clear to me that the Pythia has said, 'Go to war and be victorious.'"

Philologia, who had served as priest for ten years, stood up and said, "I differ with my distinguished colleague. To me she was saying to avoid war at all costs."

"Gentlemen," interrupted Demetrius, "what did she say about agriculture and commerce?"

Nestos of Macedonia spoke forcefully. "It is clear to me that the forecast is for bountiful agriculture and prosperous commerce."

"Nonsense!" interjected Philologia. "There will be storms at sea, shipwrecks, and serious drought."

After hours of wrangling, it became clear there could be no consensus. So Demetrius, as high priest, made his declaration: "We are not in agreement, but we must reveal the sacred oracle. So we will vote.

"How many are for war?" Hands were raised; Demetrius counted. Five in favor, four opposed.

"How many for ship trade?" He counted again. Seven in favor, two opposed.

"How many for higher taxes?" Five in favor, four opposed.

"How many for bountiful harvests?" Four in favor, five opposed.

"How many for drought?" Five in favor, four opposed.

"How many for business prosperity?" Four in favor, four opposed, one abstention; no decision.

"Tomorrow we will tell the amphictyony what the oracle inspired by the great god Apollo has revealed to us about the future."

"But wait a minute!" shouted Kostas, the youngest member of the group. "We are merely voting our own preferences and prejudices. Our task is to faithfully reveal what the oracle has told us. How can we decide matters of such importance on a five-to-four vote? We are being dishonest and deceiving the people."

"My dear Kostas," Demetrius replied gently, "of course we are under the revelation of the oracle. But you must understand that the revelation of the oracle of the great god Apollo is whatever a majority of the priests say it is."

A long blast of the ram's horn followed by the striking of a huge brass gong awakened Demetrius from his reverie. A hush fell over the crowd as he rose majestically to his full six feet then slowly extended his hands up toward heaven. The flickering lights of a hundred torches cast ghostly shadows across Demetrius and the surrounding stone columns. His face glowed. He appeared regal and wise, understanding the problems of humanity, yet malevolent and mysteriously in touch with the supernatural forces of good and evil.

And thus Demetrius spoke: "The great god Apollo has revealed himself to his priestess. Deep within the grotto of Delphi, his voice has been heard. Hear, hear, hear! Now the word that comes from on high.

"Strong armies will march and be victorious.

"Ships will sail the sea and bring much treasure.

"The great confederacy requires more funds from its people.

"Drought will cover the land and seed will perish.

"The gods have no message for the merchants.

"Hail to the great Apollo and his high priestess, the Pythia!"

There was a moment of silence before the ram's horn sounded once again, and then the priests rose from their gilded thrones high above the people and withdrew to their grotto. Slowly the crowd dispersed, murmuring and wondering about what they had heard.

Within three months of that fateful night, Odrysae, the king of Thrace, launched a war against the rival Macedonians. In the initial battle, fifty thousand Thracian soldiers were killed and the army of Thrace fled the battlefield in disgrace.

Philonius, the merchant, launched his biggest trading expedition ever. Three hundred ships loaded with rare and precious goods set sail for Sicily. But on the way a violent storm overtook them, and every ship was sent to the ocean floor, with a great loss of life.

The farmers of the confederacy, fearing the impending drought, planted no crops. By the time the rains came, it was too late to plant. Weeds rose up and choked their fields, and as a result, the price of grain tripled and thousands starved. Uncertainty then gripped the merchants of the Delphic confederacy, and their reduced business activity brought on a major economic depression. Their once-prosperous places of business were now deserted and falling into ruin. On every street corner sat emaciated beggars dressed in rags. Mobs of angry citizens gathered in front of the government buildings demanding solutions to their desperate plight. But, regrettably, the economic depression had so reduced the tax revenues that the treasuries of the confederacy and the municipalities that supported them were dangerously depleted. There was no way to help the poor or feed the starving.

Word of the plight of the Greek amphictyony soon spread far abroad. Foreign marauders, sensing easy targets of opportunity, began systematic killing and looting throughout the land. Cities were pillaged, hostages taken away as slaves, and tribute was demanded by barbarians. Kostas, the young priest at Delphi, was overcome with grief. He realized the true cause of the devastation engulfing the land. He and his fellow priests had lied to the people. In their arrogance, they had attempted to control the confederacy, and through their own stupidity they had ruined it.

Kostas could not eat. He could not sleep. He was tormented night and day by the cries of the suffering people. What could he do to make amends? First, he thought of killing himself, but what good would that accomplish? He knew that his fellow priests were blinded by arrogance and would never admit their guilt. There was only one answer, and he took it.

On a night lit only by the stars, Kostas mounted a borrowed horse and began the journey eastward to Thrace. He labored many days with little food or water, and he grew haggard and worn. His face was pale and weathered. When he arrived at the palace of the king, he had great difficulty convincing the palace guards that the gaunt, disheveled, tormented creature standing before them was truly one of the exalted priests of Delphi. But finally, the sacred amulet that he still wore around his neck convinced them that he was truly Kostas, an exalted priest of the oracle.

When he had been fed and washed, Kostas was ushered into the presence of Odrysae, the king of Thrace. He bowed low to the ground and then spoke. "Exalted King," he began, "I am Kostas, a priest of the temple of Apollo at Delphi. I have come to seek your forgiveness and to confess a terrible evil."

Odrysae was taken aback. Was this wretched creature bowing before him one of the exalted priests who sat on thrones in the temple of Delphi, whose voice was the voice of the great god Apollo, and whose pronouncements in Apollo's name controlled the life of the confederacy?

"Priest, what are you saying?" he replied. "Explain yourself."

"Your Majesty was at the temple when our high priest rendered to those assembled the words that had supposedly been spoken by the great god Apollo through his high priestess, the Pythia."

"Priest, what do you mean *supposedly*? Are you saying that the high priest was not giving us the words of the Pythia?"

"Sadly, Your Majesty, that is truly the case," Kostas answered.

"Priest!" the king exploded. "What were we hearing at that assembly if not the words of the oracle?"

Kostas hesitated and looked away. "Your Majesty heard . . . the majority opinions of the priests," he said. "In the case of war, it was a five-to-four vote: five votes in favor of war, four against . . ."

"You sniveling little worm!" Odrysae shouted. "I heard that the voice of the oracle was, 'Strong armies will march and be victorious!' Are you telling me that I went to war and lost fifty thousand brave men because of a five-to-four vote by a gang of deceitful priests trying to appear to be what they were not? Are you saying there was no oracle, no word from Apollo, only a five-to-four vote based on the opinions of nine black-robed priests?"

"Your Exalted Majesty, there was a message from the Pythia in the grotto, but we differed among ourselves as to what it meant. So we voted our opinions on the matter and disguised the vote as the voice of the oracle."

"Scoundrels! Villains! Charlatans!" Odrysae leapt to his feet in anger. "Nothing in my torture chamber is suitable punishment for deceivers like you! But," he continued, "what of the ships, the drought, the famine?"

His lips quivering in terror, Kostas continued. "We knew Philonius would be generous to the temple if the word of the oracle pleased him, so we voted seven-to-two in favor of ship trade."

"Mendacious scoundrels!" the king exclaimed. "You lied to Philonius on a seven-to-two vote, in order to gain riches for yourselves?"

Kostas fell to his knees and wept. "I bow in shame to admit it, Your Majesty, but I fear it is true."

"But what of the drought? Your priests have no knowledge of the future or the weather. Did you vote on that as well?"

"Yes, sadly, Your Majesty, that is also true. Our vote was four for good harvests, five against. Five for drought, four against it."

Odrysae threw up his hands and roared in anger, "I call the gods to witness that you priests have usurped divine power, entered into areas over which you had no knowledge, and have brought destruction on a great and proud people!"

Seizing his golden staff, King Odrysae turned furiously to his commanding general and yelled, "Prepare my elite legions! We march at dawn for Delphi."

After a long moment of silence, Odrysae stepped down from his throne and spoke softly to Kostas. "Priest," he said, "because you have been honest with me, I will spare your life. Stay in this place and I will feed and protect you. But you shall speak no more." Motioning to his servants to take Kostas away, the king withdrew abruptly to his private quarters.

It was precisely one week later when the crack legions of Thrace completed their long journey to Delphi and surrounded the temple. Demetrius, who had been told that the king's army was nearby, dressed carefully in his finest robes, combed his long beard, and then went out to the great marble portico of the temple to greet them. Haughty as ever, he looked the king of Thrace straight in the eye. "Most noble king," he said slowly, "have you once again come to seek counsel from the priestess of the great god Apollo?"

"No, Priest," Odrysae replied impatiently. "I have come to seek the truth from your lips. Did the message that sent my legions into battle and cost the lives of fifty thousand of my finest troops come from the Pythia? Or was it a five-to-four vote by you, the priests?"

For the first time in his life, Demetrius felt true fear. It stabbed like a leopard's claw at his stomach. He trembled then quickly recovered. The secrets of the grotto were inviolate. Only the priests themselves knew, and they had sworn a blood oath to secrecy. But if no one had revealed this secret, he wondered, how did this Thracian king know the precise truth? Surely the king was guessing . . . trying to trap him perhaps? If so, Demetrius thought, he would play the charade for all it was worth.

"Your Majesty," he replied unctuously, "the great god Apollo speaks in the sacred grotto through his holy priestess. The priests are here to protect her and faithfully deliver her message. This you certainly know."

"You lie!" Odrysae snarled through clenched teeth. Then to his commander, he barked, "Seize the other priests and bring them out here!" As they were brought before him, the king uttered one more question. "Priests, you must tell me: was the message for my legions to go to war given by the oracle, or was it a five-to-four vote? I warn you: if you lie, you will be stripped of power and banished forever."

Odrysae then approached Philologia, who was quaking in terror. "A simple question," the king repeated. "Was it a message from the Pythia or a five-to-four vote?"

"Your Majesty," Philologia replied cautiously, "you insult the integrity of the temple of the great god Apollo." But before the priest could utter another word, Odrysae glowered at him and shouted, "Silence! Enough of your lies! Since you won't tell the truth, my decree is that you be pulled apart by wild horses."

With a motion of his hand, four burly soldiers grabbed the priest and threw him to the ground. His hands were bound fast to a rope, as were his feet. The ropes were then tied securely around the necks of two horses facing in opposite directions. Two soldiers stood by with whips in hand to begin the process that would tear the priest from limb to limb.

"The truth, Priest!" Odrysae said in a firm but matter-of-fact fashion.

As the whip hand raised, the priest screamed in terror, "I'll tell you the truth! It was a five-to-four vote."

The king motioned to the soldiers, who then unbound Philologia and set him on his feet.

"Now, priests," Odrysae shouted as he turned to the quaking priests standing before him, "I want the truth! Was it the oracle or a five-to-four vote?" As he went down the line, each priest was quick to confess—it was a vote, a vote, a vote.

"By your own confession," the king pronounced, "you are guilty of actions that have cost the lives of countless thousands and brought ruin upon our confederacy. You are guilty of unspeakable crimes against mankind and against the gods. You have held yourselves up to the people as agents of the divine oracle. But this was all a lie. You were voting your own desires and prejudices, pretending to be representatives of the gods. For this you unjust priests will be banished forever."

With a wave of his hand, Odrysae then ordered the temple of Apollo to be burned to the ground. He had the priests of the temple bound and carried away in chains, banished forever from the land of their birth and far from the people they had wantonly abused. The disgrace that was brought upon the temple of the oracle that day was so great that, from that time to this, the shrine at Delphi has never been rebuilt.

The Greeks were wise and resourceful people. Soon word spread throughout the Mediterranean world that their troubles were not caused by farmers or merchants or rulers, and least of all by the gods, but by nine priests in black robes at the temple of Delphi. When the people realized that these priests no longer controlled their lives, they banded together as one nation, and soon they rebuilt their Greek confederation to a level of strength and prosperity, the likes of which had never been seen in the ancient world.

A Twenty-First-Century Marble Temple

The great British political commentator and satirist Malcolm Muggeridge remarked several decades ago that America is the only society in which the ruling elites turned against their own culture. Think of it. In most nations, the cultural intelligentsia seek to perpetuate their own power by reinforcing the norms of the societies they lead. They diligently guard and embellish their traditions, and then they establish institutions that not only perpetuate those traditions but transmit them to successive generations.

The traditional role of education throughout history has been to teach young people the accumulated knowledge of the culture, along with the moral and spiritual standards and common virtues that underlie their culture's formal structures and institutions. Traditional learning is designed to preserve and uphold governmental, legal, economic, social, and religious organization of the society.

From the earliest days of the American founding, from the Jamestown Colony in 1607 to the Plymouth Colony, the Revolutionary War, the Civil War, and World Wars I and II, the United States of America has been a unified nation whose culture centered on the concept of individual liberty given by God and protected by the rule of law, representative government, and a population whose private and public actions were self-regulating. American culture has served as a standard to the entire world, primarily because of near-universal acknowledgement of the importance of the Christian faith, the Ten Commandments, and the Sermon on the Mount.

Certainly America is not perfect. Until the Civil War, we allowed slavery. The working conditions of children in factories were appalling until that custom was forbidden by law. Women were denied the right to vote until the early 1900s, when the people called for constitutional changes. And at one time, our major cities had corrupt political bosses. But, despite those flaws, this nation was still the hope of the world. It was a land of boundless optimism, economic freedom, and ever-growing prosperity and power. To the rest of the world, America was a beacon—a shining city set on a hill.

America was a Christian nation, inspired by the dreams of the early settlers who came here to tame a continent for the glory of God and His Son, Jesus Christ. The entire world desired to emulate America's example of freedom, economic prosperity, high standards of education, and especially our moral compass, which shined from the smiling faces of our young men and women.

Compare the unified and admired American nation of yesterday, however, with the rancorous cry today within our nation for group identity, political correctness, and bizarre forms of self-indulgence, as well as the apparent hatred of America and its leaders by the people of many nations. Or consider the disasters of public education and the radical anti-Americanism propagated by our institutions of higher education. Once a beacon of health and prosperity, America today leads the world in almost every known social pathology. Students in our public schools score at the lowest level in standardized testing among developed nations. And the perverted world-view of some two hundred writers in the film industry—spewing forth a never-ending torrent of violence, sexuality, and materialism—has become the modern image of America that is now held by millions around the world. In the twenty-first century, does the rest of the world wish to emulate us as it once did?

The 2000 presidential election revealed a gaping chasm in America: a nation no longer unified but evenly and bitterly divided between what has come to be known as the "blue" states and the "red" states. The urban areas of the Atlantic Coast, New England, the Great Lakes, and California comprise the "blue" states, while the Midwest heartland, the South, Southeast, Southwest, and Mountain states make up the "red" states.

The dividing line between them was, without question, a matter of world-view, focused on fundamental religious, social, and family values. But rather than closing during the last four years, this chasm has only widened. The rhetoric has become more and more extreme and mean-spirited. In the halls of Congress and in the marketplace, there is rancor and vitriol.

We are in danger of becoming two Americas, not one. On one side are those who reject biblical norms and Christian values in favor of abortion-on-demand, radical feminism, intrusive central government, homosexual rights (including homosexual marriage), pornography and sexual license, weakened military defense, an ever-increasing role for nonelected judges, and the removal of our historic affirmation of faith from the public arena.

On the other side are those who believe that biblical standards are truly the glue that holds society together. They are men and women who respect human life at every stage, who stand for the sanctity of marriage, who want limited government and lower taxes, and who do not wish to give veto power over public actions to tiny, radical minorities. We believe in free enterprise and a strong defense, and we want the judges who serve in our courts to decide cases on the basis of established law rather than trying to rewrite the law to suit their own whims.

Most of those in the red states, who are generally politically conservative, want the laws that govern them to be made by freely elected representatives who are responsible to a majority of the people. Those on the other side, who are socially and politically liberal, want a social revolution. A large number of these men and women want to overthrow Christian values by a majority of nonelected judges who serve for life and answer to no one.

The filibuster battles taking place in the United States Senate over President Bush's highly qualified judicial nominees—one Hispanic, two African-American, one white woman, three white males—bear eloquent testimony to the clear truth that the core constituency of the Democratic Left is made up of radical activists who despise the processes of majority rule, preferring instead to be ruled by a pliable oligarchy who will ram a radical social agenda down the throats of the majority of Americans—under the guise of judge-made law.

As average American citizens see the tidal wave of crime and violence in our cities, failing schools, family breakups, out-of-wedlock births, the homosexual assault on the traditional family, and more than forty million abortions since the 1973 *Roe v. Wade* decision, they make their wishes known. Eighty percent of Americans favor prayer in the schools, 85 percent oppose partial-birth abortion, 65 percent are opposed to homosexual marriage, a growing majority oppose unrestricted abortion, a huge majority want the phrase "under God" to remain in the Pledge of Allegiance, 94 percent say they believe in God, and a majority want stringent regulation of pornography over the Internet.

But do the judges of the Supreme Court of the United States really care about the heart cry of the American people? Do they care enough to stop the moral disintegration of our society? Quite simply, a five-member majority of the nine judges thumb their noses at tens of millions of American citizens and their elected representatives.

Well, to that majority of black-robed tyrants we say, "We care very deeply. You have usurped power that was never given to you. Your ill-conceived decisions, more than any other cultural phenomenon, have shredded the moral fabric of this nation. The blood of millions of innocent unborn babies is on your hands. And the time has come for you unjust judges to step down, so that truth and justice may at last be restored to this land!"

This book tells that story.

PART ONE

A CRISIS OF CONFIDENCE

1
THE END OF AMERICAN DEMOCRACY

The history of liberty is a history of limitation of governmental power, not the increase of it. When we resist, therefore, the concentration of power, we are resisting the processes of death, because concentration of power is what always precedes the destruction of human liberties.

—WOODROW WILSON (1912)

Surely philosopher Lord Acton was right when he said that power corrupts and that absolute power corrupts absolutely. There is no better proof of those words than the distortion of justice and the radicalization of the courts that has taken place in this country during the past fifty years. The purpose of the courts, as the founders made clear, is to ensure that justice prevails in the land. The U.S. Constitution begins with these words: "We the People of the United States, in Order to form a more perfect Union, establish Justice, insure domestic Tranquility, provide for the common defense, promote the general Welfare, and secure the Blessings of Liberty to ourselves and our Posterity, do ordain and establish this Constitution for the United States of America."

It is no accident that, second only to the formation of the Union, justice was foremost in the thoughts of the men who built this nation. They knew, in fact, that domestic tranquility, the common defense, and the general welfare could only be assured if justice were first established. Under their British colonial masters, the early Americans came to appreciate the true meaning of justice before the law. Even earlier, in Europe, their ancestors had suffered intolerance and persecution. The law that served the Crown was harsh and unjust to the common citizen, and judges were subject to bribes and treachery of every kind. The law was certainly no friend to men and women of an independent mind, and the founders of this new republic set out from the very beginning to create a system where justice would prevail.

With such a history, it is easy to understand why the framers of the Constitution so highly prized law and order. The formation of the federal judiciary was a central concern. Nevertheless, the courts were designed to administer law, not to make it. The division of the national government into three branches—executive, legislative, and judicial—was an inspired innovation of the framers. They built into our constitutional apparatus a system of checks and balances to ensure that no single branch of government would be able to steamroll the others. Individuals chosen to serve on the bench, whether appointed or elected, whether federal or local, were to be faithful interpreters of the law. They were students of the law, with no legislative or executive functions.

Judges at all levels were expected to be experienced in jurisprudence. They were to be moral, above suspicion, circumspect in their personal behavior, highly disciplined, and defenders of the common good. They were empowered to settle disputes and to resolve matters of controversy according to known and currently existing standards of justice. As such, justices of the Supreme Court and judges in each of the inferior courts across the land would be dependent upon the executive and legislative branches—equal to them in their constitutional responsibilities but subject always to "the will of the people."

As Alexander Hamilton expressed in Federalist 78:

The judiciary, from the nature of its functions, will always be the least dangerous to the political rights of the Constitution; because it will be least in a capacity to annoy or injure them. The Executive not only dispenses the honors, but holds the sword of the community. The legislature not only commands the purse, but prescribes the rules by which the duties and rights of every citizen are to be regulated. The judiciary, on the contrary, has no influence over either the sword or the purse; no direction either of the strength or of the wealth of the society; and can take no active resolution whatever. It may truly be said to have neither force nor will, but merely judgment; and must ultimately depend upon the aid of the executive arm even for the efficacy of its judgments.

Then, with a passing reference to Baron de Montesquieu's work *The Spirit of the Laws,* Hamilton adds that "the judiciary is beyond comparison the weakest of the three departments of power." In short, the authority of the courts emanates from the lawmaking branches. Judges were never expected to take the liberties they've taken in recent years. Justices were never meant to be a power unto themselves. Yet, over time, their role has changed.

DURING GOOD BEHAVIOR

To appreciate just how much the role of the courts has changed, it will be helpful to recall briefly the manner by which the founders established our nation's judiciary. In Article III, Section 1 of the Constitution, we read:

The judicial power of the United States, shall be vested in one Supreme Court, and in such inferior courts as the Congress may from time to time ordain and establish. The judges, both of the supreme and inferior courts, shall hold their offices during good behaviour, and shall, at stated times, receive for their services, a compensation, which shall not be diminished during their continuance in office.

It was the duty of Congress to establish the Supreme Court and, through the appointment authority of the president, to see that justices were chosen to serve the people. Justices of the Supreme Court were to have a high degree of freedom and job security. They were to have life tenure and a secure income, ensuring their independence from threats or undue influence.

Nevertheless, the tenure of any Supreme Court justice was secure only so long as he or she maintained "good behaviour." On this point, Alexander Hamilton says that the precondition of good behavior is "the best expedient which can be devised in any government, to secure a steady, upright, and impartial administration of the laws." In other words, knowing that his or her actions on the bench would be under scrutiny by the other branches, as well as by the American people (who are superior in our republican form of government), would help to prevent arbitrary and improper judgments by the members of the Court. Unlike Europe, where judges were subject only to the whims of the king and Parliament, in America the people have a voice, and behavior by any justice outside the bounds of his legitimate role and authority may be grounds for impeachment.

Despite this threat, however, the courts have chosen a very different course. Through systematic reinterpretation and misreading of the Constitution, by disregarding the will of the people in dozens of politically charged cases, and by attempting to enshrine their own liberal notions of "social justice" through tortured readings of the law, justices have substantially changed the form and substance of our American democracy—and have repeatedly distorted the true meaning of the Constitution. The imbalances in the courts have placed the principle of checks and balances at risk and, in effect, handed over the government of this country to what many observers of the Court now refer to as an "imperial judiciary" and a "judicial oligarchy." Thomas Jefferson once warned that the tendency "to consider the judges as the ultimate arbiters of all constitutional questions" is "a very dangerous doctrine indeed, and one which would place us under the despotism of an oligarchy."[1] We all ought to share his concern.[2]

Anyone concerned about the apparent downward spiral of American culture during the past fifty years will no doubt be familiar with many of the disturbing cases that have come before the Court. Examples of heavy-handed judicial activism are not hard to find. In the case of *Newdow v. U.S. Congress* (2002), a three-judge panel of the Ninth Circuit Court of Appeals in San Francisco voted 2–1 to throw out the phrase "under God" in the Pledge of Allegiance. The case was heard by the Supreme Court of the United States on March 24, 2004, stirring enormous response, which I will discuss in greater detail in later chapters.

An Associated Press poll taken in the weeks just prior to Newdow's appearance before the Court revealed overwhelming support for keeping the reference to God in the Pledge. Nearly 90 percent of Americans surveyed said the words "under God" should remain, despite any questions that might arise about the so-called separation of church and state. On the day of the hearing, Sandra Banning, the mother of the child whom Michael Newdow claimed was being harmed by reciting the Pledge in her classroom, told reporters that Mr. Newdow does not have legal custody of their daughter, and he does not speak for either of them.

Furthermore, the mother told reporters outside the Supreme Court that both she and her daughter are evangelical Christians, and the child loves reciting the words "under God" in the Pledge. Yet atheists like Michael Newdow, supported by the American Civil Liberties Union (ACLU) and other left-wing groups such as the

People for the American Way and Americans United for the Separation of Church and State, have tried to use this illegitimate ploy to undermine the moral foundations of the nation. And much the same sort of moral deregulation has been unleashed in many other cases.

In the case of *Lawrence v. Texas* (2003), for example, the Court ruled that states could no longer forbid homosexual sodomy. As a direct result of that ruling, a storm of controversy erupted when homosexuals in California, Massachusetts, New York, and other places demanded the right to marry their same-sex partners. As Justice Scalia said in his blistering dissent, "It is clear from this that the Court has taken sides in the culture war." Under the logic of the Court's ruling, Scalia said, there could now be no legally defensible limit to even the most bizarre definitions of marriage and family.

Previously, in *Ashcroft v. Free Speech Coalition* (2002), the Court overturned an act of Congress, the Child Pornography Protection Act, on the grounds that prohibiting computer-generated images of children engaging in sex acts was an overly broad definition of pornography and a violation of the First Amendment. In June 2004, the Court, in a 5–4 ruling, upheld the Third Circuit Court of Appeals' injunction against enforcing another act of Congress, the Child Online Protection Act of 1998, which prescribed substantial fines and imprisonment for posting on the Internet salacious materials deemed "harmful to minors." The Court's decision in *Ashcroft v. American Civil Liberties Union* (2004) sent the case back to the lower court to determine whether the law violates the First Amendment. It's not difficult to imagine that, at the pace the Court is on today, pornography will soon be a protected right in this country.

A RELIGION OF SECULARISM

The agenda of the Supreme Court during the past five decades is unmistakable and far-reaching. In *United States v. Eichman* (1990), which was argued before the Court in combination with *United States v. Haggerty,* the tribunal ruled that another act of Congress, the Flag Protection Act of 1989, was unconstitutional because it was a suppression of the free-speech rights of an anti-American anarchist. In *Texas v. Johnson* (1989), the Court overturned a previous judgment against flag burning on the grounds that "a bedrock principle underlying the First Amendment . . . is that the Government may not prohibit the expression of an idea simply because society finds the idea itself offensive or disagreeable." Even though the will of the people and consent of the governed are even greater bedrock principles of the Constitution, the Court nevertheless held that citizens have no right to punish a dissenter for burning and, as in this case, cursing the American flag.

As disturbing as such cases may be, the greatest animus of the Court through the years has been directed, not at crime or criminals, but at the free and unfettered practice of religion. In *Santa Fe Indep. Sch. Dist. v. Doe* (2000), the Court made it illegal for students to participate in a short student-led prayer at sporting events. In *Lee v. Weisman* (1992), the Court ruled that clergy may not lead prayers at public-school events. In *Stone v. Graham* (1980), the Court struck down a Kentucky law requiring that the Ten Commandments be posted in public-school classrooms. And the list goes on.

Among the most infamous Supreme Court cases are those that stripped prayer and Bible reading from public schools. In *Engel v. Vitale* (1962) and *Murray v. Curlett* (1963), the rights of an anti-Christian minority were allowed to trump those of the Christian majority. Seemingly out of nowhere, the justices found that the Constitution forbids the free exercise of religion on public property. In *Abington v. Schempp* (1963), the Court held that public schools may not require that passages from the Bible be read or that the Lord's Prayer be recited in public schools at the beginning of the school day, even if students were excused from participation with a note from their parents. Once again, in order not to offend a contentious minority, the Court decided to trample the rights of the majority.

In his dissent to the Court's finding in *Abington*, Justice Potter Stewart said, "A refusal to permit religious exercises thus is seen, not as a realization of state neutrality, but rather as the establishment of a religion of secularism, or at the least, as government support of the beliefs of those who think that religious exercises should be conducted only in private." Stewart contended here, as he had done in the *Engel* case, that the establishment clause was meant to prevent the establishment of an official state church, not to limit religious expression altogether; and the free exercise clause was to protect religious exercises in the schools and elsewhere.

It is obvious that rulings such as *Engel, Murray,* and *Abington* are alien to the original intent of the founders. We hardly need to be reminded that it was Benjamin Franklin's remarkable call for prayer during the rancorous deliberations of the Constitutional Convention in Philadelphia that finally brought the delegates into one accord and led, as many would testify later, to the successful drafting of the Constitution. During those proceedings, George Washington challenged his fellow delegates, "Let us raise a standard to which the wise and honest can repair; the rest is in the hands of God." Almost without exception, the founders were men of deep Christian faith, and they understood not only that the hand of God was engaged in creating this nation but that divine providence would be required for its survival.

In his Farewell Address, our first president offered a bold declaration of what the founders believed: "Of all the dispositions and habits, which lead to political prosperity, religion and morality are indispensable supports. In vain would that man claim the tribute of patriotism, who should labor to subvert these great pillars of human happiness, these firmest props of the duties of men and citizens." Indeed, George Washington understood that public virtue is merely a reflection of personal virtues and that without the moral restraint that comes from within, informed by religious conviction, people must be restrained from without, by the force of law.

John Jay, the first chief justice of the Supreme Court, offered his own view of the matter. "The Bible is the best of all books," he said, "for it is the word of God and teaches us the way to be happy in this world and in the next." Then he charged his fellow citizens, "Continue therefore to read it and to regulate your life by its precepts." Are these the words of men who believed in "a wall of separation between church and state"? Certainly not. Nothing could be further from the truth.

HOSTILITY TO RELIGION

Unfortunately, Justice Stewart's strong dissent in *Abington* did not change the direction or resolve of the Court. The tribunal's record of overt hostility to religion was well established. In *McCollum v. Board of Education* (1948) and a number of other lesser cases, the Court had repeatedly ruled that religious instruction on school property is a violation of the establishment clause. And in what is perhaps the most fundamental assault on the religious freedoms of the nation, the Court's ruling in the case of *Everson v. Board of Education* (1947) set a tone that exemplifies the pernicious reasoning of the Court.

In the *Everson* case, the Court first upheld a local ordinance that authorized funds for the transportation of students attending Catholic schools in the state of New Jersey. But then, in virtually the same breath, the justices found that the Constitution does, in fact, create "a wall of separation between church and state." In an apparently gratuitous flourish at the end of the Court's majority opinion, Justice Hugo Black offered an analysis of the establishment clause and said that neither the states nor the federal government can set up a church. That much is true. But then he added, "The First Amendment has erected a wall between church and state. That wall must be kept high and impregnable. We could not approve the slightest breach."

That is certainly not true. Rather, it is a malicious mischaracterization not only of Jefferson's 1802 letter to the Danbury Baptists, in which he said that government must keep its hands off religion, but also of the original intent of the framers, who understood that the Christian religion was the surest guarantee of a virtuous nation.

But Justice Black went even further in his remarks, setting forth one of the most adversarial statements ever issued from the bench with these words:

> The "establishment of religion" clause of the First Amendment means at least this: neither a state nor the Federal Government can set up a church. Neither can pass laws which aid one religion, aid all religions, or prefer one religion over another. Neither can force nor influence a person to go to or remain away from church against his will or force him to profess a belief or disbelief in any religion. No person can be punished for entertaining or professing religious beliefs or disbeliefs, for church attendance or non-attendance. No tax in any amount, large or small, can be levied to support any religious activities or institutions, whatever they may be called, or whatever form they may adopt to teach or practice religion. Neither a state nor the Federal Government can, openly or secretly, participate in the affairs of any religious organizations or groups and *vice versa*. In the words of Jefferson, the clause against establishment of religion by law was intended to erect "a wall of separation between church and state."[3]

American University professor Daniel Dreisbach has researched Jefferson's use of the "wall of separation" metaphor and brought several startling new discoveries to light in his book on the subject. First, he found from Jefferson's original drafts of the Danbury letter that the term "wall of separation" was an entirely arbitrary phrase, never meant to convey any great message about either theology or social policy. Jefferson penned the phrase, then scratched it out and replaced it with other terms, until he eventually incorporated it in the final draft of the letter. More importantly, Dreisbach believes that Justice Black's interpretation of the phrase, and of the First Amendment, was an expression of Black's own anti-Catholic bias.

"The wall metaphor mischievously redefines constitutional principles in at least two important ways," says Dreisbach. "First, the phrase emphasizes separation between church and state—unlike the First Amendment, which speaks in terms of the non-establishment and free exercise of religion. Second, a wall is a bilateral barrier that inhibits the activities of both the civil government and religion—unlike the First Amendment, which imposes restrictions on the civil government only (specifically on Congress)." So what are the implications of the Court's misreading of the facts? Dreisbach writes:

> Today, the wall is used to separate religion from public life, thereby promoting a religion that is essentially private and a state that is strictly secular. The "high and impregnable wall" constructed by the modern Supreme Court inhibits religion's ability to inform the public ethic, deprives religious citizens of the civil liberty to participate in politics armed with ideas informed by their spiritual values, and infringes the right of religious communities and institutions to extend their ministries into the public square. The wall has been used to silence the religious voice in the public marketplace of ideas and to segregate people of faith behind a restrictive barrier.[4]

Dreisbach, who by the way is not a Catholic, has hit the nail on the head. The unavoidable implication of all these rulings, taken in context and with the attitude they so clearly convey, is that the Supreme Court of the United States has lost any sense of the connection between the authentic religious roots of the nation and the right ordering of American society. It's as if a band of nine tenured, secular judges have decided that they're in competition with the true Lawgiver and Judge of mankind.

Justice Joseph Story, who served under Chief Justice John Marshall in the first half of the nineteenth century, affirmed, "One of the beautiful boasts of our municipal jurisprudence is that Christianity is a part of the Common Law. . . . There never has been a period in which the Common Law did not recognize Christianity as lying at its foundations." Story said further, "I verily believe Christianity necessary to the support of civil society."[5] At one time, such a view would have been common in the judiciary. Yet the Court's finding in *Everson* has now passed into law, virtually unchallenged, and it continues to have an insidious effect on matters of church and state. If we follow the trajectory of federal court rulings in this area, it is terrifying to imagine what horrors may be yet to come.

RISKING EVERYTHING

In the conclusion to their compendious and insightful volume, *The Columbia History of the World,* scholars John A. Garraty and Peter Gay report that the most destructive changes in modern history have come about primarily as a result of the weakening of morality and religion in society. "Morality, like religion," they say, "has the double aspect of satisfying an emotional need and serving a social purpose. Without morality—some inner restraint—society must assign two policemen to watch every citizen day and night. And without a religion which sustains conduct or at least organizes the facts of life and the cosmos, men seek in vain for the meaning of their existence."[6] Surely the founders understood this truth as well.

Our second president, John Adams, said that "it is religion and morality alone, which can establish the principles upon which freedom can securely stand." Adams said further, "The only foundation of a free Constitution is pure virtue, and if this cannot be inspired into our people, in a greater measure, than they have it now, they may change their rulers, and the forms of government, but they will not obtain a lasting liberty." Then Adams, who had participated in every aspect of the founding of the nation, powerfully proclaimed, "We have no government armed with power capable of contending with human passions unbridled by morality and religion. . . . Our constitution was made only for a moral and religious people. It is wholly inadequate for the government of any other." Sadly, the courts of this nation, for generations now, have preferred to ignore the wisdom of the founders and have labored to enshrine, instead, their own ideals of "fairness."

In the spring of 2004, the private papers of Justice Harry Blackmun (who died in 1999) were made available for public review by the Library of Congress. It would seem that Blackmun believed he was authorized to invent law based on his own personal beliefs. His most notorious case, *Roe v. Wade* (1973), may be the greatest single example of judicial overreach in this nation's history. From start to finish, Blackmun staked his reputation and his legacy on that case. Although he had been appointed by Richard Nixon in 1970, Blackmun's moral and political world-views were far from those of his benefactor. Before coming to the Court, Blackmun had served as resident counsel for the prestigious Mayo Clinic, from 1950 to 1959. As Bob Woodward and Scott Armstrong reveal in their book, *The Brethren,* Blackmun was naturally inclined to object to any interference with a physician's prerogative, and he apparently saw abortion in that light.[7]

In a 1995 videotaped oral history, Blackmun discussed his efforts to persuade Justice Sandra Day O'Connor that the Constitution contains a "right to privacy" that gives a woman the unilateral right to terminate a pregnancy for any reason. The *Roe* decision legalized unrestricted abortion-on-demand and led to a mind-numbing slaughter that dwarfs the worst disasters in all of history. But Harry Blackmun was not shy about using the power of persuasion to get his way. He knew that Sandra Day O'Connor was a believer in states' rights. She might not like overturning Texas law, and she might not be inclined to join the gang of four "progressive" justices upholding *Roe*; but, as Justice Blackmun says in his notes, "On the other hand, she is a woman and may fear somewhat any accusation of being a traitor to her sex. Some women's organizations would so conclude."

When reporters examined the papers of Justice Blackmun in 2004, they found a note from Justice Kennedy to Justice Blackmun, which said:

Dear Harry,

I need to see you as soon as you have a few moments. I want to tell you about some developments in *Planned Parenthood v. Casey* and at least part of what I have to say should come as welcome news.

After that meeting, Justice Blackmun wrote on a pink notepad, "Roe saved." Blackmun was not the least concerned about the millions of women who believe that abortion is an act of murder. Rather, he was eager to please the minority of liberal women for whom unrestricted abortion-on-demand is a religion. Convincing Justices O'Connor and Souter to join their side in the decision assured Blackmun and Kennedy that *Roe v. Wade* would be upheld.

Even more troubling, Blackmun's private papers also reveal the power of law clerks—who are often young, liberal graduates of Eastern law schools—to influence the decisions of the justices they serve. For the most part, these young people have been taught that "original intent" and "textualist" philosophies embraced by Justices Rehnquist, Scalia, and Thomas are hopelessly out of date. A note in the Blackmun papers reveals that on January 4, 1992, law clerk Molly McUsic wrote to Blackmun about *Planned Parenthood v. Casey*, which was a major challenge to *Roe* being argued by U.S. solicitor general Kenneth Starr. In her note, McUsic said the liberal justices on the Court ought to consider the political impact of overturning *Roe* in that election year. She wrote, "If you believe that there are enough votes on the court now to overturn *Roe,* it would be better to do it this year before the election and give women the opportunity to vote their outrage."

The blatant intimidation of McUsic and Blackmun eventually worked, and *Roe* survived. Justice Anthony Kennedy—a Reagan appointee, as was Justice O'Connor—changed his vote sometime after the justices' conference and voted with Blackmun, O'Connor, David Souter, and Thurgood Marshall to uphold a ruling that was a travesty of law and logic. The Blackmun papers offer an illuminating glimpse of the attitudes and behavior of the Court, showing how elite opinion is used to shape public policy. What a dark and bitter legacy for a man appointed to serve on the nation's highest tribunal, commissioned by the nation's chief executive to preserve and defend our Constitution and values.

Roe v. Wade (1973) and its companion case, *Doe v. Bolton* (1973), will live in infamy for the immeasurable harm they have done. For as long as our nation survives, these cases will be remembered as the basis for the most ghastly holocaust in human history. By any accounting, more than forty-five million children have died in this country alone since that fiat judgment of 1973. Around the world the numbers are even higher, perhaps as high as one billion. However you measure it, the Court's record of imposing its values upon the nation, repeatedly, and in a manner that is contrary to both the will of the people and the original intent of the Constitution, is shocking and ought to elicit a universal cry of alarm.

RESTORING JUDICIAL BALANCE

For a time, some people believed that if Republican presidents could simply appoint enough conservative justices to the bench, there might be a chance of restoring balance in the Court. It is apparent now that was a mistake. With the exception of Justices Antonin Scalia, Clarence Thomas, and William Rehnquist, who have struggled against enormous odds to maintain some degree of constitutional legitimacy, the members of today's Supreme Court are hellbent on ruling from the bench without the slightest concern for what history or tradition or jurisprudence should say.

The High Court, as Judge Robert Bork has written on various occasions, is impervious to arguments about its behavior. "The illegitimacy of the Court's departure from the Constitution," Bork said in one journal article, "is underscored by the fact that no Justice has ever attempted a justification of the practice. At most, opinions have offered, as if it solved something, the observation that the Court has never felt its power confined to the intended meaning of the Constitution. True enough, but a long habit of abuse of authority does not make the abuse legitimate. That is particularly so when the representative branches of government have no effective way of resisting the Court's depredations."[8]

The controversial rulings of the Supreme Court and the federal courts almost always err on the side of "liberty without restraint," while religious principles are routinely trampled underfoot. The *Stone v. Graham* (1980) ruling that the Ten Commandments could not be posted in public schools was based on a belief, expressed in the majority opinion of the Court, that reading God's Law could be dangerous to children. In their finding, the justices declared, "If the posted copies of the Ten Commandments are to have any effect at all, it would be to induce the schoolchildren to read, meditate on, perhaps to venerate and obey, the Ten Commandments." This, they said with unfeigned passion, "is not a permissible state objective."[9]

If you think such attitudes are the exception, just recall the case of Judge Roy Moore, which has stirred such controversy during the past decade. In early 1997, Judge Moore was told to remove a copy of the Ten Commandments that had hung on his courtroom wall; furthermore, he was told to refrain from opening his court each day with prayer. But the attempt of a higher court to strip virtue, tradition, and religious values from the courtroom touched a nerve. With a promise that he would install a copy of the Ten Commandments in a place of honor in the supreme court of Alabama, Judge Moore was elected by the people of that state to serve as chief justice of the state's high court. True to his promise, Judge Moore commissioned, paid for, and erected a 5,200-pound monument engraved not only with the Ten Commandments but also with famous statements by the Founding Fathers and historic quotes from *Blackstone's Commentaries on the Law.* Predictably, the atheists demanded that a federal judge enter the fray and order Moore to remove the monument from the premises. Moore refused, and subsequently, in the midst of enormous controversy, he was removed from office by judicial fiat.

In his dissent to the Supreme Court's anti-religious ruling in the case of *Santa Fe Indep. Sch. Dist. v. Doe* (2000), which proscribed student-initiated prayer at high school sporting events, Chief Justice William Rehnquist wrote, "even more disturbing than its holding is the tone of the Court's opinion; it *bristles with hostility to all things religious* in public life. Neither the holding nor the tone of the opinion is faithful to the meaning of the Establishment Clause" (emphasis added).

The same may be said for almost all the religious rulings of the federal courts since the 1940s. Something seems to happen to the nation's judges once they are seated on the High Court bench. Over the years, Justices Scalia and Thomas have taken a beating in the press, but they have remained true to their convictions. Such men deserve our support, and they certainly need our prayers. But the battle is not altogether lost.

THE SEPARATION OF POWERS

In *The Columbia History of the World,* scholars John A. Garraty and Peter Gay tell us that civilization is an expression of the collective life of a nation, which rests on a "tacit individual faith in certain ideals and ways of life, seconded by a general faith in the rightness of the whole."[10] That is, a great nation is not just the ideas of the so-called elites but of the people who work, raise their families, and participate in the day-to-day reality of that nation. Truly there is no better description of the uniform faith of the founders, who first dreamed and then forged a nation into existence out of their shared belief in God and their reverence for the ideal of human liberty. The Founding Fathers understood the challenges, of course, and there were many. But their vision was much greater than the obstacles they had to overcome.

For that vision to be restored in our time, we, the people of the United States, must come together in common cause to bring forth that reality. Most of all, we must recommit ourselves to the self-evident truths enshrined in the Declaration of Independence. If we do that, I believe that, with God's help, we will see changes that would boggle the mind. But if we do not take that risk, we will face the prospect of losing everything, as Professors Garraty and Gay make very clear. "It follows," they write in the conclusion of their work, "that widespread disbelief in those intangibles and the habits they produce in day-to-day existence brings on the dissolution of the whole."[11] In the end, they say, disbelief in our great national vision, informed by our resolute faith in God, is a sure recipe for disaster.

Do we still understand that reality? Do we realize that by relentlessly changing the ordering of society and corrupting the fundamental beliefs of the American people, as the courts have done, we are witnessing the destruction of our nation and our future? I'm convinced this is, indeed, the risk we face, and we simply cannot allow that to happen. While the broad general subject of this book is the Supreme Court and the distortion of law and order, the real motivation for this work is my deep concern that American society is in trouble, and the courts are as much to blame as any other institution.

We have come to a time and place where nothing short of national revival, accompanied by a radical overhaul of our justice system, can save us. In their efforts to institute their liberal vision of "the rights of man," the courts, abetted by the media, liberal politicians, the atheistic counterculture, and others who make up that large group called the "cultural elites," have done this nation a grave disservice. But the American people have resources and rights, and we may yet be able to turn the tables.

While he was still serving in Congress, former president Gerald Ford drafted a writ of impeachment against the extremely liberal justice William O. Douglas. Commenting on that bold step, Ford said, "An impeachable offense is whatever a majority of the House of Representatives considers it to be at a given moment in history." He added that, when a justice is impeached, "conviction results from whatever offense or offenses two-thirds of the other body [meaning the Senate] considers to be sufficiently serious to require removal of the accused from office." That idea was not new with Ford; it comes straight from the Constitution.

Perhaps we should be asking, is it possible that the Republican majority in Congress today, supported by a conservative majority in the nation, might have the strength of will to call this out-of-control judiciary to task? Obviously, that remains to be seen. Even Justice Stevens, in his decision in the Pledge of Allegiance case, noted the concerns of "the constitutional and prudential limits to the powers of an unelected, unrepresentative judiciary" in our kind of government. Regardless of your view of the courts or judicial authority, it should be apparent by now that the founders never intended for judges to rule this nation, to promote their own anti-religious agenda, or to overrule national, state, or local legislatures that are exercising their legitimate democratic authority.

Thomas Jefferson once said, "The opinion which gives to the judges the right to decide what laws are constitutional and what are not, not only for themselves in their own sphere of action but for the legislature and the executive also in their spheres, would make the judiciary a despotic branch." Representative Tom DeLay of Texas, who is now the majority leader of the House of Representatives, said in an April 3, 1997, letter to the *New York Times*, "I advocate impeaching judges who consistently ignore their constitutional role, violate their oath of office and breach the separation of powers. The Framers provided the tool of impeachment to keep the power of the judiciary in check. It is a tool Congress should explore using."

THE FUNCTION OF THE CITIZEN

The congressman's point is well taken. Whenever the subject of impeachment is mentioned, as we saw during the trial of President Clinton, there is an immediate outcry from the Left, and especially from the liberal media, claiming that conservatives are trying to legislate their own morality. But that is not the case, and we should not be intimidated. Judges must be held accountable, and the standard by which judges hold tenure ought to be the will of the people, not the unfettered will of the liberal elite. The founders did not give federal judges life tenure so that they could hold forth as a judicial oligarchy.

In our constitutional system of checks and balances, both the legislative and executive branches are accountable to the voters, by means of frequent elections. But if there is to be any hope of reversing this fifty-year trend of judicial tyranny, then judges must be held accountable to a standard of "good behaviour," as provided by the Constitution. Justice John Jay said it well: "Providence has given to our people the choice of their rulers, and it is the duty as well as the privilege and interest of our Christian nation to select and prefer Christians for their rulers." Justice Robert Jackson offered sage counsel as well when he said, "It is not the function of our Government to keep the citizen from falling into error; it is the function of the citizen to keep the government from falling into error."[12]

The overwhelming motivation for this book is a desire to provoke a discussion that would allow the American people to put restraints on a judicial system that is out of control and to restore the appropriate role for the nation's courts. In subsequent chapters, I will look in greater depth at bills currently being considered in Congress that are designed to prevent the Court from ruling on matters of religion and to keep them from incorporating rhetoric, language, or logic from foreign courts in their rulings. I will also look in greater depth at the Court's liberal agenda overall, at some of the most troubling social and political issues threatening us now, and at what's being done to stop the abuse of law. Finally, I will offer my own analysis of where our nation stands and what can be done to end this distortion of democracy and return the government to the people.

But there's something else you should know. In each instance, and on every front, you are as much a part of this controversy as anyone else. As a citizen of a free and independent republic, you are charged with the responsibility of preserving the democratic process and using your voice and your vote to make a difference. You have an implicit challenge from the founders to hold public officials accountable to a higher standard. This is both a privilege and a solemn duty that none of us should ignore.

As you read this book, I hope you will decide to join me in this bold and important endeavor. With God's help, we can make a difference.

TABLE OF CASES

Abington Sch. Dist. v. Schempp, 374 U.S. 203 (1963).
Am. Communications Ass'n v. Douds, 339 U.S. 382 (1950).
Ashcroft v. Free Speech Coalition, 535 U.S. 234 (2002).
Doe v. Bolton, 410 U.S. 179 (1973).
Engel v. Vitale, 370 U.S. 421 (1962).
Everson v. Bd. of Educ., 330 U.S. 1 (1947).

Lawrence v. Texas, 539 U.S. 558 (2003).

Lee v. Weisman, 505 U.S. 577 (1992).

McCollum v. Bd. of Educ., 333 U.S. 203 (1948).

Newdow v. Elk Grove Unified Sch. Dist., 2004 U.S. LEXIS 4178.

Newdow v. U.S. Congress, 292 F.3d 597 (9th Cir. 2002).

Roe v. Wade, 410 U.S. 113 (1973).

Santa Fe Indep. Sch. Dist. v. Doe, 530 U.S. 290 (2000).

Stone v. Graham, 449 U.S. 39 (1980).

Texas v. Johnson, 491 U.S. 397 (1989).

United States v. Eichman, 496 U.S. 310 (1990).

2

THE ORIGINAL INTENT
OF THE FOUNDERS

Now the Lord is the Spirit; and where the Spirit of the Lord is, there is liberty.

—2 CORINTHIANS 3:17

Before anyone can understand the beliefs and values that are woven into the fabric of American jurisprudence, it's important to know the history of the American people and how they came by their ideas. Had the founders been widely divided in their views, the Constitution would have been many times its size; they would have needed volumes to explain all the principles enumerated so succinctly in that remarkable document. But the founders were not divided.

It's true that a majority of Americans were hesitant to consider the prospect of separating from Great Britain, which they saw as their lifeline and connection to the rest of the world. Initially, the move toward independence was a source of contention. But the colonists were not divided on matters of conscience and conviction.

In their view of honor, truth, justice, and law, the founders were of one mind: they had a biblical world-view. To better understand how that came to be, let's look back briefly and remember the circumstances of America's birth.

Starting a new nation, by any standard, is a genuinely radical idea, and it was certainly not something that most of the original settlers of New England had contemplated in coming to this new land. Even in the face of frequent humiliations and abuses by their rulers, the colonists were naturally inclined to remain steadfast subjects of the British Crown. They had come to America voluntarily. They made their own choices, and for a considerable period of time they were content to leave matters as they were.

For more than one hundred years, colonial Americans pursued their livelihoods with dignity and discipline. Even when troubles over taxation and the quartering of British troops stretched the colonists' loyalty and resolve to the breaking point, they were nevertheless inclined to remain loyal to the English king. As Thomas Jefferson phrased it, "all experience hath shown, that mankind are more disposed to suffer, while evils are sufferable, than to right themselves by abolishing the forms to which they are accustomed."

During the seventeenth and eighteenth centuries, England was the most powerful nation on earth, with the most fearsome military in Europe and the most dynamic impact on world events of any nation. The colonists knew that even casual threats to British sovereignty could provoke fierce reprisals; and King George, who saw the New World primarily as a means of increasing his wealth and power, certainly would not hesitate to clamp down at the slightest hint of insurrection.

Accordingly, the majority of colonial Americans saw the benefits of their status as subjects of the British Empire as being of greater value than the risks of any foolhardy endeavor to gain independence. On the other hand, they were also self-assured, industrious, and pious people, and as the provocations from London and the intimidation by the king's governors and administrators increased over the years—accompanied by more and more egregious offenses against the dignity and will of the people—an atmosphere of defiance began to develop.

A Heritage of Faith

Matters of conscience were very important to the colonists. After all, it was religious intolerance that had brought the first settlers to these shores. From England, Scotland, Holland, and other parts of Europe, entire families left behind their homes and customs, sacrificing everything to cross a hostile ocean and conquer a savage wilderness. Why? For the right to think and believe as they wished.

On April 26, 1607, after four long months at sea, 104 English colonists led by Captain Christopher Newport stepped ashore on the south coast of Virginia, making camp on a sandy point of land near what is now Virginia Beach. They had been sent by the Virginia Company of London to establish a new colony, and what they discovered, as George Percy, a member of the ship's company, described, was "fair meadows and goodly tall trees, with such fresh waters running through the woods as I was almost ravished at the first sight thereof."

Percy's journal also reports, "The nine and twentieth day we set up a cross at Chesupioc Bay, and named the place Cape Henry." They called their settlement Jamestown, in honor of the English king, James I, and then kneeled to dedicate the new land to Jesus Christ. Their chaplain, Rev. Robert Hunt, led the settlers in prayer that day, and he continued to conduct daily prayers and religious services until his death, just over a year later. When Captain John Smith described these services, he wrote, "When I first went to Virginia, I well remember we did hang an awning . . . to three or four trees to shadow us from the sun. Our walls were rails of wood, our seats unhewn trees till we cut planks, our pulpit a bar of wood nailed to two neighboring trees." From the very first hours of this nation, prayer, Bible reading, and religious observance were essential features of American daily life.

The Mayflower Compact, which was written and signed aboard ship prior to the landing at Plymouth in 1620, has been called the birth certificate of America. Having sailed up the Hudson and anchored at Provincetown on November 21, 1620, at the northern tip of Cape Cod, forty-one men of the ship's company signed an accord modeled after a Separatist church covenant, in which they agreed mutually to establish a "Civil Body Politic" and to be bound by its laws. In their unanimous confession, they said:

> In the name of God, Amen. We, whose names are underwritten, the Loyal Subjects of our dread Sovereign Lord, King James, by the Grace of God, of England, France and Ireland, King, Defender of the Faith, e&.
>
> Having undertaken for the Glory of God, and Advancement of the Christian Faith, and the Honour of our King and Country, a voyage to plant the first colony in the northern parts of Virginia; do by these presents, solemnly and mutually in the Presence of God and one of another, covenant and combine ourselves together into a civil Body Politick, for our better Ordering and Preservation, and Furtherance of the Ends aforesaid; And by Virtue hereof to enact, constitute, and frame, such just and equal Laws, Ordinances, Acts, Constitutions and Offices, from time to time, as shall be thought most meet and convenient for the General good of the Colony; unto which we promise all due submission and obedience.
>
> In Witness whereof we have hereunto subscribed our names at Cape Cod the eleventh of November, in the Reign of our Sovereign Lord, King James of England, France and Ireland, the eighteenth, and of Scotland the fifty-fourth, Anno Domini, 1620.

Among those who made the arduous journey to the New World were Congregationalists, Separatists, Quakers, Baptists, Presbyterians, Lutherans, Anglicans, and many other Christians of an independent mind. For these people, the proper function of government was to preserve and protect individual liberty. As expressed later by John Locke and certain Enlightenment figures, the essential rights of "life, liberty, and property" were God-given and "unalienable." Samuel Rutherford's remarkable treatise, *Lex Rex* [Law is King], was published in 1644 and offered a stirring rebuttal to the idea of the divine right of kings.

In *Lex Rex,* Rutherford expressed two cardinal points. First, there must be a codified statement of the laws and covenants to bind a ruler to his people. In other words, a constitution is essential. His second point was a statement of the universal equality of men. Since all men are sinners, Rutherford said, no man can claim to be superior to another. By compelling logic, drawing upon Christian teachings about individual liberty and man's accountability before God, Rutherford identified the principles of liberty and equality that would be popularized later in Locke's essays.

Throughout the drafting of the colonial covenants, the founders held to the idea that government authority comes from the "consent of the governed." They expressed this sense of autonomy in each of the charters and accords that were enacted. Yes, they were prepared to suffer certain hardships under colonial rule, and they did; but they made it known that there were limits to the indignities they would willingly endure. This sense of justice was not born of pride but of faith. The founders' understanding of the dignity of man and the sanctity of human life came straight from the pages of Scripture.

Public life in America had, from the first, a distinctly religious character. The New England Confederation Constitution of 1643 states that the aim of the colonists was "to advance the Kingdom of our Lord Jesus Christ, and to enjoy the liberties of the Gospel thereof in purities and peace." The communities they established were of utilitarian design; and while the settlers were hardworking and practical people, they nevertheless took religious life very seriously, with a sense that they were building "the New Jerusalem" on the shores of the New World.

When French statesman Alexis de Tocqueville visited this country two hundred years later, in 1831, he was struck by the fact that faith and devotion remained so strong among the Americans. After traveling across this country for the better part of a year, de Tocqueville wrote in his book *Democracy in America,* "I do not know if all Americans have faith in their religion—for who can read the secrets of the heart?—but I am sure that they think it necessary to the maintenance of republican institutions. That is not the view of one class or party among the citizens, but of the whole nation; it is found in all ranks."[1]

By the early nineteenth century, Europe had already begun a long, disastrous flight from its heritage of faith. The Age of Reason and the European Enlightenment had spawned revolutionary ideas about the "rights of man" that left little room for traditional ideas of reverence and worship. Outward symbols of Christianity remained, but inwardly the people were changing. The influence of philosophers such as Rousseau, Voltaire, and Diderot in France, and Hume, Locke, and Bentham in England, helped to breed a secular spirit and a radical skepticism that would have a disabling effect on religion and life in Europe.

Enlightenment rationalism taught Europeans to distrust the church, but in America the Christian religion was still widespread and strong. Alexis de Tocqueville could see the benefits of the American way, not only in the high level of prosperity among the people but in their cheery nature and sense of common purpose. America, he wrote to his European audience, is "the place where the Christian religion has kept the greatest real power over men's souls; and nothing better demonstrates how useful and natural it is to man, since the country where it now has the widest sway is both the most enlightened and the freest."[2]

RUMBLINGS OF DISCONTENT

Christianity reinforced the habits and character of the American people, and it taught them the value of independence and self-reliance. Ultimately, it was this sense of intrinsic personal value, combined with an understanding of the Bible's teachings about liberty, that made the people begin to question the abuses they were being forced to endure. Jesus, reading from the words of the prophet Isaiah, announced that He had come "to proclaim liberty to the captives and . . . to set at liberty those who are oppressed" (Luke 4:18). The colonists, who were beginning to feel less like respected citizens and more like captives every day, took those words to heart. Furthermore, they recalled the words of the apostle Paul, who said, "the Lord is the Spirit; and where the Spirit of the Lord is, there is liberty" (2 Corinthians 3:17). As they were beginning to chafe under the English yoke, these settlers longed to be free.

History rightly recalls that it was the Stamp Act, the Townshend Acts, the Sugar Act, and other similar provocations that stirred the citizens to revolt. The Boston Port Act that barricaded Boston Harbor in order to punish the colonists for the Boston Tea Party led, in turn, to other acts of sedition. Altogether, the efforts of the English Crown to intimidate and punish Americans came to be known by the colonists as the Intolerable Acts. Members of the English Parliament had enacted these insults primarily to prevent disorder in Massachusetts, they said. But each new outrage only served to fan the flames of rebellion.

Because the church was such a central feature of colonial life, much of the information about the state of affairs in those revolutionary times came from the pulpits of New England. It has been estimated that as much as 80 percent of the political literature of that era was published first in the form of pamphlets and tracts based on popular sermons of the day. Thanks to bustling commerce among printers such as Benjamin Franklin and John Campbell, who was the publisher of the first successful newspaper in America, a rousing sermon could be set in type, pushed through the presses, and passed into the hands of thousands of patriots within hours of its delivery.

Among the men who fired the imagination of the patriots, perhaps the best known is Rev. Jonathan Mayhew, who was a graduate of the seminary at Harvard and pastor of Boston's historic West Church. Mayhew is considered by many to be one of the prophets of the American Revolution. Then, as now, there were many people in the churches who resisted such practical theology. Rather than facing up to the political realities of their situation, these sedentary churchgoers called for modest homilies, pleasant hymns, and readings from the Psalms; they had little patience with sermons that confronted the issues of the day. Jonathan Mayhew was scolded by some of his congregants and told to stick to his preaching, but the young man would not be dissuaded.

Reprints of Mayhew's sermons found their way, along with various other documents, to the Court of King George, where they were read studiously by members of Parliament. Rather than acknowledging the concerns of the colonists, the monarch and his subjects were enraged. In response to the growing discontent abroad, Parliament voted in 1762 to garrison ten thousand British troops in America. On arrival, English commanders informed the citizens they had come to bring added protection for the colonies. But it was no secret they had come to enforce the trade laws and to punish anyone who spoke out against the king.

The crowning blow, however, was news from Canterbury that the archbishop had issued a formal recommendation to the king to begin appointing colonial bishops, in order to stifle the independent spirit being spread by men like Mayhew. From that moment,

American pulpits were ablaze with indignation, accusing the English clergy of "establishing tyrannies over the bodies and souls of men." In his most famous sermon, called "A Discourse Concerning Unlimited Submission,"[3] Reverend Mayhew responded to those who had recited from Romans 13, in which Paul instructs Christians to be subject to the governing authority. Passive submission to tyranny, Mayhew exclaimed, is not a principle of Scripture. Rather, he said:

> Rulers have no authority from God to do mischief. . . . It is blasphemy to call tyrants and oppressors God's ministers. . . . No rulers are properly God's ministers but such as are "just, ruling in the fear of God." When once magistrates act contrary to their office, and the end of their institution—when they rob and ruin the public, instead of being guardians of its peace and welfare—they immediately cease to be the ordinance and ministers of God, and no more deserve that glorious character than common pirates and highwaymen.[4]

The principle of justice was Mayhew's and the colonists' real concern. Furthermore, to those who had questioned his right to speak of politics from the pulpit, Mayhew quoted 2 Timothy 3:16: "All Scripture is given by inspiration of God, and is profitable for doctrine, for reproof, for correction, for instruction in righteousness." And if this be so, "then should not those parts of Scripture which relate to civil government be examined and explained from the desk? . . . Civil tyranny is usually small in its beginning, like 'the drop of a bucket,' till at length, like a mighty torrent, or the raging waves of the sea, it bears down on all before it, and deluges whole countries and empires." Some would say later that this sermon was the first volley of the American Revolution, setting forth the intellectual and scriptural justification for rebellion against the Crown.[5]

FANNING THE FLAMES

Samuel Adams, a strict Calvinist who was a second cousin of John Adams and founder of the Sons of Liberty, was one of the first public-spirited citizens of Boston to recognize that a break with Britain was inevitable. His inspired talks and harangues to his fellow patriots grew more frequent and more impassioned with each passing day. A member of the Caucus Club, Adams spoke to all who would listen and worked tirelessly to push the people of Boston to action. As the most influential member of the Massachusetts legislature, he drafted protest documents, such as the Circular Letter of 1768, that denounced the Townshend Acts. He also wrote pamphlets and inflammatory newspaper editorials defending the rights of colonists.

Adams, who was the son of a prominent businessman and brewer, understood the power of theater to rouse people into action. He helped stage the Boston Tea Party and organized public demonstrations, including hanging in effigy the British governor and the colonial tax collector at the Liberty Tree, which was an ancient elm tree on the Boston Common.

Meanwhile, far from those pivotal events in Boston and other parts of New England, Patrick Henry was a member of the oldest legislature in the country, the Virginia House of Burgesses, which had been dissolved abruptly by English governor Lord Dunmore in 1774. The atmosphere in Virginia was very different from that in Boston or Philadelphia, but British demands were no less onerous there, and it was apparent that matters were coming to a head in Virginia too.

By March 23, 1775, when members of the assembly gathered privately to discuss the growing rumors of war and rebellion, a number of distinguished citizens spoke at length about the need for caution and humility. Patrick Henry listened in silence for some time. At last, when he could listen no more, he motioned to the president of the assembly for the right to speak, then he rose to his feet.

It is difficult to abbreviate his magnificent speech—it is so eloquent and powerful—but nothing better illustrates the original intent of the founders or the passion of their plea for justice than these historic words. Patrick Henry said:

> Mr. President, it is natural to man to indulge in the illusions of hope. We are apt to shut our eyes against a painful truth, and listen to the song of that siren till she transforms us into beasts. Is this the part of wise men, engaged in a great and arduous struggle for liberty? Are we disposed to be of the number of those who, having eyes, see not, and, having ears, hear not, the things which so nearly concern their temporal salvation? . . .
>
> If we wish to be free—if we mean to preserve inviolate those inestimable privileges for which we have been so long contending —if we mean not basely to abandon the noble struggle in which we have been so long engaged, and which we have pledged ourselves never to abandon until the glorious object of our contest shall be obtained—we must fight! I repeat it, sir, we must fight! An appeal to arms and to the God of hosts is all that is left us! They tell us, sir, that we are weak; unable to cope with so formidable an adversary. But when shall we be stronger? Will it be the next week, or the next year? Will it be when we are totally disarmed, and when a British guard shall be stationed in every house? Shall we gather strength by irresolution and inaction?
>
> Shall we acquire the means of effectual resistance by lying supinely on our backs and hugging the delusive phantom of hope, until our enemies shall have bound us hand and foot? Sir, we are not weak if we make a proper use of those means which the God of nature hath placed in our power. The millions of people, armed in the holy cause of liberty, and in such a country as that which we possess, are invincible by any force which our enemy can send against us. Besides, sir, we shall not fight our battles alone. There is a just God who presides over the destinies of nations, and who will

raise up friends to fight our battles for us. The battle, sir, is not to the strong alone; it is to the vigilant, the active, the brave. . . .

Gentlemen may cry, Peace, Peace—but there is no peace. The war is actually begun! The next gale that sweeps from the north will bring to our ears the clash of resounding arms! Our brethren are already in the field! Why stand we here idle? What is it that gentlemen wish? What would they have? Is life so dear, or peace so sweet, as to be purchased at the price of chains and slavery? Forbid it, Almighty God!

I know not what course others may take but as for me: Give me liberty or give me death.

It is reported that when Patrick Henry returned to his seat, a stunned silence hung over the room for several minutes. Then, slowly, one by one, the members of the house rose to their feet with the cry, "To arms! To arms!" on every lip. From that moment, there could be no denying that the American Revolution had finally and irrevocably come.

In order to deal with the growing restlessness, it was decided that each colony would dispatch delegates to Philadelphia to examine the issues in greater depth and try to bring closure to the issue. The first meeting of the Continental Congress ended inconclusively, as did the second. Each colony's wishes were seemingly different, but one thing was apparent: there was no way to avoid conflict with Great Britain. Once that fact was allowed, on June 10, 1776, a committee was chosen to write a summary of grievances—a document outlining in brief the reasons for separating from England. Five men were selected for the task: Benjamin Franklin of Pennsylvania, John Adams of Massachusetts, Thomas Jefferson of Virginia, Roger Sherman of Connecticut, and Robert Livingston of New York. Each provided input for the initial draft, but in the end it was agreed that Jefferson would compose the final version of the document.

Jefferson labored for two weeks on the declaration, but his first draft made no mention of the deeply held religious motivations of the colonists, and Adams insisted that this be added. Jefferson had said that the Americans were subject to "the laws of Nature and of Nature's God," but the committee felt this statement to be insufficient. Jefferson's sense of pride was wounded by what he perceived as heavy-handed editing of his work; but he was mollified, and eventually the draft was revised to include one of the most memorable paragraphs in the literature of freedom:

> We hold these truths to be self-evident, that all men are created equal, that they are endowed by their Creator with certain unalienable rights, that among these are life, liberty, and the pursuit of happiness. That to secure these rights, governments are instituted among men, deriving their just powers from the consent of the governed.

In subsequent deliberations, other members of the Continental Congress proposed adding further recognition of the religious dimensions of their undertaking. Thus they documented that they were "appealing to the Supreme Judge of the World for the rectitude of our intentions" and acting in "firm reliance on the protection of divine Providence."

Jefferson had also drawn on the Virginia Declaration of Rights, which was written by his friend George Mason and distributed in the first week of June 1776. In that document, Mason had said that "all men are by nature equally free and independent, and have certain inherent rights, of which, when they enter into a state of society, they cannot, by any compact, deprive or divest their posterity; namely, the enjoyment of life and liberty, with the means of acquiring and possessing property, and pursuing and obtaining happiness and safety." Jefferson's draft was more poetic and persuasive, but Mason had given him the inspiration.[6]

Eventually, and only after a series of colorful exchanges between Jefferson and Adams, the final draft of the Declaration of Independence was approved by all but Livingston, who decided he didn't want to be a part of the proceedings and returned to his family estate in New York. Members of the Congress debated the document, arguing over every item, particularly Jefferson's remarks about the evils of slavery. Southerners would not support those remarks, so further revisions were made. Then, on July 2, 1776, delegates of all the states except New York approved the new Declaration of Independence. John Adams wrote home to his wife, Abigail, saying that the second day of July would be forever remembered as the day America's liberty was gained. As it turned out, of course, the Declaration was actually approved and signed two days later.

THE ROAD TO FREEDOM

The road to freedom and independence, however, would be a perilous and unpredictable adventure for the patriots for years to come, and we cannot help but feel the passion and anxiety of that monumental predicament in the language of Jefferson's declaration. Separating from the mother country was difficult in itself, but how would the colonists explain this urge for freedom and independence? How would they present their case to the court of public opinion, to posterity, to future generations who would certainly look back and wonder what strange madness had overcome the colonists? This is the spirit that animates Jefferson's powerful words: a sense of their accountability to the eyes of history. To reply to King George and to those peering eyes, Jefferson writes:

> When in the course of human events, it becomes necessary for one people to dissolve the political bands which have connected them with another, and to assume among the powers of the earth, the separate and equal status to which the laws of nature and of nature's God entitle them, a decent respect to the opinions of mankind requires that they should declare the causes which impel them to the separation.

Just reading these words gives us a sense of the emotion that motivated our ancestors so many years ago. Yet the question hangs in the air: by what authority have you done this? By what right? Jefferson's answer to those haunting questions turns to the language of Samuel Rutherford and John Locke as he asserts that the rights of "life, liberty, and the pursuit of happiness" are, in fact, God-given and "unalienable."

In his statement of grievances, Jefferson rehearses "a long train of abuses and usurpations," describing the manner in which the colonists have suffered patiently in hopes that relief might come from the king. One by one, Jefferson lists twenty-eight grievances, solemnly, deliberately, and fully, emphasizing by sheer repetition and insistence that every effort to make peace had been rebuffed by the Crown and followed by insult and injury. Coming to his summation, Jefferson declares, "A prince, whose character is thus marked by every act which may define a tyrant, is unfit to be the ruler of a free people."

From this comes the actual declaration that "these United Colonies are, and of right ought to be Free and Independent States; and that they are Absolved from all Allegiance to the British Crown, and that all political connection between them and the State of Great Britain, is and ought to be totally dissolved." As a summary of the authority and guarantee of liberty on which they make such a declaration, the document says that "with a firm reliance on the protection of divine Providence, we mutually pledge to each other our Lives, our Fortunes, and our sacred Honor."

Surely King George could not have failed to feel the force of those words. Nothing could prevent him, of course, from sending his armies and navies to crush the rebels. But no one could have read those words without being moved, and the king must have sensed that this would be no easy victory. Today, in newly liberated countries around the world, and in many other lands still under the iron heel of dictators and tyrants of many creeds, the United States Declaration of Independence is revered as a sacred text. All across

Eastern Europe during the 1980s and '90s, men and women longing to breathe free carried copies of our Declaration in their pockets and purses as a silent witness to their aspirations and hopes.

In his essay "What I Saw in America," English author and broadcaster G. K. Chesterton observes, "America is the only nation in the world that is founded on a creed. That creed is set forth with dogmatic and even theological lucidity in the Declaration of Independence." No one reading the words of that august document can miss it: "We hold these truths to be self-evident, that all men are created equal, that they are endowed by their Creator with certain unalienable rights, that among these are life, liberty and the pursuit of happiness." Merely pausing to consider the long odds against the colonists in their confrontation with the mightiest army on earth, it's impossible to imagine that they could have won that contest were it not for the fact that God was on their side.

In his tracts *The Rights of the Colonists*, Samuel Adams wrote, "The right of freedom being a gift of God Almighty. . . . The rights of the colonists as Christians . . . may be best understood by reading and carefully studying the institutes of the Great Law Giver . . . which are to be found clearly written and promulgated in the New Testament." The colonists had placed their trust in that great hope, and God saw fit to miraculously grant their petitions. Later, John Quincy Adams, son of John Adams and the sixth president of the United States, would offer an apt assessment. He said, "The highest glory of the American Revolution was this: it connected in one indissoluble bond the principles of civil government with the principles of Christianity."

THE HIGHER LAW

It's important to know that the allegiance of the founders was not to king or congress or courts of law but to the one eternal God, who judges men and nations and sets at liberty the captives. The reason they were emboldened to cut their ties to Great Britain was that by a "train of usurpations" the Crown had violated the "laws of Nature and of Nature's God." The colonists certainly knew the term: they had read it in *Blackstone's Commentaries on the Law*. That book, published in 1765, sold more copies on this side of the Atlantic than the other, and Blackstone had defined the "law of nature" as "the will of God."

Had they not believed in a law that established God's justice among men, the signers of the Declaration would have risked their lives, fortunes, and sacred honor in vain. They paid a high price for their actions. Of the fifty-seven signers of the Declaration, nine were killed, two lost sons, five were taken prisoner by the British, twelve had their homes sacked or destroyed, and at least seventeen lost everything they owned and were branded as outlaws and traitors. Many who had been among the most prosperous in America were reduced to poverty because they dared to stand on principle. They willingly made the sacrifice and sustained their faith in the glorious cause of liberty, because they knew there was a "higher law."

The founders also understood the concept of original sin, that men do wrong because they are predisposed by nature to do so. Gouverneur Morris of New York, a signer of the Constitution, offered this assessment:

> The reflection and experience of many years have led me to consider the holy writings not only as the most authentic and instructive in themselves, but as the clue to all other history. They tell us what man is, and they alone tell us why he is what he is: a contradictory creature that seeing and approving of what is good, pursues and performs what is evil. All of private and of public life is there displayed. . . . From the same pure fountain of wisdom we learn that vice destroys freedom; that arbitrary power is founded on public immorality.

Morris and his colleagues deplored evil, but they were not shocked by it because they knew there is a higher law instituted by God that offers men a way of redemption. And, in any case, the courts had been instituted to keep the peace and preserve public order.

The belief in a higher law that compels even kings to obey goes still further back, having entered the Common Law at Runnymede in the twelfth century, when King John was forced to sign England's first declaration of liberties, the Magna Carta. That great charter proclaims, "The King himself ought not to be under a man but under God and under the law, because the law makes the king for there is no king where will governs and not law." In the charter's sixty-three clauses we read, "Know ye that we, in the presence of God, and for the salvation of our souls, and the souls of all our ancestors and heirs, and unto the honor of God and the advancement of Holy Church . . . have in the first place granted to God, and by this our present charter confirmed for us and our heirs forever." Here again was the recognition that God's authority is over all.

Decades after the Revolution, at a time when America stood on the brink of another great war, William Henry Seward, a member of Congress and later secretary of state under Lincoln, offered an eloquent tribute to this higher law. In one of his most eloquent speeches before Congress, Seward said, "There is a higher law than the Constitution, which regulates our authority over the domain, and devotes it to the same noble purposes. The territory is a part, no inconsiderable part, of the common heritage of mankind, bestowed upon them by the Creator of the universe. We are his stewards, and must so discharge our trust as to secure in the highest attainable degree their happiness."

Sadly, other philosophies and theories have crept into the public discourse over time, and the once-high ideals of the founders have been all but lost. As early as 1907, we could see signs of this erosion of ideals when Justice Charles Evans Hughes declared that "the Constitution is what the judges say it is." In his view, the Court of nine unelected judges was able to establish justice, ensure domestic tranquility, provide for the common defense, and promote the general welfare all on their own, and by any means necessary. Those who hold comparable views today apparently see themselves as a higher law than the codified laws of the land.

The liberal media play a big part in the undoing of justice as well. As columnist Thomas Sowell writes, "One of the reasons judicial activists get away with ignoring the law and imposing their own pet notions instead is that much of the mainstream media treat the actions of judges as automatically legitimate and all criticism of them as undermining the rule of law." He goes on to say, "The time is long overdue to stop regarding judges as little tin gods who can do no wrong. An independent judiciary does not mean a judiciary independent of the law. If it does, then we can forget about being a free and democratic nation. We are just the serfs of whoever happens to be on the bench."[7]

DISORDER IN THE COURT

Nowhere are the distortions of America's modern justice system more apparent than in the statements of those, like former justices William Brennan and Thurgood Marshall, who preferred to ignore the beliefs of the founders and the sacrifices they made. In 1963, Brennan said, "A too literal quest for the advice of the founding fathers seems to me futile and misdirected." And Marshall said in 1987, "I do not believe that the meaning of the Constitution was forever fixed at the Philadelphia convention. Nor do I find the wisdom, foresight and sense of justice exhibited by the framers particularly profound. To the contrary, the government they devised was defective from the start." One has to wonder how men who held such contempt for American traditions and values ever arrived at the High Court.

We need to thank God that this nation was founded at a time when there was still a consensus among people about what is good and just and true. Sadly, that consensus no longer exists on a broad scale, and we often feel helpless in the face of the tyranny that now passes for justice. What we recognize today as the clash of cultures— the culture wars in America—is actually a pitched battle between those who still believe that God is the Source of truth and justice, and those who believe that man is all the god we need.[8] It is a struggle, as the apostle Paul phrased it, "against principalities, against powers, against the rulers of the darkness of this age, against spiritual hosts of wickedness in the heavenly places" (Ephesians 6:12).

The First Amendment to the Constitution, written by James Madison as a safeguard of essential liberties, has become a club in the hands of today's judges used to silence religious expression. Throughout the last century, liberals on the High Court took Jefferson's phrase "a wall of separation between church and state" and consciously erected a fortress against the free exercise of religion. Before we acquiesce to this act of bad faith, we ought to pause to consider what Jefferson actually said in his letter to the Danbury Baptists. He wrote:

> Believing with you that religion is a matter which lies solely between man and his God; that he owes account to none other for his faith or his worship; that the legitimate powers of the government reach actions only, and not opinions, I contemplate with sovereign reverence that act of the whole American people which declared that their legislature should "make no law respecting an establishment of religion, or prohibiting the free exercise thereof," thus building a wall of separation between church and state.

Jefferson then concluded his letter with the words, "I reciprocate your kind prayers for the protection and blessings of the common Father and Creator of man, and tender you for yourselves and your religious association, assurances of my high respect and esteem."

Clearly, these are not the words of a man who meant to shove religious observance out of public places. The clear implication of

Jefferson's statement is that the federal government may not create a national church, as in England. This letter was his assurance, as president, to Baptist believers that their right of independence would be respected. Subsequently, in a letter to a Presbyterian clergyman, Jefferson said, "Certainly, no power to prescribe any religious exercise or to assume authority and religious discipline has been delegated to the general government. It must then rest with the states as far as it can be in any human authority."

Jefferson was certainly not neutral in the matter of religion. After all, he used federal monies to hold religious services, to build Christian churches, and to support missions to the Indians. The only limitation on government was prescribing a particular denomination or hampering the unfettered proclamation of the gospel. One of the first acts of the first Congress was to appoint Rev. William Linn as chaplain of the House of Representatives. Linn was paid a salary of five hundred dollars out of federal funds. James Madison, the principal author of the Constitution and the First Amendment, served on the committee that hired Linn. Immediately after adoption of the First Amendment, Congress called for a "national day of prayer and thanksgiving" to honor the Author of liberty.

A SPIRITUAL CHALLENGE

Many years later, in a commemorative service at Plymouth Rock, on December 22, 1820, the great orator Daniel Webster challenged his fellow citizens not to forget the religious nature of our nation's origins. He said, "Our fathers were brought hither by their high veneration for the Christian religion. They journeyed by its light and labored in its hope. They sought to incorporate its principles with the elements of their society and to diffuse its influence through all their institutions, civil, political, or literary. Let us cherish these sentiments, and extend this influence still more widely, in the full conviction that that is the happiest society which partakes in the highest degree of the mild and peaceful spirit of Christianity."

That challenge still stands. But how will America respond? Are we still capable of recognizing our debt to those principles? Are we capable of renewing our great heritage and extending its influence in society? English jurist Lord Devlin said, "History shows that the loosening of moral bonds is the first stage of disintegration." Others, from Edward Gibbon to Francis Schaeffer, have said much the same, and there's no doubt they're right.

As we review in these pages the many corruptions that are eating away at American society in this first decade of the twenty-first century, we can hardly deny that signs of disintegration are all around us: the assault on marriage and family, the deregulation of pornography and the celebration of homosexuality, the assault on religious expression in every public place, as well as the attempt to take God out of the Pledge of Allegiance and to scrub His name and the Ten Commandments from our public buildings and monuments. And this is all being done in the name of liberty and law?

In light of all these warning signs, we can only come to one conclusion: we are engaged in a struggle of enormous spiritual proportions. The spiritual nature of America's founding is only too apparent. The hand of providence was on the founders at every step. No ordinary army could have conquered the British legions unless providence had intervened. George Washington, the hero of York-town, surely believed that, and he said as much.

But today we are engaged in a contest of wills and a struggle for survival of even greater consequence, and the outcome of this clash is very uncertain. Toward the end of the eighteenth century, Ezra Stiles, one of the great former presidents of my alma mater, Yale University, made this charge: "The United States are under peculiar obligations to become a holy people unto the Lord our God." Stiles knew what he was talking about. Whether this nation can restore justice, overcome its enemies, and continue to prosper in the years to come will depend on whether we are willing to accept Dr. Stiles's challenge.

I believe this with all my heart. If we are able to restore the foundations of liberty and law in America and return to the bedrock of devotion our forefathers enjoyed, then nothing can harm us. But if we merely surrender to lawlessness and to the godless moral deregulation that has made a mockery of everything the founders stood for, then we cannot hope to survive. The original intent of the founders can be read on every page of the history they gave us. They left us a clear prescription for national success. But do we still have the courage and the discipline to make their principles our own?

Posterity will judge our answer.

3

DEFYING
THE WILL OF THE PEOPLE

The fabric of American empire ought to rest on the solid basis of the consent of the people. The streams of national power ought to flow immediately from that pure, original fountain of all legitimate authority.

—ALEXANDER HAMILTON
FEDERALIST 22 (1787)

From the earliest days of the Republic, Americans have had a high view of justice and the law. The founders were very aware of their obligation to create a government that would outlast them, that would be just and fair—"a government of laws and not of men" that would endure for centuries to come. They did not take this trust lightly. As students of both ancient and modern history, they often looked to great minds of the past, as well as to the Bible, for moral guidance and for a practical philosophy of jurisprudence upon which to build a new nation.

Roman statesman and orator Cicero defined justice this way: "Law is the highest reason, implanted in Nature, which commands what ought to be done and forbids the opposite. This reason, when firmly fixed and fully developed in the human mind, is Law." One hundred and fifty years later, the apostle Paul put forth a similar view when he told the Christians at Rome that "the requirements of the law are written on their hearts" (Romans 2:15 NIV). He said that the invisible attributes of God, which lead to righteousness and purity before the law, are clearly seen in the laws of nature, so that no one can claim immunity by virtue of ignorance (see Romans 2:14–15).

Thomas Jefferson, who admired Cicero's wisdom and his aristocratic country life, was familiar with both of these quotations, as were an astonishing number of the founders. Contrary to the revisionist history being taught in today's classrooms, the first settlers were not ignorant rustics or country bumpkins. There were a great many who pursued common trades, but as Oxford historian A. L. Rowse reports, among the first two thousand families who came to the New World, there were 138 graduates of Oxford and Cambridge Universities—a group that social critic Martin Gross has called "the largest concentration of brains in one place in the history of mankind." The children of these educated men and women would become, as Alexis de Tocqueville phrased it, the beacon that lit the New World.[1]

As the young nation grew and families began moving westward, most Americans had great respect for education. They wanted their children to be competent and competitive, and to know not just the three Rs but the Holy Bible and other moral literature. On the other hand, some pioneers felt that too much book learning could be counterproductive, often making a man unfit for the practical and harsh realities of life on the frontier. But, virtually without exception, these early settlers were schooled in the Bible. They knew right from wrong. Like Abraham Lincoln, they understood the importance of justice and the law, and even in the remotest villages they had a code of morals that allowed them to prosper and maintain order.

The first American settlers brought their ideas of right and wrong with them. There wasn't much in the way of codified law in the beginning. There were no police departments in this country until the mid-nineteenth century. For many years, the law of the land was simply understood, based on common sense, English common law, the Ten Commandments, and New Testament teachings on morality and good behavior. During the colonial period, law enforcement and adjudication had been managed mainly by the British. Later, as distinctively American conventions were still being established, the justice system was often on an ad hoc basis. It wasn't until several years after the Revolution that a legitimate court system began to take shape.

The British had seen America primarily as an economic resource—a colony that produced wealth for those who funded the great trading companies. Consequently, British justice in the colonies often relied upon martial law, along with edicts from Parliament or the king. Later, enforcement was provided by volunteers, wardens, or local constables and sheriffs, along with the cooperation of citizens whose primary occupations were normally something other than law enforcement. When the settlers grew impatient with the protection they received for their families and property from these local officials, they sometimes turned to vigilance committees, which, especially on the frontier, acted as judge, jury, and executioner. Thus grew the legends of the Wild West.

THE JUSTICE SYSTEM

The American people were entirely capable of establishing local policies, but something more was needed, and that something came on March 4, 1789, when the newly created government of the United States officially opened its doors for business. On that day, the first legislature of thirteen representatives and eight senators was seated. The presidential inauguration had also been scheduled for that day, but neither house of Congress had enough members present for a quorum, which meant that the electoral ballots from the recent elections could not be counted. Since President

Washington needed time to make the long journey from his home in Virginia to the new federal capital of New York City, the inauguration was postponed until April 30.

In the interval, Congress debated such questions as what to call the new chief executive. Would it be "Your Excellency," "Your Highness," or perhaps "Your Republican Majesty"? It was finally decided that the president would be addressed as "Mr. President" or simply "Sir." George Washington wanted no hint of English aristocracy, and for the most part his Federalist colleagues agreed. This and many other matters were eventually ironed out, and the general framework of the system the founders created is still in place today.

Since Congress had no formal rules to follow, they borrowed from the procedures of the English Parliament. The president had no staff, no bureaucracy, no policies to administer, and no one was quite sure what jobs would need to be created. Secretary of State Thomas Jefferson hired a couple of clerks. But the most pressing matter was the fact that the Constitution required Congress to create a federal judiciary, and it was up to the newly installed senators and representatives to decide what the judiciary would entail. The Constitution had named only one court, the Supreme Court, along with "such inferior courts as the Congress may from time to time ordain and establish." From there the congressmen were on their own.

Once matters of staff, workspace, and statutory procedures were settled, the first major act of Congress was to create the federal court system, which they did by means of the Judiciary Act of 1789. According to Article II, Section 2 of the Constitution, justices of the Supreme Court were to be appointed by the president and confirmed by the Senate, but the Constitution did not stipulate the size of the Court. It was eventually decided that six was a good number, and that's where it remained until 1863, when four new seats were added. Three years later the Court was reduced to its current size of nine justices.

Under the Judiciary Act, Congress established two lower levels of federal courts. There were to be thirteen district courts and three circuit courts to hear appeals from the district courts. The act also provided that the federal judiciary would have power of review over actions of the state legislatures, meaning that acts of the state governments shown to be in violation of the Constitution or other federal statutes could be overturned.

The Judiciary Act also established the office of attorney general, but it wasn't until 1870 that Congress finally created what we recognize today as the primary agency of justice in America, the Department of Justice (DOJ). The essential purpose of the DOJ was to serve as the legal office of government. Attached to the executive branch, the DOJ is headed by the attorney general, who is the cabinet officer responsible for enforcement of federal laws and who represents the federal government in all legal actions.

The attorney general advises the president and other department heads. He supervises the office of solicitor general, the FBI, and six other offices, including the criminal, antitrust, civil rights, tax, and land and natural resources divisions. The DOJ was also responsible for the Federal Bureau of Prisons, the Board of Parole, the Immigration and Naturalization Service, the Board of Immigration Appeals, the Drug Enforcement Administration, and the Law Enforcement Assistance Administration. Since the 9/11 terror attacks, many of these offices have been reorganized or combined under a new Office of Homeland Security, the configuration of which is still in transition.

Most of the time, cases come to the Supreme Court by means of a writ of certiorari, which is an appeal to be heard by the High Court from a litigant who has lost a case in a lower court. Approximately 90 percent of the cases heard by the Court come in this way; however, of the approximately seven thousand writs that reach the Supreme Court each year, only about one hundred will actually be accepted for hearing. The Court has absolute and final discretion over the cases it hears and makes its selection generally based on the extent to which the case involves a question of law that may help to resolve other constitutional issues. At least, that's the reasoning.

Under Court rules, certiorari is granted only "where there are special and important reasons therefor." Among these reasons is when two federal courts of appeals or two district courts have rendered conflicting rulings. In some cases, the Supreme Court will take a case when a state court or a federal appellate court has passed on an important matter of law on which the Supreme Court has not yet made a pronouncement, or perhaps when a federal court has departed from recognized standards of law in rendering a judgment.

The Supreme Court is in session from October through April each year and will hear up to four oral arguments per day, three days a week, in two-week intervals. Major decisions are sometimes rendered as late as June or July, and like Congress, which may be called back into special session by matters of great urgency, the Supreme Court may be called on to decide issues of consequence at other times as well. This happened in 1971 when the Court heard arguments concerning the Pentagon Papers, and again in 1974 with regard to the release of President Nixon's private tape recordings. Prior to oral arguments, attorneys for both sides submit written briefs to the Court. These may be supported by any number of amicus curiae (friend of the court) briefs submitted by parties who wish to go on record in support of one side or the other.

HOW THE COURT WORKS

During the past several years, I've attended sessions of the Supreme Court when cases were being argued by the American Center for Law and Justice (ACLJ). In *Bray v. Alexandria Women's Health* (1993), for example, chief counsel Jay Sekulow and his team challenged a group of abortion supporters who claimed that a pro-life protest at an abortion clinic was "discrimination against women." In that case, the

Supreme Court sustained the ACLJ argument, guaranteeing that pro-life demonstrators would be free to express their views without the threat of censorship or recrimination through the misuse of federal antidiscrimination laws. In the majority opinion, Justice Scalia specifically noted that opposition to abortion does not constitute discrimination against women; thus rejecting the entire argument raised by the National Organization for Women and others.

The ACLJ was founded in 1990 for this purpose, in order to counteract the insidious advances of groups such as the American Civil Liberties Union, People for the American Way, and other left-wing organizations that were successfully attacking and dismantling the nation's heritage of faith. There was no one at that time with the capacity to stand up against these anti-Christian bullies, so the ACLJ was created to restore balance to these important debates. Within the first few years of its existence, the ACLJ was recognized as one of the most successful public-interest law firms in the country and has been winning cases in courts at all levels that would have been lost just a few years ago.

Along with its activities in the courts, the ACLJ was also designed as an educational organization dedicated to advancing the cause of religious liberty, so that's another aspect of what Jay Sekulow and his team are doing. During the past fifteen years, the ACLJ has defended the rights of students and adult believers, the unborn, the elderly and infirm, and the rights of parents and the traditional two-parent family. On several occasions, members of the ACLU have candidly admitted that they've never faced such a fierce and well-armed opponent.

In the case of *Lamb's Chapel v. Center Moriches School District* (1993), the ACLJ challenged a local school board that would not rent its facilities to a neighborhood church because of the "religious content" of the church's message. The ruling in that case guaranteed religious groups "equal access" to public facilities. All in all, the ACLJ has a remarkable track record, particularly in cases involving equal access in public schools. In cases where students were told they couldn't have Bible clubs in their schools, or when Bible clubs were denied equal treatment with other student groups, the ACLJ has stepped in to defend the believers' rights. This usually means taking on liberal activist groups such as the ACLU, People for the American Way, Planned Parenthood, and others. But that has never been a deterrent to Jay and his team.

No matter how familiar anyone may be with the Court itself, the proceedings are always somber and very impressive—they're designed to be that way. As I said earlier, the Court loves to create an aura of mystery. The justices first enter the spacious robing room behind the bench, where they greet one another with a traditional handshake, and then they await the marshal's announcement of their arrival. The courtroom, with its grand marble columns, elegant pews, and velvet curtains, has the feel of a magnificent cathedral. Visitors whisper in respectful tones as they await the justices' arrival.

When the nine are about to enter the chamber, a police officer calls for quiet, saying, "All rise!" The marshal raps his gavel on the bench and pronounces the solemn ritual:

The honorable, the chief justice and associate justices of the Supreme Court of the United States! *Oyez, oyez, oyez!* All persons having business before the honorable, the Supreme Court of the United States are admonished to draw near and give their attention, for the Court is now sitting. God save the United States and this honorable Court!

With the words of that ancient prayer still in the air, the justices enter the great chamber and proceed from behind the red velvet curtain in groups of three, from the left, center, and right side of the bench, regaled in their black robes. The chief justice sits in the middle, and the associate justices take their seats in strict order of seniority, on either side of the chief justice.

During oral arguments, which are generally limited to thirty minutes for each side, the justices generally ask probing (and sometimes confrontational) questions about the issues involved. The Court's most important work begins afterward, usually from one to six days later, when they meet in conference to vote on the case. The justices meet privately, behind locked conference room doors, and with no other staff members present, to deliberate and vote.

During the conference, the chief justice presents the cases for discussion. After each justice, in order of seniority, has expressed his or her candid opinion on the case in question, there will generally be a sense of "the will of the Court." The chief justice makes a tally of pro and con votes, and then he assigns the task of writing the Court's majority opinion to one of the justices, or perhaps to himself. As a rule, the justices never comment publicly on their opinions after they've been announced, so all the relevant legal implications of a case must be inferred from what appears in these lengthy documents. In some cases concurring opinions will be read as well, by those justices who have another perspective on the case that they want to be heard. Unless the verdict is unanimous, there will generally be at least one dissenting opinion.

Whenever the chief justice is in the majority, he may either write the Court's opinion himself or assign it to one of the associate justices. If he is in dissent, however, he will select the most senior justice in the majority to write the opinion. Chief Justice Earl Warren, who presided over the most liberal period in the history of the Court, wrote the majority opinion in many highly controversial cases, including those involving school desegregation, reapportionment of Congress, a defendant's right against self-incrimination, and a defendant's right to counsel during police interrogation.

Announcement of the Court's finding is done in a public hearing that may take place anywhere from a few weeks to six months after oral arguments are made. As in all sessions of the Court, the announcement of decisions is also done in a formal and stately manner. The justice who has written the majority opinion (which becomes the official opinion of the Court) delivers an oral summary from the bench.

THE RIGHT OF JUDICIAL REVIEW

The first session of the Supreme Court took place in February 1790, and for the first ten years the caseload was very light. But the case that most people refer to as the most far-reaching in the Court's 215-year history was heard in 1803: *Marbury v. Madison.* This case is important not because of the issues involved but because of what the case led to: the right of judicial review. The issue at law began during the final hours of President John Adams's administration. Adams, a member of the Federalist party, wasn't thrilled to be succeeded by his intellectual sparring partner and political adversary, Thomas Jefferson, who was a member of the Democratic-Republican Party. So, in order to seed Jefferson's administration with as many judicial appointees from his own party as possible, Adams made several "midnight appointments."

One of those was William Marbury, a prosperous land speculator from Maryland, whom Adams named to serve as justice of the peace for Washington, D.C. Adams signed the documents, but subsequent to his leaving office several letters of appointment, including Marbury's, were never physically delivered. Chances are they were simply overlooked during the transition of administrations. However, when Jefferson took office in March 1801, he instructed Secretary of State James Madison to ignore all those commissions. When William Marbury learned of this, he took his case to the Supreme Court, asking for a writ of mandamus, which is a direct order issued by the Court requiring Madison to carry out his duties.

Chief Justice John Marshall, sometimes referred to as simply "the great chief justice," decided that the Court would consider three questions in the case: Did Marbury have a right to the commission?

Did the law actually give him a means to obtain his commission? And could the Supreme Court, with original jurisdiction in Marbury's case, issue a writ of mandamus? When the opinion was announced, Marshall said that Marbury was, in fact, due his commission. They also decided that the writ of mandamus, which the Court was authorized to issue under Section 13 of the Judiciary Act of 1789, would be the proper legal procedure to follow.

However, to everyone's surprise, they said that according to Article III, Section 2, Clause 2 of the Constitution, the Court did not have original jurisdiction. Therefore, Section 13 of the Judiciary Act of 1789 violated the Constitution, and, in consequence, the law enacted by Congress was unconstitutional. Marbury did not receive his commission because the federal statute by which he brought his case to the Court was automatically nullified. The most far-reaching implication of all this was that, unless challenged by the president or Congress, a previously unimaginable precedent had been established whereby the Court would have the power of "judicial review" over all acts of Congress.

This means that laws duly enacted by the elected representatives of the people could be struck down by nine unelected justices on the basis of their own authority and judgment. In due time, this would come to mean that the Supreme Court could overrule the chief executive, and even make law from the bench essentially created out of whole cloth, as in a number of outrageous cases in the twentieth century that I will discuss in greater detail in the next chapter.

Needless to say, the *Marbury* decision has had an enormous impact not only on the role of the Court but also on the relationship of Congress and the Court. After *Marbury,* the Court didn't declare any more acts of Congress unconstitutional until 1857, when their ruling in the *Dred Scott* case declared the Missouri Compromise of 1820 unconstitutional. That was a very troubling case in many respects, but since that time the Court has often ventured into uncharted water in the name of "judicial review" and has continued to expand its authority not only beyond anything the founders envisioned but beyond anything the Constitution allows.

The legitimate decision in the *Marbury* case, and in other cases since that time, should have been to remand any discrepancies in the language of a particular law or act of Congress back to the Congress for correction or revision. Legislation is the duty of Congress, not the courts. If the Supreme Court, on review of a particular case, found errors in the way a bill was constructed or in the manner of execution of a law, then it should be the responsibility of Congress to address the problem and resolve it.[2] But that was not Justice Marshall's approach.

There are many permutations and extenuations to all of this, but one thing we do know is that Marshall's influence was larger than life, both then and now. As one writer said, Marshall's power to persuade was due in large part to his "political canniness, disarming charm, and a riveted focus on his unvarying long-term strategic objective: establishing the supremacy of the federal judiciary." In other words, Marshall was never content for the federal judiciary and the Supreme Court to be, as Alexander Hamilton described it, "the least dangerous branch" of government. In Federalist 78, the framers said that "the judiciary is beyond comparison the weakest of the three departments of power." But that was not Marshall's view.

When Marshall took over in 1801, each of the six justices wrote his own opinion for each case, but Marshall changed that. He wanted the Court to speak with one voice. In his first three years on the bench, Marshall decided forty-two cases. In every case, the Court's opinion was unanimous, and Marshall wrote every opinion himself. In *Gibbons v. Ogden* (1824), he nullified a commercial agreement between the state of New York and Robert Fulton's steamship company, rewriting the authority the Constitution gives to Congress to regulate interstate commerce. In *McCulloch v. Maryland* (1819), Marshall created the "doctrine of implied powers," giving the federal government authority over the states and chipping away at the constitutional guarantee of states' rights contained in the Tenth Amendment.

INTO STORMY WATERS

In the post-Civil War period, the Court waded into other even more controversial issues dealing with state regulatory authority and the due process provisions of the Fourteenth Amendment. As the industrial might of the nation continued to grow and prosper during the late nineteenth and early twentieth centuries, there were more and more cases before the Court focused on modifying the powers of Congress and regulating interstate commerce. The most serious challenge facing the Court, however, would come in the aftermath of the stock market crash of 1929 and the onset of the Great Depression.

In his efforts to control the effects of the Depression and provide relief for the millions who were suddenly out of work, President Franklin D. Roosevelt set out to create a host of government agencies to deal with the problems. We know now that the experiment pushed the nation down a dangerous road toward socialism. Roosevelt began by regulating business, investment, and banking practices, then he added wage and price supports to stabilize production and assist the farmers. During the next four years, Congress created the Public Works Administration, the Works Progress Administration, and the Civilian Conservation Corps to provide jobs for displaced workers. The Social Security Administration, established in 1935, provided unemployment insurance and old-age pensions.

Roosevelt's New Deal did, in fact, stimulate the economy; but at the outset of his second term, the nation discovered that this president had even bolder plans up his sleeve—ideas that pushed the nation much closer to state socialism than they were willing to go. Between 1936 and 1939, Roosevelt ran into nothing but obstacles, both in Congress and the courts. When his National Industrial

Recovery Act and Agricultural Adjustment Act were blocked by the Supreme Court in 1937, he came up with an outlandish scheme.

Since the number of justices wasn't specified by the Constitution, Roosevelt asked Congress to increase the size from nine to fifteen justices. The purpose of Roosevelt's plan was to pack the Court with handpicked judges who would take his side in legal disputes. There were supporters and defenders on both sides. But after much debate, Congress refused. The pretext on which the president had made his pitch directly to the American people—that the Court was over-worked and needed help—was proved to be false, and there the matter died.

Or so it seemed for a time. In fact, during the years immediately following the court-packing scheme, the Supreme Court suddenly began rubber-stamping most of Roosevelt's programs. Their decision in *National Labor Relations Board v. Jones & Laughlin Steel Corporation* (1937) apparently convinced some justices who had resisted Roosevelt's agenda that the commerce clause, in Article I, Section 8 of the Constitution, gave them power to regulate all business that affected interstate commerce. From that time on, the Court ruled consistently against business and in favor of big government programs. In fact, it wasn't until the attack on Pearl Harbor on December 7, 1941, and America's entry into World War II, that the emphasis began to shift.

Charles Evans Hughes, who was promoted to chief justice in 1930, was both friend and nemesis to Roosevelt. When Hughes retired in 1941, he was succeeded during the Truman era by Chief Justices Harlan F. Stone and Fred Vinson. Then in 1953, President Dwight Eisenhower made one of the most contentious judicial appointments in history, later admitting that it was the worst decision of his career.[3] He appointed the former governor of California, Earl Warren, who served as chief justice from 1953 to 1969 and ran the Court during the era of civil rights and the most liberal epoch in the history of the Court. The most far-reaching ruling of the period, *Brown v. Board of Education* (1954), ended segregation in the public schools but became a flashpoint for a very public debate over control of the public schools: a battle that was waged in the media and in riots coast to coast throughout the following decade.

In a recent assessment of the *Brown* decision, columnist Thomas Sowell observes that the Court's reasoning in that case was based not so much on real issues confronting black students in the public schools but on a sort of wishful utopian idealism. Of even greater concern is the way that case set a pattern for the judicial activism that continues to this day. Sowell writes:

> The flimsy and cavalier reasoning used by the Supreme Court, which based its decision on grounds that would hardly sustain a conviction for jay-walking, set a pattern of judicial activism that has put American law in disarray on all sorts of issues that extend far beyond racial cases. The pretense that the Court was interpreting the Constitution of the United States added insult to injury. The Court got away with this, despite some calls for impeachment, because it was outlawing a set of racial practices that the country as a whole found abhorrent. If the Justices took a few liberties with the law and the facts, who cared?[4]

Even by the simpler standards of the 1950s, the Court was known for its liberal activism and was seemingly above approach. Today, however, we can see how far the Court's logic has taken us. As distinguished African-American scholar Thomas Sowell concludes, "If the Justices took a few liberties with the law and the facts, who cared?" After half a century of unbridled judicial activism on many fronts, we now know that victims of frivolous lawsuits and violent crime care, among others. And restoring law to our courts may take another 50 years—if it can be done at all."[5] As we've seen in so many cases, it's often under the banner of the noblest of causes that the greatest of mischief has been done.

In *Baker v. Carr* (1962), a Supreme Court composed of nine

lawyers, none of whom had ever served as a judge at any level, went even further in regulating the states by ordering the reapportionment of the state legislatures. The Constitution requires a census every ten years to determine how many seats each state will have in the House of Representatives. It says nothing, however, about the apportionment of districts, since this is not a federal issue. However, in *Baker* and in *Reynolds v. Sims* (1964), the Court established the so-called one-man-one-vote principle, by which states were told to make certain that electoral districts were of approximately equal size, in terms of population.

There is no better example of the Court acting as an unelected legislature than the case of *Miranda v. Arizona* (1966), in which the Warren Court required police officers, regardless of the particular circumstances or the nature of the crime, to inform suspects of their "rights" before interrogating them. In that case, twenty-three-year-old Ernesto Miranda, an uneducated drifter, kidnapped and raped an eighteen-year-old girl. Later, at the police station, the victim picked Miranda from a lineup, and he was interrogated.

After two hours, Miranda gave a detailed oral confession and signed a statement admitting the crime. Miranda was convicted by a jury. But when his appeal reached the Supreme Court, Chief Justice Earl Warren wrote the majority opinion, which held that evidence obtained during interrogation is inadmissible unless the perpetrator has first been informed of his or her "rights." The Court provided no option for law enforcement to correct procedural errors or to ensure that a known criminal was not mischievously set loose on society. Instead, it *excluded* all evidence obtained by police and demanded that the suspect be released.

There was an excellent chance to revisit this issue and correct the excesses of the Warren Court in 2000, when *Dickerson v. U.S.* came to the Court on certiorari. In that case, a bank robber who confessed to police and led them to his accomplices, appealed his conviction on the grounds that he had confessed prior to being read his Miranda rights. Predictably, the Court voted 7–2 to uphold *Miranda,* but not without dissent. Professor Paul Cassell, who submitted an amicus brief in the case, pointed out that more than seventy thousand violent criminal cases go unsolved each year because of this rule. The problem, Cassell said, is the exclusionary rule of the *Miranda* decision, which throws out hard evidence simply because a procedural error was made.[6] In a just system, guilt should weigh more heavily than technicalities. But the Court was not swayed.

Writing in dissent to the *Dickerson* ruling, Justice Scalia pointed out, "There is a world of difference . . . between compelling a suspect to incriminate himself and preventing him from foolishly doing so of his own accord." In other words, the only logical basis for the Court's actions in upholding *Miranda* was to prevent criminals from foolishly incriminating themselves, and that should not be the Court's concern. By such logic, criminals are set free to commit more crimes, and they almost always do. Whether or not reading a suspect his rights is a good idea, *Miranda* is clearly Court-made law that involves no act of Congress, no statute of a state legislature, and no remedial processes. The "least dangerous" branch of government has taken on the role of Congress, once again, and ordered federal, state, and local law enforcement to do whatever nine unelected judges demand.

DEPENDING ON PRECEDENT

The doctrine of stare decisis (meaning "to stand by decided matters") is one of the most ancient principles of law. By design and by mandate of the Constitution, the courts are not lawmaking entities. Courts interpret laws and offer advice on principles that ought to be considered in the legislative process. By looking at case law and by reviewing the policies by which other courts have decided important issues at various levels, attorneys have a better sense of how to approach the issues—and, more importantly, judges have grounds for rendering their opinions. That's how it's supposed to be. But, sadly, that's not the way it is anymore. Far too often, today's Supreme Court decisions are out of step with the will of the people, reading more like something from the legislative branch than the judicial one.

Since *Marbury v. Madison,* the floodgates of moral relativism have been thrown wide open. Looking back at cases such as *Brown v. Board of Education, Miranda v. Arizona,* and *Gideon v. Wainwright* (1963)—a case that pushed the Fourteenth Amendment's guarantee of due process to all new limits—they seem more like test cases. As controversial as those decisions have been through the years, it's tempting to believe that justices were really testing to see how far they could go without getting caught. Judging from what we've seen from cases such as *Lawrence v. Texas* (2003) and *Newdow v. U.S. Congress* (2002), the worst may be yet to come.

One of the somber side effects of the *Brown* decision was forced busing, which destroyed schools and communities, further enflamed racial tensions, and led to "white flight" and other urban problems. The underlying principle of that decision was sound, declaring that blacks and whites ought to have equal access to the public schools in this country. But the means of implementation have not always been appropriate and have led to a dramatic shift in the racial makeup of not only the public schools but of communities all across America.

One of the most pernicious, unethical, and ungodly rulings in the history of the United States (if not in the history of mankind) were the Court's rulings in *Roe v. Wade* (1973) and its companion case, *Doe v. Bolton* (1973). I'm convinced history will one day regard these cases on the same level as the infamous *Dred Scott* decision of 1857, which continued the practice of slavery. In the first chapter, I spoke about the flawed ruling of the Warren Court in *Engel v. Vitale* (1962) and *Murray v. Curlett* (1963), and I will come back to them again later. The animosity of the liberal, activist Supreme Court to the free exercise of religion became supremely clear in those and related cases. By judicial fiat, three hundred years of history and the beliefs of the overwhelming majority of the American people were nullified and rejected. The evil of the *Roe* decision, even by that standard, is unrivaled.

President Reagan attempted to push through an amendment to reverse the *Roe* decision during his two terms in the White House, but the outcry from the Left—especially the howls of the media—short-circuited the process. There were a few judicial victories during the Reagan years, however. The Court upheld the principle of seniority over racial quotas in promotions in the case of *Firefighters v. Stotts* (1984); and in *Lynch v. Donnelly* (1984), citizens of Pawtucket, Rhode Island, won the right to have a Nativity scene in the town's public Christmas display.

Furthermore, *Miranda's* exclusionary rule, which prevents police from using evidence obtained without a warrant, or even evidence discovered by accident during an investigation, was relaxed in certain types of cases. In *United States v. Leon* and *Nix v. Williams* (1984), the Court allowed evidence that comes to light after the fact or by nonstandard means to be admitted in some cases. These were important victories for law enforcement, in part because these rulings were so contrary to the liberal, anti-law enforcement agenda of the Warren Court.

The brooding darkness that has hovered over the Court and the nation ever since Justice Blackmun's tragic ruling in *Roe v. Wade* has only grown darker and more oppressive with time. This fact has not been lost on Norma McCorvey, the plaintiff in that case, who is now a dynamic pro-life activist working to overturn the *Roe* decision. Norma stunned the pro-abortion world when she became a Christian in 1995 and described the "pro-choice" movement as a web of "lies and deception." She has said more recently, "I am dedicated to spending the rest of my life undoing the law that bears my name. I would like nothing more than to have this law overturned."

Chief Justice Warren Burger succeeded Earl Warren in 1969 and was succeeded, in turn, by William Rehnquist, who was promoted by President Reagan from associate to chief justice. For many Court watchers, this was a positive note. For those who supported the idea of judicial restraint, there was reason to hope that Rehnquist might be a moderating influence on the leftist bias of the Court. Unfortunately, there's no reason yet for rejoicing. Many had thought that the retirement of justices Lewis Powell, William Brennan, and Thurgood Marshall would provide the long-hoped-for opportunity for Presidents Reagan and Bush Sr. to appoint conservatives who would be true to their charge. In fact, two of those appointments, Antonin Scalia in 1986 and Clarence Thomas in 1991, were well worth the wait. But others have been disappointing.

Sandra Day O'Connor was named as the first female justice of the Supreme Court by Ronald Reagan in 1981. Anthony Kennedy was appointed in 1988, and David Souter was named to the Court by George H. W. Bush in 1990. Many of the decisions from these justices have stunned conservatives and the American people in general. Their rulings are certainly inconsistent with the principles of the presidents who appointed them.

A CHANGE OF PHILOSOPHY

Part I, Article XXX, of the Massachusetts Constitution, written in 1780, makes this declaration: "In the government of this commonwealth, the legislative department shall never exercise the executive and judicial powers, or either of them: the executive shall never exercise the legislative and judicial powers, or either of them: the judicial shall never exercise the legislative and executive powers, or either of them: to the end it may be a government of laws and not of men." This is very much what the framers intended in the national Constitution as well. From the Supreme Court's first session in 1790 until the first decade of the nineteenth century, all Americans believed this was the proper relationship of the branches of government.

The balance of powers created by the framers was meant to ensure that neither the courts, the legislature, or the executive branch would be able to invade the territory of the other branches. In Federalist 51, James Madison wrote these famous words:

> If men were angels, no government would be necessary. If angels were to govern men, neither external nor internal controls on government would be necessary. In framing a government which is to be administered by men over men, the great difficulty lies in this: you must first enable the government to control the governed; and in the next place oblige it to control itself.

The problem for us today is that the "least dangerous" branch of government cannot control its ambition and refuses to be restrained. As columnist Thomas Sowell has written:

> One of the tragedies of our time, and a harbinger of future tragedies, is that court decisions at all levels have come to be judged by whether we agree or disagree with the policy that is upheld or overturned. Recent controversies over gay marriage have been a classic example of failing to see the woods for the trees. The most fundamental issue is not gay marriage. The most fundamental issue is who is to decide whether or not to legalize gay marriage—and all the other decisions that define a free, self-governing people, as distinguished from people living under dictators in black robes.[7]

The problem is complicated further by the fact that those on the political Left—especially in government, universities, law schools, and the media—are very much in favor of an activist court, and they vigorously defend the Court's usurpation of power. They know that Congress would never be able to convince the American people to support their liberal agenda—unlimited abortions, gay marriage, racial preferences, flag burning, banning the Ten Commandments, and discriminating against the free exercise of religion—so they do it through the courts.

According to Title 28, Part I, Chapter 21, Sec. 453 of the United States Code, each Supreme Court justice must swear to uphold the Constitution with these words: "I, [Name], do solemnly swear (or affirm) that I will administer justice without respect to persons, and do equal right to the poor and to the rich, and that I will faithfully and impartially discharge and perform all the duties incumbent upon me as [Title] under the Constitution and laws of the United States. So help me God." Yet, despite this solemn pledge, a majority of the justices on today's Supreme Court have chosen to interpret the laws, and even to invent new ones, based not on constitutional principles or precedents but, as Justice Scalia phrased it, out of their alignment in the culture war.

To those who support moral relativism and legal realism, the ideologies that dominate most leftist thinking, the Constitution is simply whatever the judges say it is. And the law, by implication, is whatever nine unelected justices can get away with. For them, there is no logical connection between law and morals. Justice is based on feelings. Time-honored principles such as stare decisis, enumerated powers, and judicial restraint are merely inconvenient distractions. For these men and women, everything is "relative" and nothing is "absolute." But the legal realists can only win their cases if no one challenges them; and that's why it's essential that Christians and everyone else who believes in American justice must stand on history and principle, and demand a stop to the radical activism that's being carried out in the courts in the name of "fairness," "sensitivity," and "social equity."

During the deliberations of the Virginia Constitutional Convention in 1788, James Madison said, "Since the general civiliza- tion of mankind, I believe there are more instances of the abridgment of the freedom of the people by gradual and silent encroachments of those in power, than by violent . . . and sudden usurpations." Madison was wary of the tendency of the majority to overpower the minority, and he worked to make laws that would help maintain a healthy balance. But equitable laws mean nothing if the highest court in the land is allowed to legislate from the bench.

In a document written a few years after the Court's abortion rulings in 1973, Rev. Edward Melvin offered a stirring assessment of where we stand as a nation. He said:

> In *Roe v. Wade* and *Planned Parenthood v. Danforth* [which allows abortions after the first trimester in some cases] the Supreme Court has entered forbidden territory, the natural rights reserved to the people in the minds of the original writers of the Constitution and later specifically implied in the Ninth Amendment. The Court is attacking the foundation of American society, American civilization. The Fathers bled to establish the American nation and exerted the fullness of their genius to build a legal superstructure, national and state constitutions, which would protect and perpetuate natural human rights and human dignity. The Justices are using the beams from the superstructure to pry loose its foundation stones.[8]

This is really a wise and insightful analysis of the problem. When we look at the destruction and demoralization that have been unleashed on this nation by liberal jurists, eaten up with their own power and importance, we have to wonder where it will end. Where are we headed when the innocent unborn can be slaughtered in the womb, when a mother can murder her own child in the name of convenience or self-fulfillment? Where will we be if we allow the courts to toss out the Ten Commandments and to authorize homosexual sodomy and every other perversion the Left admires? Historian Clinton Rossiter offers this perspective:

> Americans may eventually take the advice of their advanced philosophers and adopt a political theory that pays more attention to groups, classes, public opinion, power-elites, positive law, public administration, and other realities of twentieth-century America.

Yet it seems safe to predict that the people, who occasionally prove themselves wiser than their philosophers, will go on thinking about the political community in terms of unalienable rights, popular sovereignty, consent, constitutionalism, separation of powers, morality, and limited government. The political theory of the American Revolution—a theory of ethical, ordered liberty— remains the political tradition of the American people.[9]

We can only hope that Dr. Rossiter is right. But how do we awaken the voice of the people? That seems to be the real challenge. To this point in our history, liberal Supreme Court justices have trampled the will of the people, making a mockery of the fundamental principles of American democracy. Without the consent of the governed, the will of the people, or apparently any notion of the principles of limited government and judicial restraint, the federal courts have turned our "government of laws" back into a "government of men," with the Supreme Court leading the way.

The only question now is, what are we going to do about it?

TABLE OF CASES

Baker v. Carr, 369 U.S. 186 (1962).
Bray v. Alexandria Women's Health, 506 U.S. 263 (1993).
Brown v. Bd. of Educ., 347 U.S. 483 (1954).
Dickerson v. United States, 530 U.S. 428 (2000).
Doe v. Bolton, 410 U.S. 179 (1973).
Engel v. Vitale, 370 U.S. 421(1962).
Firefighters v. Stotts, 467 U.S. 561 (1984).
Gibbons v. Ogden, 22 U.S. 1 (1824).
Gideon v. Wainwright, 372 U.S. 335 (1963).
Lamb's Chapel v. Ctr. Moriches Sch. Dist., 508 U.S. 384 (1993).
Lawrence v. Texas, 539 U.S. 558 (2003).
Leon v. United States, 124 S. Ct. 496 (1984).

Lynch v. Donnelly, 465 U.S. 668 (1984).

Marbury v. Madison, 5 U.S. 137 (1803).

McCulloch v. Maryland, 17 U.S. 316 (1819).

Miranda v. Arizona, 384 U.S. 436 (1966).

Murray v. Curlett, 374 U.S. 203 (1963).

Newdow v. U.S. Cong., 292 F.3d 597 (9th Cir. 2002).

Nix v. Williams, 467 U.S. 431 (1984).

NLRB v. Jones & Laughlin Steel Corp., 301 U.S. 1 (1937).

Planned Parenthood v. Danforth, 428 U.S. 52 (1976).

Reynolds v. Sims, 377 U.S. 533 (1964).

Roe v. Wade, 410 U.S. 113 (1973).

United States v. Leon, 468 U.S. 897 (1984).

4

THE COURT'S
LIBERAL AGENDA

Liberty lies in the hearts of men and women;
when it dies there, no constitution, no law,
no court can save it.

—JUDGE LEARNED HAND
THE SPIRIT OF LIBERTY (1944)

To boldly go where no man has gone before." For years, that legend scrolling off into outer space at the start of each new *Star Trek* film alerted moviegoers that they were in for a wild ride into uncharted territory. It was an effective device, but long before *Star Trek* author Gene Rodenberry plotted a course for Captain Kirk and his intergalactic crew, the Supreme Court was already doing much the same, taking this nation, our Constitution, and the law of the land into places no one had ever dreamed they could go.

If you think any of this has happened by accident or that it's merely the natural evolution of the American justice system during the past two hundred years, think again. Ever since creating the right of judicial review in *Marbury v. Madison* in 1803, the Court has been absolutely giddy with its power. Justices addicted to the ideas of incremental change and social progress have been on a mission to transform the structures of American democracy. Along the way, the courts have invented rights and mandated social policies that are completely outside the bounds of the Supreme Court's legitimate function or authority. They have alienated millions; given aid to criminals, sociopaths, and social engineers; and erected obstacles to law and order that trouble every city and state, and cloud the future of the Republic.

The purpose of activists in the courts, as elsewhere in society, is to win cases by judicial overreach that they could never win at the ballot box. Because of the pomp and ceremony of the Supreme Court, ensconced in architect Cass Gilbert's magnificent marble mausoleum on First Street right across from the United States Capitol, these justices have been able to give their liberal agenda an aura of legitimacy. Robed in black and surrounded by all the symbolism of their high office, the justices pronounce from the bench like Zeus from Olympus.

The Court's liberal agenda is driven by two revolutionary ideologies favored by the political Left: egalitarianism and radical individualism. At its root, egalitarianism is a form of envy that manifests itself as a deep resentment of the natural differences between individuals. This is the driving force behind feminism and every other attempt to force absolute uniformity on individuals and institutions that are inherently dissimilar. Radical individualism, on the other hand, is a distortion of the American ideal of liberty, transforming it into a type of unprincipled "liberation" that makes a mockery of our legitimate constitutional rights and freedoms. Both of these are fueled, in turn, by the moral relativism that has saturated American culture since the 1960s.

Judge Robert Bork, who has written persuasively about this fatal combination, points out that the inevitable consequences of this type of thinking are such things as "special rights" for homosexuals, the assault on single-sex colleges and academies, the demand for forced equality of men and women in the military and the workplace, the assault on the traditional family, the court-ordered "right" to flag burning and desecration of our national monuments, and the removal of restrictions from pornography, and the discovery of a previously unknown constitutional "right to privacy" that has led to today's holocaust of abortion-on-demand.

WHO MAKES THE RULES?

Where does all this come from? And how have such disreputable notions managed to creep into the framework of modern justice? These questions are not easy to answer since they point us back even further, to the foundations of constitutional law. As I said earlier, there's a spiritual component to the attack on Judeo-Christian beliefs and the ceaseless undermining of America's moral heritage that is as ancient as civilization itself. But there's no better illustration of the moral relativism and arrogance of the justice system today than the Supreme Court's majority opinion in the case of *Planned Parenthood v. Casey* (1992).

In the original case, a group of abortionists brought suit against Pennsylvania governor Bob Casey and the Pennsylvania state legislature in order to overrule a newly enacted law that revised abortion laws to require "informed consent" and a twenty-four-hour waiting period before an abortion. According to the statute, minors would need the consent of at least one parent, and married women would need to notify their husbands if they planned to abort a child. When the statute was challenged by Planned Parenthood, a federal appeals court upheld all the provisions of the statute except the requirement to notify the husband. At that point the case was appealed to the next level.

At the Supreme Court, Justices O'Connor, Kennedy, and Souter, in a plurality decision joined by Justices Blackmun and Stevens, didn't just address the legal question but announced a brand-new test to determine the constitutionality of state laws restricting abortions. If any law imposes an "undue burden" on the woman, they held, or if it places a "substantial obstacle in the path of a woman seeking an abortion before the fetus attains viability," the law is ipso facto unconstitutional and, therefore, illegal. What was the basis for this surprising new test? There was none. The justices just felt it was a good idea; they had inferred it from their reading of the Constitution.

To say the least, the Court's opinion was unique. What was most disturbing, however, wasn't just that the Supreme Court had again trounced the will of the people and overruled the duly elected representatives of the people, but that a three-judge triumvirate felt free to wander off into la-la land and come back with one of the strangest and most injudicious statements ever made from the bench. In what is now known as the "mystery clause" of the *Casey* decision, the justices offered their view that "at the heart of liberty is the right to define one's own concept of existence, of meaning, of the universe, and of the mystery of human life."

The pronouncement was sheer lunacy. With no reference to science or history or theology, or any other standard—particularly the Constitution—the justices were babbling nonsense: it was more like an utterance from Baba Ram Dass than the nation's high tribunal. It's a perfect example of what has happened to law in America. All the high-sounding rhetoric in the world couldn't disguise what the justices were really saying. As legal scholar Hadley Arkes points out:

> The words of the judges were philosophically untethered, but they were not inadvertent. This bantering, this rhetorical play with relativism, had been at work for many years. It ran back to the end of the nineteenth century, when law schools became the vehicles for a new science of law that enshrined legal "positivism" as the reigning orthodoxy in the profession.[1]

76

If we had known what to look for, perhaps the American people might have seen these things coming much sooner. There were signs as long ago as the Lincoln-Douglas debates of 1858. During those now-famous clashes, Abraham Lincoln argued from a perspective of natural law, which is the idea that there is a greater law that precedes the written law. Natural law is an unwritten code of justice that, as constitutional scholar J. Budziszewski had said, is "written on the heart."[2] Because that unwritten law is a free gift to all men from the Creator, it is the people of the nation who are the real power behind the law. The founders understood that it is the people who grant the government the authority to rule, not the other way around. The Constitution, then, is simply a codified expression of the commonly held beliefs of the governed, and to the extent to which any constitution or code or legal pronouncement violates this natural law, it is morally unjust and, therefore, illegitimate.

Stephen Douglas, however, took the other side of the question and argued from the positivist or relativist perspective, a view that refuses to recognize any absolute standards of truth or moral judgment. Legal positivists were forerunners of realists, who say that truth and justice are merely arbitrary judgments based on convention and expedience. In Douglas's view, any notion of "right and wrong" had to be judged by the values of the culture at any given moment, especially as interpreted by those best qualified to speak for the people: in his judgment, the cultural elites.

THE RELIGION OF THE ELITE

Lincoln won the election of 1860 and the heart of the common man, but he lost the debate among the leading lights of the legal profession. Consequently, by the end of the century, legal positivism, supported by a philosophy of moral relativism, had become the reigning dogma of the intelligentsia. Oliver Wendell Holmes, another popular exponent of this doctrine, served as a justice of the Supreme Court from

1902 to 1932 and influenced the direction of the Court for decades afterward. As Hadley Arkes points out, Justice Holmes was no friend of either "natural law" or "original intent." Rather, Holmes said, "I often doubt whether it would not be a gain if every word of moral significance could be banished from the law altogether, and other words adopted which should convey legal ideas uncolored by anything outside the law."[3]

In his dissenting opinion in *Lochner v. New York* (1905), Justice Holmes argued that laws develop along with society and the ever-changing habits of the people. According to Holmes, the law is not based on a fixed standard but is subtle and subject to change. "General propositions do not decide concrete cases," he said. "The decision will depend on a judgment or intuition more subtle than any articulate major premise." And the Constitution in no way forbids governments the right to experiment with social legislation.

In his majority opinion in *Schenck v. United States* (1919), Justice Holmes declared the supremacy of judicial review and said that in cases involving "freedom of speech," the courts must determine if there is a "clear and present danger" that may weigh on a defendant's behalf. Some types of inflammatory speech, such as yelling "Fire!" in a crowded theater, may not be lawful. But there are exceptions that the courts must decide.

Justice Louis Brandeis, incidentally, was a frequent ally of Justice Holmes and an advocate of broad protections for free speech, particularly speech of a political nature, and he shared Justice Holmes's view of a "living Constitution." In a statement written for *United States v. Moreland* (1922), Justice Brandeis said, "Our Constitution is not a strait-jacket. It is a living organism. As such it is capable of growth—of expansion and adaptation to new conditions. Growth implies changes, political, economic, and social. Growth which is significant manifests itself rather in intellectual and moral conceptions than in material things."[4]

In the volatile political climate of that era, five years after the

Communist Revolution, such words could easily have ignited a firestorm—after all, "political, economic, and social" change suggested all sorts of troubling possibilities. At the last minute, the statement was removed from the Court's opinion and surfaced only years later in Brandeis's private papers. But there's no doubt about what sort of Court that Brandeis and Holmes had in mind. In each of these statements, Holmes and his so-called progressive colleagues did not hesitate to roam far beyond the law and well off into the realm of social policy legislation, thus giving both precedent and sanction to the kinds of legal and moral relativism that dominate the Court today.

TAKING SIDES IN THE CULTURE WAR

Most people have a pretty good idea of what justice is supposed to be, and we don't need the Supreme Court to tell us the meaning of right and wrong. Justice is such a fundamental human concept that even the smallest child knows instinctively when standards of good behavior have been violated. C. S. Lewis said in *Mere Christianity* that we can hear this in the child's protest, "That's my seat, I was there first!" or, "Come on, you promised!" A sense of fairness and equity are as natural to human nature as water, sunlight, and the air we breathe. This "moral sense" is innate and universal, though you wouldn't know it from what the courts have said.

Conservative philosopher and social critic Russell Kirk tells us that "we learn the meaning of justice by acquaintance with just persons." Our Western concepts of justice, Kirk believed, "are derived from the Decalogue, Platonic religious philosophy, and the teachings of the Christ. Somewhere there must exist an authority for beliefs about justice; and the authority of merely human, and therefore fallible, courts of law is insufficient to command popular assent and obedience."[5]

Most Americans still believe this. We recognize that the concept of justice is greater than the law; or as former attorney general Ed Meese said famously in a speech at Tulane University in 1986, "the Constitution cannot be reduced to constitutional law."[6]

For relativists, however, justice is simply the plaything of the courts. Or, in the words of Charles Evans Hughes, "the Constitution is what the judges say it is." Even more disturbing were the words of Chief Justice Fred Vinson, in the case of *Dennis v. United States* (1951), when he offered this dictum: "Nothing is more certain in modern society than the principle that there are no absolutes."

To cement that expression of moral relativism, which I believe was actually penned by one of Vinson's left-leaning law clerks, he said, "To those who would paralyze our Government in the face of impending threat by encasing it in a semantic straitjacket we must reply that all concepts are relative." The idea that everything is relative is anathema to law and order.[7] If such a view were actually true and were thrust on the nation by the highest court in the land, there could be no standards of truth or judgment whatsoever. To claim that there are *absolutely no absolutes* is not merely logically implausible, but it is the most absurd non sequitur imaginable.

This struggle between those who hold to original intent and those on the Left who favor a "living, breathing Constitution," was the focal point of a widely publicized debate in the mid-1980s between Attorney General Meese and Justice William Brennan. Meese has spoken about the need for a jurisprudence founded on "first principles" on many occasions over the years. He believes that original intent ought to be the guiding light for lawyers and the courts. As Madison and Jefferson certainly concurred, a textual interpretation of the Constitution based on the aims and beliefs of the founders is the only legitimate means of construing law correctly. It's only by adhering to the content of the Constitution as it was meant to be understood, Meese has argued, that the courts are able to "produce defensible principles of government that would not be tainted by ideological predilection."[8]

We don't need to look very far, however, to see the extent to which the "predilections" of today's judges have overwhelmed the clear and logical structures of the law. In the case of *Mapp v. Ohio* (1961), another decision from the Warren Court, a woman named Dollree Mapp had been convicted in a state court of possessing obscene books and photographs. She challenged the conviction on the grounds that evidence had been seized illegally by police officers who entered her home without a warrant. In their decision over-turning the case, the Supreme Court not only freed Mapp to go back to her porn business, but they created the so-called exclusionary rule, meaning that evidence obtained without a specific warrant would be inadmissible in court. In fact, as Justice Benjamin Cardozo once quipped, the exclusionary rule means that "the criminal is to go free because the constable has blundered."

That decision, and the new rule the Court created out of whole cloth, has been a thorn in the side for law enforcement ever since. One member of the bench, Judge Harold J. Rothwax, a twenty-five-year veteran of the New York Supreme Court, was so outraged by what he saw—corrupt lawyers, activist judges, and the liberalized appeals process—that he penned a hard-hitting exposé that quickly jumped to the top of the bestseller list.[9] Especially troubling, he said, were decisions of the Supreme Court of the United States, such as the exclusionary rule, that undermined the justice system and made prosecution of hardened criminals almost impossible.

In one case he cited, New York City police stopped a car because the driver and passenger acted suspiciously when police drove by. When the officers opened the trunk of the suspect vehicle, they found more than thirty pounds of marijuana and drug paraphernalia. They arrested the men, read them their rights, and took them to jail. But when the case came to trial, a judge of the criminal court freed the men because the officers didn't present a search warrant, and, he said further, in that neighborhood, suspicious behavior was only natural because most residents feared the police. In other

words, clear evidence of crime and criminal behavior was less important than following procedures that are guaranteed to put criminals
back on the streets.

That's how it is far too often. Under the guise of constitutional
adjudication, Judge Rothwax said, the courts contrive rules and
technicalities that allow defense attorneys to distort the truth and
skim "the edge of ethics." In the process, thousands of criminals have
been allowed to commit further crimes. Among needed changes,
Rothwax proposed limiting the "rights" of the accused during investigation, overturning the infamous *Miranda* ruling, and stopping the
insidious process of jury nullification. Whether by impeachment, by
action of Congress, by civil disobedience, or by internal reform,
Rothwax said, something has to change, and he's right about that.

In the *Miranda* ruling, discussed briefly in the previous chapter,
the Court created a rule requiring police to read every suspect his
rights before apprehension. If the accused or a shrewd lawyer could
simply convince the court he hadn't been read his rights, or even that
he simply didn't understand them, then the criminal could go free.
Anyone who has ever watched a cops-and-robbers show on television knows all about this, of course. But we have to wonder whom
these judges are really trying to protect: the criminal or the victim?
On second thought, maybe we know the answer to that.

EVOLVING STANDARDS

In the case of *Griswold v. Connecticut* (1965), Justice William O.
Douglas discovered a right to privacy in what he described as the
"penumbras" and "emanations" of the Constitution. In the original
action, Estelle Griswold, executive director of the Planned
Parenthood League of Connecticut, and her associate, Dr. Lee Bux-
ton, a professor at Yale and an adviser to Planned Parenthood, were
convicted and fined one hundred dollars each for dispensing birth-
control information to married couples. A former Yale professor

himself, Justice Douglas rendered the majority opinion, which reversed both convictions and declared the Connecticut statute null and void.

Even though the Constitution does not explicitly protect a general "right to privacy," said Justice Douglas, the marital relationship is protected by rights that may be found in the "penumbras" of the Bill of Rights. Taken together, he said, the First, Third, Fourth, and Ninth Amendments create a *new* constitutional right to privacy. While the facts in the *Griswold* case may seem minor today, the real impact of the case would show up eight years later, when Justice Harry Blackmun expanded on that "fundamental right to privacy" in order to give women a "right" to abort an unwanted child under virtually any circumstances, in the horrendous *Roe* decision of 1973.

This is just a sample of how liberal justice works, in which law-abiding citizens are often at greater risk than the perpetrators of crimes. The hostility to law enforcement is obvious in many of the Court's decisions during the era of Chief Justice Earl Warren, but the reality of our predicament really struck home when the courts began their undeclared war on the free exercise of religion. Suddenly we witnessed the animus of the Supreme Court in such cases as *Engel v. Vitale, Murray v. Curlett,* and *Abington v. Schempp:* a hostility that was undeniable when the Court stripped prayer and Bible reading from the schools. It is obvious that the founders believed in the value of religious instruction; they funded and encouraged it in every imaginable way. But that hasn't dissuaded the courts from preying on the rights of Christians, denying the majority of the American people the right to live and worship as they please.

If anything, the predictable public protest against such rulings only intensified the fervor of liberal Supreme Court justices in their vendetta against religion. In the days following another speech by Ed Meese, this time to the American Bar Association in 1985, Justice Brennan was quick to attack, saying that "judicial power resides in the authority to give meaning to the Constitution," not in its history or the intent of the framers. It's not possible, Justice Brennan claimed, to discern the original intent of the founders; but if it were, it would be absurd to bind the law to their views. Like Justice Holmes, Brennan had no faith in an inviolable moral standard. The Constitution, he proclaimed, is simply an expression of "the evolving aspirations of human dignity," and he added, the "demands of human dignity will never cease to evolve."[10]

Drawing on a famous quip by Judge Learned Hand, Brennan said that judges are not "platonic guardians appointed to wield authority according to their personal moral predilections." But in virtually the next breath, he went on to say that those who hold to the doctrine of original intent have missed the point. The Bill of Rights, Brennan said, is actually a vehicle for the "transformation of social conditions and [the] evolution of our concepts of human dignity."

Justice Brennan said, "We current Justices read the Constitution in the only way that we can: as Twentieth Century Americans. We look to the history of the time of framing and to the intervening history of interpretation. But the ultimate question must be, what do the words of the text mean in our time[?] . . . What the constitutional fundamentals meant to the wisdom of other times cannot be their measure to the vision of our time."

Justice Brennan had already clarified his view of the Constitution two years earlier, in an op-ed piece in the *New York Times,* in which he wrote, "I approached my responsibility of interpreting it as a 20th-century American . . . for the genius of the Constitution rests not in any static meaning it may have had in a world dead and gone but in its evolving character."[11]

WHO'S TO SAY NO?

In *Marbury v. Madison,* John Marshall announced three new propositions: first, he said, the Constitution is the supreme law of the land; second, he added, the Constitution is "the fundamental and paramount law of the nation"; but then, rushing out on a limb, he added that "it is emphatically the province and duty of the judicial department to say what the law is." And no one dissented. Thus, the doctrine of judicial supremacy was announced in utter defiance of the executive and legislative branches.

Adding more weight to this power grab, the Court's unanimous decision in *McCulloch v. Maryland* (1819), read by Chief Justice Marshall, held that "the constitution . . . declares, that the constitution itself, and the laws passed in pursuance of its provisions, shall be the supreme law of the land, and shall control all State legislation and State constitutions, which may be incompatible therewith; and *it confides to this court the ultimate power* of deciding all questions arising under the constitution and laws of the United States . . . anything in the laws of any State to the contrary notwithstanding" (emphasis added). Thus, with the blessing of "the great chief justice," William Brennan could argue later that *Marbury* "declared the basic principle that *the federal judiciary is supreme* in the exposition of the law of the Constitution, and that principle has ever since been respected by this Court and the Country as *a permanent and indispensable feature* of our constitutional system" (emphasis added).

According to Justice Brennan's logic, the "emanations" and "penumbras" of the Constitution are what really matter, while the vision of the framers—available to anyone who will simply pause to consider the counsel of Hamilton, Madison, and Jay in *The Federalist*—is of no lasting value. Behind such a view is a level of arrogance and contempt for "the consent of the governed" that is utterly shocking. The essential meaning of what Justice Brennan and his liberal colleagues had to say was that Supreme Court justices are free to go beyond the Constitution in formulating the law, however they see fit.

So what is justice? What is the fundamental law of the land? Supreme Court justices know very well that they're defying the will of the people in most of these controversial decisions. They read the headlines, which show that the American people overwhelmingly reject the idea of homosexual marriage. Yet because the federal judges always run ahead of the people, pushing the most wild-eyed liberal ideas, they're determined to continue pushing us against our will. Judges are entrusted with interpreting the Constitution, but they regularly violate that trust.

Criminals are not punished for their crimes because of the Court's fixation on procedures and because of the soft spot in every liberal's heart for those who violate the law. The minute that robbers, thieves, and rapists are brought into today's courts, they're immediately sent back onto the streets, where they're free to rob, steal, and rape again. They can commit the most heinous crimes—especially in dealing drugs—but the liberal courts are unwilling to say that anything is wrong, since their "value-neutral" belief system simply doesn't allow for wrongdoing. The stark reality of this situation has only been complicated by the ridiculous sentencing guidelines put into place by Congress, which have filled the jails with people who've done minimal crimes.

But the man on the street is not the only one who sees what's happening. In responding to the Court's majority opinion in *Lawrence v. Texas,* which overturned that state's sodomy laws and of every other state (thanks to the "full faith and credit" provisions contained in Article IV of the Constitution), Justice Scalia penned a stinging rebuke. Since his remarks here, as in other cases where the Court has patently overreached its authority, are so trenchant and so relevant to the concerns of this book, I would like to quote portions of them at length.

In the *Lawrence* dissent, Justice Scalia said, "Today's opinion is the product of a Court, which is the product of a law-profession culture, that has largely signed on to the so-called homosexual agenda, by which I mean the agenda promoted by some homosexual activists directed at eliminating the moral opprobrium that has traditionally attached to homosexual conduct." As the entire world could see, the

Supreme Court was not neutral on the matter, and Justice Scalia took pains to point that out.

Then, going a step further, the brilliant associate justice pointed to the real source of the problem, adding, "It is clear from this that the Court has taken sides in the culture war, departing from its role of assuring, as neutral observer, that the democratic rules of engagement are observed. Many Americans do not want persons who openly engage in homosexual conduct as partners in their business, as scoutmasters for their children, as teachers in their children's schools, or as boarders in their home. They view this as protecting themselves and their families from a lifestyle that they believe to be immoral and destructive.

"The Court views it as 'discrimination,'" Justice Scalia continued, "which it is the function of our judgments to deter. So imbued is the Court with the law profession's anti-anti-homosexual culture, that it is seemingly unaware that the attitudes of that culture are not obviously 'mainstream'; that in most States what the Court calls 'discrimination' against those who engage in homosexual acts is perfectly legal."

Predictably, the liberal media, the universities, the law schools, and other haunts of the cultural establishment were scandalized by Justice Scalia's words. Hadn't he heard that sexual crimes are no longer crimes in our value-neutral society? Hadn't the judge yet gotten the message that morality is a thing of the past? But Justice Scalia wasn't finished—not by a long shot. He assured his critics that he wasn't just being closed-minded. He said, "Let me be clear that I have nothing against homosexuals, or any other group, promoting their agenda through normal democratic means. Social perceptions of sexual and other morality change over time, and every group has the right to persuade its fellow citizens that its view of such matters is the best. That homosexuals have achieved some success in that enterprise is attested to by the fact that Texas is one of the few remaining States that criminalize private, consensual homosexual acts.

"But persuading one's fellow citizens is one thing," he said, "and imposing one's views in absence of democratic majority will is something else. I would no more *require* a State to criminalize homosexual acts—or, for that matter, display *any* moral disapprobation of them— than I would *forbid* it to do so. What Texas has chosen to do is well within the range of traditional democratic action, and its hand should not be stayed through the invention of a brand-new 'constitutional right' by a Court that is *impatient of democratic change*" (emphasis added).

Then Justice Scalia powerfully concluded, "It is indeed true that 'later generations can see that laws once thought necessary and proper in fact serve only to oppress,' and when that happens, later generations can repeal those laws. But it is the premise of our system that those judgments are to be made by the people, and not imposed by a governing caste that knows best."

REDEFINING MORALITY

Justice Scalia's words, which were joined by Justice Clarence Thomas, were logical, powerful, and right to the heart of the matter. Unfortunately, such wisdom is generally lost on the liberal mind. Pundits on the Left, along with the predictable tirades of the homosexual lobby, viciously attacked what this honest man had to say. The defenders of the Court's liberal agenda were much too comfortable with the doctrines of cultural and moral relativism to let one outspoken conservative impede their "social progress," and they weren't about to let Justice Scalia's dissent slow them down. As the justice had said, it was precisely the Left's "impatience with democratic change" that was driving their entire agenda, and nothing better proved the point.

Chief Justice Earl Warren, in the case of *Trop v. Dulles* (1958), said that the Bill of Rights, along with the Eighth Amendment protection against "cruel and unusual punishment," ought to be interpreted according to "the evolving standards of decency that mark the progress of a maturing society." Neither the phrase nor even the idea of "evolving standards" had any standing or precedent in American law, but the exact phrase showed up two decades later in the Court's opinion in *Rhodes v. Chapman* (1981), announced by Justice Lewis Powell.

Then, more recently, the idea of "evolving standards of decency" was incorporated again by Justice Sandra Day O'Connor in the majority opinion in the case of *Hudson v. McMillan* (1992). The Court's logic in each of these cases is so transparent: "imposing one's views in absence of democratic majority will," as Justice Scalia phrased it, demands legal precedent. Sure enough, by sheer repetition, those "evolving standards of decency" were firmly established as a principle of law, no matter how ridiculous the notion may have been.

To accomplish all that the Left has in mind for America in years to come, it was important for these activist judges to make sure that such doctrines were given the appearance of legitimacy. How better to accomplish that than to incorporate their own moral relativism into a long series of rulings from the highest court in the land? With each new victory securely in hand, left-wing activists were at liberty to continue their march through every cultural institution in the nation, banishing moral standards and time-honored traditions at every bend in the road.

One of the most important victories in that campaign would be delivered by the case of *Lemon v. Kurtzman* (1971). In the original case, a group of Rhode Island and Pennsylvania taxpayers challenged a statute that had provided financial support for teacher salaries, textbooks, and instructional materials for secular subjects to be taught in non-public schools. In the majority opinion, Chief Justice Burger created yet another test for laws dealing with religion.

To be constitutional, Burger said, the law must have "a secular legislative purpose," it must "neither advance nor inhibit religion," and it must not foster "an excessive government entanglement with religion." There was a certain rationale to the approach, but any way they put it, the *Lemon* test was just one more assault on the First Amendment guarantee of the free exercise of religion. Chief Justice Warren Burger in subsequent Court opinions recognized that the *Lemon* test had provided inconsistent, conflicting, and irreconcilable decisions. He later backed away from using it and even questioned the test's ongoing viability.

Although Justice Scalia voted with the majority in the *Lamb's Chapel* case, which had been argued and won by ACLJ chief counsel Jay Sekulow, he also wrote a separate concurrence in which he pounded the logic of the *Lemon* test invented by Justice Burger. This was just one more attempt by the Court to regulate free exercise of religion, and Justice Scalia's colorful statement made the point very well. He said, "As to the Court's invocation of the *Lemon* Test: like some ghoul in a late-night horror movie that repeatedly sits up in its grave and shuffles abroad after being repeatedly killed and buried, *Lemon* stalks our Establishment Clause jurisprudence once again, frightening the little children and school attorneys of Center Moriches Union Free School District.

"Its most recent burial, only last Term, was, to be sure, not fully six feet under: Our decision in *Lee v. Weisman* conspicuously avoided using the supposed 'test,' but also declined the invitation to repudiate it. Over the years, however, no fewer than five of the currently sitting justices have, in their own opinions, personally driven pencils through the creature's heart (the author of today's opinion repeatedly), and a sixth has joined an opinion doing so."

Justice Scalia then added, "The secret of the *Lemon* Test's survival, I think, is that it is so easy to kill. It is there to scare us (and our audience) when we wish it to do so, but we can command it to return to the tomb at will. . . . Such a docile and useful monster is worth keeping around, at least in a somnolent state; one never knows when one might need him." And he then concluded his wonderful statement with the words, "I will decline to apply *Lemon*—whether it validates [the law in question] or invalidates the government action in question—and therefore cannot join the opinion of the Court today."

At that point, most felt the dissent, joined again by Justice Thomas, was sufficient; but Justice Scalia had something else on his mind. He continued, "I cannot join for yet another reason: the Court's statement that the proposed use of the school's facilities is constitutional because (among other things) it would not signal endorsement of religion in general. What a strange notion, that a Constitution which itself gives 'religion in general' preferential treatment (I refer to the Free Exercise Clause) forbids endorsement of religion in general.

"The attorney general of New York," Justice Scalia continued, "not only agrees with that strange notion, he has an explanation for it: 'Religious advocacy,' he writes, 'serves the community only in the eyes of its adherents and yields a benefit only to those who already believe.'" That was *not* the view of those who adopted our Constitution, who believed that the public virtues inculcated by religion are a public good.

"It suffices to point out that during the summer of 1789, when it was in the process of drafting the First Amendment, Congress enacted the famous Northwest Territory Ordinance that the Continental Congress had adopted in 1789 Article III of which provides, 'Religion, morality, and knowledge, *being necessary to good government and the happiness of mankind,* schools and the means of education shall forever be encouraged.' Unsurprisingly, then, indifference to 'religion in general' is not what our cases, both old and recent, demand" (emphasis in original).

Point made, brilliantly, once again.[12]

THE DIRECTION OF THE COURT

By definition, a liberal is someone devoted to liberty—to human rights, human dignity, and the freedom of conscience. Liberals through the years have portrayed themselves as defenders of the common man. But, as we have seen in these pages, that is not what liberalism has become in our time, and that is not where the liberal judiciary is taking us. As Hadley Arkes asserts, "The deeper secret that dared not speak its name was that liberalism had converted itself from a public doctrine, proclaimed and defended in public, into a covert doctrine, whose ends were to be articulated and imposed only through the courts."[13]

Alfred Goodwin and Stephen Reinhardt, the two justices on the three-member panel of the Ninth Circuit Court in San Francisco who declared the words "under God" in the Pledge of Allegiance to be unconstitutional, knew very well that no legislature in the land would ever propose such a law. But like Michael Newdow, the atheist lawyer who brought the case, and like the majority of the Left who have nothing but contempt for America's spiritual heritage, they believed they could trump the will of the people through the courts. Fortunately, when news of what they had done was broadcast on CBN and Fox News and emblazoned on the Internet, there was a tremendous backlash from the American heartland.

Seeing that their constituents all across America were outraged at the court's actions, both houses of Congress set aside regular business to join together in support of the Pledge of Allegiance and the words "under God." Chaplains of both the House and Senate were on hand, and various members of Congress who were recognized as religious leaders prayed together on the floor of those chambers. As a packed gallery looked on, they stood together with their hands over their hearts to recite the Pledge, loudly and in unison. When the members of the House of Representatives finished saying the Pledge, the room erupted in a two-minute-long standing ovation. Then, led by Speaker Dennis Hastert and Majority Leader Tom DeLay, they sang spontaneously, "God Bless America."

Later, the *Washington Times* reported, "The Senate responded to the court ruling by passing a bill 99–0 reaffirming the 1954 law that added the words 'under God' to the Pledge, and the House over-whelmingly passed a resolution condemning the court's majority opinion on a 416–3 vote."[14] Surprisingly, the measure was approved by a bipartisan majority of 220 Republicans and 194 Democrats. Senator Joe Lieberman said that if the Court didn't reverse the ruling of the Ninth Circuit, he would personally draft a constitutional amendment banning any future court from meddling with such an important part of our national heritage.

Were the justices of the Ninth Circuit suitably rebuked and humbled by this outpouring of patriotic fervor? Not in the least. Despite the uproar they had created, and despite the overwhelming reaction of both houses of Congress, the circuit court simply stayed their previous ruling, meaning that the judgment would not be enforced until the full eleven-member panel could meet to reconsider the case. Ultimately, the case worked its way through the system and was eventually heard by the Supreme Court in March 2004.

All over America, people who had never realized just how pernicious the Court's liberal agenda had become, suddenly realized it was high time to speak out. Local newspapers reported on spontaneous protests and rallies in many places where men, women, and children came together to defend the Pledge. My friend Tim Wildmon, who is president of the American Family Association, was quoted in several places as saying, "Americans will no longer remain silent in the face of such judicial arrogance." In attempting to undermine the nation's religious traditions, Wildmon said, the Court "seems to be on a search-and-destroy mission to remove any and all vestiges of our religious heritage from the public square." And, of course, he was absolutely right.

RESTRAINING THE COURTS

If there is any good news in all of this, it's that the American people still have the courage to rise up when they're pushed too far. The

Court's liberal agenda can only succeed in transforming our laws if "we the people" fail to use our constitutional authority to stand up and say no, demanding a halt to the unauthorized usurpation of authority. But are we willing to do that? And do we understand what a truly unique instrument we have in our magnificent Constitution?

When given a chance to rule on the importance of the words "under God" in our Pledge of Allegiance, the Supreme Court of the United States simply punted, postponing their ultimate decision on this matter until another day. Faced by so much controversy, they took the easy way, holding that *Newdow* lacked standing, in the certain knowledge that later, sometime after the 2004 presidential election, there would be another atheist, another challenge, and another occasion to flex their judicial muscles. But maybe America has learned a lesson from all of this. Maybe it takes a Michael Newdow to remind us what we have and what we're in danger of losing. And perhaps we also need to be reminded of what others have said about our great democratic treasure.

Toward the end of the nineteenth century, the English statesman William Gladstone, who served four terms as prime minister, gave a speech in which he talked about the great heritage of English common law—which is based on an unwritten constitution that embodies, through parliamentary procedure, almost one thousand years of tradition. But no sooner had he made those remarks than he added that "the American Constitution is, so far as I can see, the most wonderful work ever struck off at a given time by the brain and purpose of man."

That marvelous tribute should be a reminder to all of us of what the founders gave us to work with. And what an incredible document it is! The Constitution, as it was designed to do, distributes the rights and responsibilities of government broadly, so that no single entity can wield exclusive power over the others. As the supreme law of the land, the Constitution gives power to the people, not to the courts, not to the president, and not to the Congress alone or any other department. And equally important, the document gives citizens the right to choose their leaders and to remove from office by impeachment any who betray their trust.

The author of the Declaration of Independence certainly believed that we have a right to censure unjust judges, to remove them from office, and to protest loudly when power-hungry justices attempt to exceed their authority. In a letter to his friend William Jarvis, written in 1820, Thomas Jefferson expressed grave concern with the tendency of some of his colleagues to trust the courts to settle all matters of law. This view, he wrote, is "a very dangerous doctrine indeed, and one which would place us under the despotism of an oligarchy." He added, "The Constitution has erected no such single tribunal, knowing that to whatever hands confided, with corruptions of time and party, its members would become despots."

Unfortunately, we know now that Jefferson was right about the risks, for that's precisely what's happening today. By allowing the courts to rule over us, we are in danger of surrendering our sovereignty to a gang of judicial despots. In another letter, this time to Judge Spencer Roane, Jefferson blasted the notion of giving authority to the Court that the Constitution never intended. "For intending to establish three departments, coordinate and independent, that they might check and balance one another, it has given, according to this opinion, to one of them alone the right to prescribe rules for the government of the others, and to that one, too, which is unelected by and independent of the nation." And he added, even more strongly, "The Constitution on this hypothesis is a mere thing of wax in the hands of the judiciary, which they may twist and shape into any form they please."

Jefferson and the founding fathers risked everything to give us our incredible legacy, but they recognized the dangers that lay ahead for the American people if we ever failed to restrain the courts and stand up for our rights as citizens. It is said that when Benjamin Franklin and his colleagues walked out of Independence Hall on

September 17, 1787, having just signed the new Constitution minutes earlier, a woman in the crowd called out to the old man, "Well, Doctor, what have we got: a republic or a monarchy?" To which Franklin replied, "A republic, if you can keep it." Now more than ever, that is our challenge.

In our republican form of government, the people are supreme, not the courts. We lend authority to our elected representatives. The executive, legislative, and judicial branches are the bureaucracy empowered by government to execute the will of the people. Therefore, government, at all levels, exists to serve, and not to rule. And whenever liberal judges begin to "twist and shape" the Constitution into any form they please, as Jefferson warned, we are no longer a free people but slaves of a dangerous liberal agenda.

That's why changes are needed now. And that's the issue I want to address in the next section. So far we've looked at the history of the federal judiciary and some of the ways the courts have been usurping the power of Congress and the people on a fairly broad scale. In the next few chapters, I want to focus on some of the specific issues facing us today, and especially the individuals and organizations that are involved, briefly tracing the way these problems have developed and the role the courts have played. From there, I will return to an assessment of the situation today, where we stand at this hour, and what we can do about it.

TABLE OF CASES

Abington Sch. Dist. v. Schempp, 374 U.S. 203 (1963)
  (together with *Murray v. Curlett*).
Dennis v. United States, 341 U.S. 494 (1951).
Engel v. Vitale, 370 U.S. 421 (1962).
Griswold v. Connecticut, 381 U.S. 479 (1965).
Hudson v. McMillian, 503 U.S. 1 (1992).

Lamb's Chapel v. Ctr. Moriches Union Free Sch. Dist., 508 U.S. 384 (1993).

Lawrence v. Texas, 539 U.S. 558 (2003).

Lemon v. Kurtzman, 403 U.S. 602 (1971).

Lochner v. New York, 198 U.S. 45 (1905).

Mapp v. Ohio, 367 U.S. 643 (1961).

Marbury v. Madison, 5 U.S. 137 (1803).

McCulloch v. Maryland, 17 U.S. 316 (1819).

Newdow v. U.S. Cong., 292 F.3d 597 (2002).

Planned Parenthood v. Casey, 505 U.S. 833 (1992).

Rhodes v. Chapman, 452 U.S. 337 (1981).

Schenck v. United States, 249 U.S. 47 (1919).

Trop v. Dulles, 356 U.S. 86 (1958).

United States v. Moreland, 258 U.S. 433 (1922).

PART TWO

AN OUT-OF-CONTROL COURT

5

PRAYER AND BIBLE READING

*Why may not the Bible and especially the New Testament . . . be read
and taught as a divine revelation in school? . . . Where can the purest principles of
morality be learned so clearly or so perfectly as from the New Testament?*

—JUSTICE JOSEPH STORY
UNANIMOUS OPINION OF THE COURT IN
Vidal v. Girard's Executors (1844)

When delegates to the Constitutional Convention of 1787 completed the solemn task of drafting a code of government to last for the ages, they were finally able to return to their homes and families, and get back to the ordinary business of daily life. They were citizens of a free and independent nation, but each of these men must have waited with a sense of uneasy anticipation, for the real test of the Constitution was still to come.

By the terms of Article VII, which they had written, nine of the original thirteen states had to ratify the new Constitution for it to be legally binding. So the document was printed, published, and sent out to the constitutional conventions in each of the states. Word eventually came back to the provisional government on June 21, 1788, that nine states had recognized and adopted the new

Constitution; and despite the protests of the Antifederalists, who feared losing local autonomy to the federal government, by 1790 all thirteen states had followed suit.

The Bill of Rights, which is made up of the first ten amendments, was a matter of great importance to many of the framers. Lack of a statement of "first freedoms" had provoked angry debates throughout the constitutional conventions and at times threatened to shut down the entire process. After being persuaded by Jefferson of the need for a "bill of rights," James Madison led the debates and took an active role in the political maneuvering between the House and Senate. The House approved the Bill of Rights on September 24, 1789, and the Senate gave its approval the next day. The state legislatures ratified them on December 15, 1791.

Simultaneously with this process, the first Congress began working on other matters of urgency, including the appointment of chaplains for the House of Representatives, the Senate, and the army and navy. The members had not forgotten Benjamin Franklin's call to prayer or President Washington's example of reverence for the providence of God throughout their long ordeal. From that time to this, every American president has followed the tradition of issuing a Thanksgiving proclamation, calling for a national day of prayer.

George Washington issued the first one at the request of the first Congress, sending them a letter asking that a day be set aside, "devoted by the people of these States to the service of that great and glorious Being who is the beneficent author of all the good that was, that is, or that will be," so that "we may then unite in most humbly offering our prayers and supplications to the great Lord and Ruler of Nations, and beseech Him . . . to . . . promote the knowledge and practice of true religion and virtue."

One hundred and fifty years later, when America found itself in World War II, President Franklin D. Roosevelt took an even bolder step and called upon the American people to take part in "reading of the Holy Scriptures during the period from Thanksgiving Day to

Christmas," so that "we may bear more earnest witness to our gratitude to Almighty God." Federal law now directs the president to "issue each year a proclamation designating the first Thursday in May . . . as a National Day of Prayer, on which the people of the United States may turn to God in prayer and meditation at churches, in groups, and as individuals."[1]

Presidential inaugurations open and close with prayer. The Supreme Court and other courts around the nation traditionally seek divine protection over their proceedings. The United States Supreme Court opens each session with the invocation, "God save the United States and this honorable Court!" And Congress has gone even further, setting aside not only a prayer room in the Capitol for members of the House and Senate, but appointing full-time chaplains to open each session with prayer and to help deal with the personal and spiritual needs of the members.

Most people are surprised to learn that there is a chapel in the U.S. Capitol for the use of congressmen and senators. The room is decorated with a stained-glass panel showing President Washington kneeling in prayer. Surrounding the mosaic are the words, "Preserve me, O God, for in Thee do I put my trust," with the Scripture reference Psalm 16:1. Below the picture is a copy of the Bible on a bookstand, and standing right beside it, an American flag. There's no war of ideologies here—just a silent tribute to the legitimate heritage of the American people.

THE FREE EXERCISE OF RELIGION

The point is that prayer and reverence have always been a vital part of our national heritage. Prior to the 1960s, it was common for students in public schools to participate in a morning prayer, Bible reading, or some other type of devotional, usually presented by students over the intercom. But a tiny minority of people who despised religion began a campaign to take away those freedoms, and throughout that troubled era the Supreme Court consistently struck down the right of free exercise, allowing the ACLU and others to declare that religious activities of any kind violated the "separation of church and state."

The American people were outraged, as they should have been, by the pronouncements from the Court. More than 150 separate bills and amendments were proposed by members of both houses of Congress in an effort to overturn those out-of-touch rulings. But the Court held firm and has consistently supported the Left's agenda to eradicate all evidence of religious expression from the public square—most recently from high school graduations and sporting events.

The first Supreme Court rulings concerning religious exercise in the schools involved released-time programs, which allowed students to take time from regular classroom activities, usually once a week, to receive religious instruction. In *McCollum v. Board of Education* (1948), the Court voted 8–1 to strike down programs in which teachers came into the public schools to provide religious instruction to volunteer participants. But four years later, in *Zorach v. Clauson* (1952), the Court voted 6–3 to uphold released-time programs in which religious instruction was available to students during class hours but generally outside the classroom, in trailers.

As Robert Bork has said, "The framers and ratifiers could not conceivably have anticipated that the Supreme Court, sitting in a courtroom with a painting of Moses and the Ten Commandments, would hold it an unconstitutional establishment of religion for a high school to have a copy of the Ten Commandments on a wall. Nor could they have supposed that when a public school system provided remedial education to educationally deprived children, these children from religious schools would have to leave the premises and receive the instruction in trailers."[2] But, in fact, that's what happened, along with other assaults on religious liberty that would no doubt be even more shocking to the founders.

Most Christians are aware of these things and have kept a

weather eye to changes in the climate for religious freedom. Even as we've prayed for a new atmosphere of respect for our heritage of faith, we've watched the environment grow progressively worse during the past forty years. And while many on the Left continue to call for "tolerance" and "diversity" toward their own causes, we've witnessed growing hostility to all things religious. In the meantime, American public schools have changed in ways none of us could ever have imagined.

In the 1950s and '60s, these schools turned out graduates who were the best informed, most literate, and most competitive in the world. They were truly "the best and the brightest." Today, however, more often the news of American public schools is about plummeting SAT scores, gay and lesbian clubs, body piercings, robbery and sexual assaults of teachers and students, along with an infusion of the radical anti-American and antiwar bias of the liberal teachers' unions, Hollywood, MTV, and the rest of the morally challenged popular culture. And sometimes we see news of other things that are heartbreaking, such as the tragedies at Columbine, Jonesboro, Springfield, Paducah, Pearl, and other places. And, yes, we know where it all comes from.

Even as the Supreme Court is busily casting prayer, Bible reading, and religious instruction as the greatest threats to civil liberty, America's young people are being deprived of any exposure to that great repository of moral strength that the founders believed to be essential to the maintenance of good government and to the survival of the nation. The greatest tragedy, it seems to me, is that Congress and the courts have outlawed the very beliefs that could have given Eric Harris and Dylan Klebold (the disturbed young shooters at Columbine High School) and other emotionally troubled young people in many similar cases a reason to live, and a reason even to love their neighbors.

Will it always be this way? Is there any hope that things may change? Many Christian parents aren't waiting around to find out:

they've abandoned the public schools altogether, with all the benefits and all the repercussions that entails. Homeschoolers, most of whom participate in Bible study as a part of their education, are blowing the doors off the SAT and every other test of learning and being admitted to the nation's most prestigious universities in record numbers. Private Christian schools are right behind them. Sadly, there is almost no good news out of the public schools anymore, as social engineers struggle to stop the bleeding.

Most of us know quite a bit about this struggle. We've seen the news on TV and in the headlines. The battle over prayer and Bible reading is not yet over, but rather than simply giving you a recitation of the battles and the various court cases in this struggle, I'd like to do something a little different in this chapter. In the next few pages, I will offer two documents that address these problems in a slightly different light. The first is the congressional testimony of my friend William Murray, an evangelical minister and the son of the late Madalyn Murray O'Hair. Madalyn O'Hair was, of course, the atheist who brought the 1962 suit that ended Bible reading in the schools. William Murray's story is fascinating, and his presentation is moving.

After that, I've included a copy of a letter that I wrote to the editor of *The Virginian-Pilot* daily newspaper in 1963, concerning prayer and Bible reading in the schools. That letter was subsequently published in the Congressional Record at the request of then senator John Stennis, and it addressed the national debates currently taking place regarding these same issues. Both of these documents concern religious freedom and the efforts of Congress to pass legislation to restore the rights of Americans of faith, to exercise their beliefs as they see fit. I think you will find both of them of interest.

Public Testimony

House of Representatives, Committee on the Judiciary
Subcommittee on the Constitution

Subcommittee Hearing on H. J. Res. 78:
"Proposing an Amendment to the Constitution Restoring
Religious Freedom."
Testimony of William J. Murray, of Americans for School Prayer

Tuesday, July 22, 1997

Honorable Chairman, distinguished members of the committee:

My name is William J. Murray. I am the president of a Christian
evangelistic association, the chairman of the Religious Freedom
Coalition and the chairman of Government Is Not God, a political
action committee for social conservatives. None of the organizations I represent have ever received federal funding and the PAC of
which I am chairman has never contributed funds to the campaigns
of any member of this committee.

Allow me to give you a brief background:

I personally came from a bizarre, dysfunctional family. I was one
of two illegitimate children in a fatherless home. Both my half
brother and myself were raised in a background antagonistic toward
God simply because our mother did not want the constraints of the
Ten Commandments. There were no real ideological arguments for
her opposition to school prayer. She simply did not want her two
sons taught that out-of-wedlock sex was improper. At one point,
before filing the lawsuit to remove prayer from the public schools,
she even attempted to defect to the Soviet Union to find a home
where the Commandments of God were not taught. As a one-
woman minority her will was indeed imposed upon our schools.

Most of the philosophy she propounded while writing for *Hustler* magazine is now a part of mainstream education in America.

I was taught as a child a totally materialistic, hedonistic philosophy in which the individual should have complete freedom and almost no responsibility to society. Living according to this belief system will eventually destroy an individual—or a society. At what some would call the late age of 33 I committed my life to Christ. Since that time I have worked to undo the damage I believe my family perpetrated upon America and the world. To that end I even founded a Bible publishing company in 1991, in what was then the Soviet Union.

Some two years ago I had the honor to testify before the committee at hearings held on a similar subject in Oklahoma City. I will never forget the testimony that day of one young lady, a high school student. This young woman had been a member of a school choir and had objected to some of the songs as being intolerant of her family's beliefs. Her demand was simple: she wanted all songs sung by the choir to be approved by her father. Her father would be the final judge of the music to be performed by the entire choir. She proclaimed that this could be the only "just" solution in her case. The feelings and the beliefs of the other students were of no concern to her or to her family. In America, she was convinced, only minority opinions count.

If this girl's father should have veto power over the choir, then should not each member of this committee have full and complete veto power over any actual vote in which the majority is against him? That is the logical conclusion to the statements set forth by some who have testified.

I find much of what the Congress does distasteful and wasteful. As an Irish-American Protestant I am a minority. As a Southern Baptist I am a minority. Since I am at least a dual minority should I not have final veto power over anything the Congress does that I dislike?

Both the examples I have given are indeed foolish. No one

congressman can have veto power over the majority. Were that the case, no law would ever be passed and no tax could ever be levied.

The rule of law, the rule of democracy, requires that the majority must make the basic decisions for the role of the society and of government.

We would not give one congressman or one senator veto power. Not even the President of the United Sates has unlimited veto power. Yet, the Supreme Court of the United States has appropriated veto power time and again, telling both the citizens of this nation and its elected representatives that the Court and the Court alone has veto power over majority belief.

Having moved from the irrational ravings of the communism I was taught as a child to a more rational belief in a democratic system, I now find myself accused of 'majoritarianism.' In truth neither I nor any other supporter of the Religious Freedom Amendment desires to force a majority religion on anyone. I do believe, however, that the majority does have a right to express their beliefs.

The framers of the Constitution did not give the young lady I mentioned above the right to suppress the desires of the majority. They did, however, give her the right not to participate. This concept has been lost on our court system. As a teenager in Baltimore, I was given the right by school officials not to participate in classroom prayer. This was not enough for my mother, though. Free expression by the other students had to be totally silenced. The Supreme Court agreed. But this was never the intention of those who wrote the Constitution, nor was it the will of the majority of Americans.

I am not asking this Congress to force anyone to utter a state-authored prayer. I am asking that the Congress pass the Religious Freedom Amendment so that the various states can cast their lot for it and end the usurpation of the religious freedoms of the people by the Supreme Court.

The time has come for the passage of the Religious Freedom Amendment because of a recent disastrous ruling by the Supreme Court.

The final blow to religious liberty in this nation came on June 26th of this year [1997] when the Supreme Court again cast its lot against religious liberty by holding the Religious Freedom Restoration Act (RFRA) unconstitutional. This decision will ultimately lead to the taxation of churches and the stripping away of all religious liberty in America. The church now has equal legal standing with the tobacco companies, as far as government is concerned. I stood with Senator Ted Kennedy and Chairman Canady at a news conference that same day. I recall Senator Kennedy's remark: "The decision is disappointing. The law struck down a good faith bipartisan effort by Congress to enable persons to practice their religion without the unnecessary interference by the federal government or by state and local governments."

With the Court's ruling against RFRA, the Religious Freedom Amendment to the Constitution is now the only solution to the continued attack on religious belief and freedom in this nation.

In light of the Supreme Court's RFRA ruling, I believe that the language of RFRA must now be codified into the Religious Freedom Amendment itself. I do not believe the current language of the RFA should be changed, but rather, RFRA should be added as a second section even if there is redundancy. This is one case in which redundancy would help, not hinder, as it appears the Supreme Court has extreme difficulty in understanding the people or the Congress.

Whatever the final language, the membership of the Religious Freedom Coalition believes that the following items must be covered:

1. Protect the religious heritage of the nation. City seals, state flags and statues of a religious nature on city, county or state property could not be removed by the courts.

2. Allow acknowledgment of God on public property. No mayor, congressman or other public official could be banned from public participation in a religious event. God could and would be acknowledged at such events as school baccalaureates. [Note: This does not permit promoting religion, only acknowledging religion.]

3. Allow the public expression of all religious beliefs in the school house, the courthouse and the workplace. No employer, not even the federal government, could order an employee not to express his religious beliefs.

4. Allow students to pray at school as long as the prayer is initiated and led by students.

5. Prohibit the government from discriminating against any organization in the dissemination of aid because of the religious nature of the group. This would include the issuance of vouchers to students to use at ANY school of the parents' choice (if a state chooses to create a voucher system). No Christian school would be forced to accept a voucher.

An example of the need for the benefits language may be seen in the recent situation in Oklahoma City. There, many downtown buildings were damaged by the bombing of the Murrah building. Government assistance was made available to the owners of all privately owned buildings that were damaged—except churches. Congress had to pass a special law to allow for repairs! Another example is that in times of disaster, religious organizations may not distribute federal aid even if it means the aid cannot be distributed and people may die. I need not go into the horrible state of our schools, particularly our inner city schools, to further justify item number five. The first four, I believe, speak for themselves, as does the language of the Amendment itself.

The religious heritage of our nation is being hidden from the youth of today. Textbooks now teach that the Pilgrims came to America for economic reasons. Schools cannot have a "Thanksgiving" dinner; and if they do, no prayer of thanks may be offered. The concepts that led this nation to exist in the first place are being replaced by a political correctness that makes us accept all forms of depravity as normal while turning our backs upon thousands of years of history and the beliefs of those who established this great nation.

I urge you to pass the Religious Freedom Amendment as promptly as possible to the full House for debate and a vote. Let *the will of the people*—the vast majority of the people—be heard [emphasis added].

Thank you for allowing me to testify before this distinguished body.

FROM THE CONGRESSIONAL RECORD

One Nation Under God

Extension of Remarks of Hon. John Stennis of Mississippi
In the Senate of the United States
Tuesday, September 17, 1963

Mr. Stennis:

Mr. President, the splendid letter written by the Reverend Marion Gordon Robertson, associate pastor of the Freemason Street Baptist Church, Norfolk, Virginia, to the editor of *The Virginian-Pilot*, Norfolk, has come to my attention. In his letter, Mr. Robertson discusses the recent Supreme Court decision banning prayer and Bible reading from the public schools, and presents a forceful argument indeed that our children should be taught at least that we are "one nation under God."

Mr. Robertson, the son of our distinguished colleague, the

junior Senator from Virginia (Mr. [A. Willis] Robertson), has an unusual, if not unique, background. He received his B.A. degree from Washington and Lee University, magna cum laude, just after his 20th birthday, and went on to receive his LL.B. degree from Yale Law School, and then his theological degree from one of the outstanding nonsectarian theological seminaries in the nation.

Mr. Robertson is thus able to discuss and view the recent Court decision from both the legal and theological background, and his splendid letter is worthy of the special reading of every member of the Congress and the entire nation. I ask unanimous consent that the letter from Mr. Robertson, appearing in the September 8 *Virginian-Pilot,* be inserted in the appendix of the Record.

There being no objection, the article was ordered to be printed in the Record as follows:

UNITED STATES RESTS SQUARELY ON BIBLE

From *The Virginian-Pilot,* Sept. 8, 1963

Editor:

In your editorial of September 2 you took Virginia's Senators to task for criticizing the recent Supreme Court decision banning prayer and Bible reading from the public schools, while at the same time you affirm that these decisions are a true support of our liberties. I must disagree with you on both philosophic and legal grounds.

In the first place, we must recognize that every pragmatic expression of government rests on certain underlying philosophic principles. The Governments of Soviet Russia and Red China rest squarely on a materialistic view of history which is regarded as a religion. The Fascism of Hitler's Germany grew out of a distorted view of racial supremacy, and the wars of aggression came from

Hitler's desire for *lebensraum* for the master race. The monarchies of the 17th century rested on the theory of the divine right of kings. Even today a new nation of Israel is being founded squarely on the principles of the Old Testament.

In the case of the United States of America there is no question that our ideas of government, individual liberty, private property and initiative, education, and personal morality rest squarely in a personal God and the Holy Bible as the revelation of that God. It is in these things, and not in our material prosperity, that we differ from reactionary communism. How utterly absurd it is to tell our children that our country is good, while at the same time denying them the experiential understanding of how it got that way.

Schools in Russia and Red China teach the Marxist-Leninist "religion" day in and day out. In Israel children are indoctrinated in the Old Testament principles. In almost every other nation children are shown the reasons behind their way of life. Yet in the United States, by Supreme Court fiat, some 80 percent of the population is being told that ethical humanism is now replacing theism in our public life. And make no mistake about it, ethical humanism is a religion.

In the second place, the Supreme Court decision does not rest on sound constitutional law. It has always been the prevailing constitutional rule that the task of the Supreme Court was not to write laws but to interpret a document and the decisions flowing from it. In order to do this the justices were to examine certain historical papers shedding light on the intent of the framers of the Constitution. It is the height of folly to believe that the men who brought forth this document out of a prayer meeting ever intended that there should be no devotional expression in schools. If this was what the framers of the Constitution intended, why has it taken 170 years for this fact to come to light?

Instead, the Supreme Court has read into the establishment of religion clause a meaning totally alien to the framers, past history and tradition, as well as the prevailing American folkways. I assure you our liberties have not been safeguarded when the judiciary usurps the role of the legislature in order to take away the things on which our liberty is predicated.

M. G. Robertson
President
The Christian Broadcasting Network, Inc.

As I hope you will appreciate from the context and tone of these documents, while Mr. Murray and I are both deeply concerned for what's happening to the nation in the absence of public support for the "faith of our fathers," our concerns are motivated not by bitterness or bias or animosity but by a deep love for this country and its people. Is this an "eccentric view of religion," as some would have it, or is the view taken by government and the Supreme Court really the eccentric view?

An editorial in the journal *First Things,* dealing with these same issues, along with the general climate of animosity toward religion in official Washington, expresses this perspective very well:

Voluntary school prayer is not a constitutionally forbidden "establishment" of religion, unless one believes that government policies that favor religion constitute an establishment of religion. Regrettably, the Supreme Court has at times indicated that it believes just that. The Court has said that, between religion and irreligion, the state must be neutral. Sometimes it has gone further, suggesting that religion, unlike irreligion, poses a threat to society and deserves, at most, legal protection as an individual choice or private eccentricity. That was not the view of those who wrote and ratified the Constitution, and it is not the view of the overwhelming majority of Americans today. It is the Court that has promulgated an eccentric view of religion, and it is the Constitution that provides the means for preventing the Court from imposing that view on the society, namely, a constitutional amendment.[3]

Richard Neuhaus and the editors of that journal understood that the problem had been created by the courts in the first place: In the years immediately prior to Earl Warren's rise to the position of chief justice of the Supreme Court, only about 6 percent of all cases before the Court dealt with religious issues. During Warren's sixteen years on the bench, the figure went up to 8.8 percent, and it continued upward to 10.3 percent and 9.3 percent, respectively, under Chief Justices Burger and Rehnquist. And fully 77 percent of those cases dealt with First Amendment issues.

Obviously, something has been happening to American culture that is much bigger than prayer in the schools. As the *First Things* editorial concludes, "The debate about the school prayer amendment, then, is not about school prayer. It is about returning to the people a right and responsibility that was arrogantly usurped by an imperial judiciary. It is about the restoration of democratic self-governance." Exactly, and it's about time that all Americans knew it.

TABLE OF CASES

McCollum v. Bd. of Educ., 333 U.S. 203 (1948).
Zorach v. Clauson, 343 U.S. 306 (1952).

6

FREE SPEECH
AND EQUAL RIGHTS

In the United States the lawyers constitute a power which is little dreaded and hardly noticed . . . but it enwraps the whole of society, penetrating each component class and constantly working in secret upon its unconscious patient, till in the end it has molded it to its desire.

—ALEXIS DE TOCQUEVILLE
DEMOCRACY IN AMERICA (1835)

How quickly things change! In just a few short years, we've gone from "one nation, under God, with liberty and justice for all" to a nation divided, under judges, with unrestrained license instead of liberty and justice for no one. Thanks to the hubris of the Supreme Court, along with a priesthood of unelected federal judges and a new breed of trial lawyers who will stop at nothing in their frenzy to benefit themselves, the high ideals of America's founders have almost vanished, replaced by arrogance, greed, and the moral relativism of the Left. On top of all this, the inspired language of the United States Constitution is being systematically reinterpreted by judges to imply that justice is whatever the judges say it is.

People ask me how all of this could have happened in such a short time, and my answer is, how could it be otherwise? Today we have more than eight hundred thousand lawyers, law professors, legal administrators, and government attorneys who control practically every breath we take. Among them are six thousand legal scholars and twenty-seven thousand judges, most of whom hold very liberal views. Every large company in America has at least one lawyer on its payroll—or, more likely, a fleet of them on retainer—and at least eighteen million families now have some sort of prepaid legal plan to protect them from litigation of one kind or another. The amount of litigation, at all levels of the system, is increasing at a breathtaking pace. In this environment, it's little wonder that the dean of the International Academy of Trial Lawyers would declare, more than twenty years ago, that "we have become the most litigious society in all history."[1]

One of the most troubling developments in recent years has been the rapid increase in tort litigation, which involves lawsuits claiming damage or injury, or some other wrongful act done willfully. Criminal and civil courts are necessary, of course, and when functioning properly they provide important assurances that wrongs against citizens or against the community can be dealt with judiciously. Unfortunately, the system doesn't always function properly, and there are too many judges at all levels who are either ignorant, incompetent, or malicious, and they allow cases to be heard and tried that have no legitimate business in a court of law.

In this category we find cases like the one filed by eighty-one-year-old Stella Liebeck, who spilled hot coffee in her lap and sued McDonald's for bodily and emotional injury, winning an outrageous judgment of $2.9 million.[2] That case made international headlines, and the actual award was ultimately reduced, but there are dozens of cases just as ludicrous that most of us will never see. In his book *The Product Liability Mess: How Business Can Be Rescued from the Politics of State Courts,* Judge Richard Neely, formerly of the West Virginia Court of Appeals, suggested that judges dealing with tort cases often feel they have liberty to interpret tort laws loosely, or even in their own favor. As an example, Neely said, "As long as I am allowed to redistribute wealth from out-of-state companies to injured in-state plaintiffs, I shall continue to do so. Not only is my sleep enhanced when I give someone else's money away, but so is my job security, because the in-state plaintiffs, their families and their friends will reelect me."[3]

No doubt such thinking is a factor in some of the outrageous jury awards of recent years. In June 2004, a San Diego jury awarded a woman paralyzed in a rollover accident in a Ford Explorer $246 million in punitive damages and $122 million in compensatory damages. Even though the plaintiff, Benetta Buell-Wilson, and her attorneys were only seeking $27 million in compensatory damages, the jury decided to make an example of the SUV manufacturer. Meanwhile, in the same month, a Houston jury awarded $2.4 million in actual damages and $5 million in punitive damages to another woman, Rhea McAllister, who suffered brain damage in a stroke after taking a diet supplement that contained the herbal stimulant ephedra.

In the 2001 case of *Barnes v. Daly and University Psychiatric Associates,* a North Carolina jury awarded $8.1 million to the family of an IBM executive who killed himself two weeks after a psychiatrist refused to put him in the hospital.[4] The award in the *Barnes* case was primarily based upon the family's loss of the "love and companionship" of the decedent. In the case of *Rissolo v. Sloop,* a jury awarded $5 million to the plaintiff, who had suffered serious medical complications after a dentist pulled her wisdom teeth. And in *Waters v. Jarman,* another North Carolina jury awarded $4.5 million to a patient whose physician had misdiagnosed a ruptured appendix.

Senator Bill Frist, Republican from Tennessee, has been a strong advocate for tort reform in the Senate. In a recent speech, Senator Frist said, "Abuse of our tort system is also undermining our public institutions. Every time a jury delivers an outrageous verdict, every time a trial lawyer files a frivolous lawsuit, every time a victim fails to receive fair, just and timely compensation, confidence in and the integrity of our judicial system suffers. The American people lose faith that the scales of justice are fairly balanced."[5]

The tort system in American courts, Frist said, consistently fails to compensate victims who have legitimate complaints. In fact, less than half of the cost of running the tort system is returned to the injured party; 21 percent of the system's costs go toward administrative functions, and fully one-third of the cost goes to the lawyers. This means that more than half of all tort-system costs go for lawyers and administration, not to the person who has been injured. In 2001 alone, these costs rose 14 percent from the previous year.[6] In 2002, they grew another 13 percent, pushing the total to more than $230 billion, a figure that has a potentially crippling impact on business and the economy. This total represents an astonishing 2.23 percent of the entire United States gross domestic product, and, as Frist says, is more than the entire economy of his home state of Tennessee—and growing at a pace substantially faster than the nation's rate of economic growth.

Madison County, Illinois, provides a perfect illustration of the problems of the current tort system, as lawyers there filed more than one hundred class-action lawsuits in 2003. Their decisions were certainly affected by the fact that past awards in other class-action cases in that area had reached $250 million, $350 million, and even $10 billion. In 2003, the tort system cost American taxpayers an average of $809 per person, and that total is expected to expand to $1,000 per person by 2005.[7]

Most people understand that many of these cases are absurd, and we realize that unreasonable monetary judgments make a mockery of the law. But this is just a tiny sample of the insanity that passes for justice in many places. According to the National Center for State Courts, more than fifteen million civil lawsuits were filed in this country in 1999 alone.

EXPLOITING THE SYSTEM

Commenting on these findings, economist Bruce Bartlett says that the impact of today's out-of-control tort litigation, including outrageous damage awards like the ones on the previous pages, is about the same as putting a 2 percent tax on everything bought or sold in this country. It's a tax we all have to pay. The long-term effect of accumulated tort losses, in the form of bankruptcies, lost jobs, reduced investments, higher prices for medical insurance, and the increased cost of goods and services of every kind, hits every one of us to the tune of $721 a year.[8]

Problems throughout the legal system are, in fact, a reflection of the growing disunity and disharmony in American culture. Reckless litigation of "rights" by unscrupulous lawyers means that the law is no longer an inviolable standard: we've all seen the headlines, and we've laughed at the lawyer jokes. But more and more, it seems, the law is not just what the judges say; it's whatever you can get away with. As a law school graduate myself, I'm acutely aware of the public's attitude about these things, and it troubles me to see so much disrespect and disarray surrounding the law profession. Regard for lawyers and legal professionals has dropped tremendously during the past thirty years. As a result, people with an ax to grind simply dismiss the whole concept of personal responsibility—but they all know their "rights"!

Thanks to the hedonism and self-indulgence of the baby boom generation, which has worked its way through the culture and is now entering middle age, ours has become the most permissive and promiscuous society in history. MTV and other raunchy cable channels, along with magazines such as *Us, Self, People,* and a host of others, are only too eager to feed America's insatiable desire for self-gratification. Purveyors of pop culture and slick TV advertising tell us, "You deserve it!" and "You're worth it!" Millions of people flock to that message—especially young people, for whom the idea of deferred gratification doesn't exist.

But to make matters worse, we've become what Georgetown University professor and best-selling author Deborah Tannen calls "the argument culture." In this adversarial environment, Tannen writes, "The best way to discuss an idea is to set up a debate. The best way to cover news is to find people who express the most extreme views and present them as 'both sides.' The best way to begin an essay is to attack someone. The best way to show you're really thoughtful is to criticize. The best way to settle disputes is to litigate them."[9] And the best way to exhibit your sophistication, we might add, is to express contempt for American values and to ridicule the beliefs that made this nation great.

Obviously, Deborah Tannen is onto something. A lot of people are angry most of the time, and it's always the other guy's fault. This is an environment tailor-made for litigation. If you're unhappy, sue somebody. If you're broke, sue somebody big. And more and more these days, if somebody hurts your feelings, take him to court. Unfortunately, thanks to "political correctness" and the Orwellian "speech codes" promoted by the Left, liberals who once made a fetish out of free-speech rights are suddenly on the prowl, looking for ways to keep conservatives and Christians from speaking their minds.

If conservatives want to curb public indecency or vulgar language, or if they try to limit the exposure of their children to behaviors that any moral person would perceive as vulgar and obscene, they're accused of being fascists or of using Nazi tactics. Hiding behind the First Amendment—which liberals use now as a cover for every type of indecent behavior—loud, profane people are able to get away with the most offensive behaviors imaginable.

To offer a nonsectarian prayer at a public-school football game is a violation of "separation of church and state." To complain about the nastiness of gangsta rappers is "racism, bigotry, and prejudice." Free speech for these people is strictly one-sided: liberal opinion is fine, but traditional moral values are forbidden. As columnist John Leo puts it, "The rhetoric of the censors is drenched in concern about hate and violence." But in reality, practically all of that hate speech comes from the Left, and it's focused on people who still believe that some things are sacred.

Explaining free speech to the cultural Left, Leo says, gets harder every day. "The rise of identity politics has produced the attitude that hurt feelings and fear of hurtful expression trump free speech. At colleges, when campus orthodoxy is about to be challenged, speakers are disinvited, student newspapers are stolen, and student cartoonists are fired, all without much of a ripple." And to no one's surprise, the ACLU, which bills itself as a free-speech watchdog, looks the other way or, more often, takes the side of the censors in order to eradicate traditional values and Christian morals from the public square. The Left is not really interested in free speech anymore. "For defenders of free speech," says Leo, "look to the center and to the right."[10]

An old maxim says that hard cases make bad law, and that's where the American court system seems to be stuck: making and enforcing bad laws. In an adversarial culture like the one described by Professor Tannen, petty grievances, minor disturbances, unjustified claims, and other "hard cases" not only make it to the justice system but often lead to prolonged trials and unreasonable judgments. And far too often these cases make it through the appeals process, all the way to the Supreme Court, where they, indeed, become "bad law." Unscrupulous lawyers know this, of course, and they do everything in their power to exploit the system. But there are well-funded groups in this country whose entire agenda is focused on this exact formula, and the most notorious of these is the American Civil Liberties Union.[11]

POISONING THE WELL

Whenever you hear about courts overturning laws and making judgments that undermine the foundations of American culture, you don't have to look far to see who's behind it. More often than not you'll find the ACLU, which has been a wrecking ball in the American culture for more than eighty years. As I've said in previous chapters (and in previous books, for that matter), the ACLU has never been a friend to those who cherish civil liberties. In case after case, left-wing lawyers recruited by the ACLU are on the offensive, attacking every expression of faith, independence, and traditional values they can find—often under the guise of a "separation of church and state" that never existed.

Where the ACLU really excels, however, is in cases making claims under the First and Fourteenth Amendments, where the ACLU can do the most damage. Cases involving free-speech issues under the First Amendment, and due process or equal-access claims under the Fourteenth, are the ones that end up most often in the Supreme Court, and this is the root of many of the problems we've covered in these pages. As just an example of the harm they've done, in June 1997, the ACLU claimed major credit for their Supreme Court defeat of the Communications Decency Act, which had been passed by Congress in order to restrict display and availability of pornographic materials on the Internet.

That same year, ACLU lawyers in Chicago managed to get an injunction to stop drug searches in the city's high-crime, inner-city housing projects, claiming that the searches were a violation of tenants' rights. Consider the logic of such a ruling in a city that had the highest violent crime rate of the eight largest cities in America. In 1998 alone, Chicago had 703 homicides, nearly double the murder rate in New York City. As Chicago's district attorney tried to show, drugs and alcohol are almost always implicated in violent crimes such as murder, rape, and robbery, but the courts ignored all of that and held for the ACLU. And the list goes on.

In Mississippi, ACLU lawyers obtained a court order to block student-initiated prayer; in New Jersey they were able to ban voluntary prayers at high school graduations. In Bossier Parish, Louisiana, the ACLU filed a federal suit to prevent schoolteachers from participating in out-of-class prayer groups, at which children did not attend. But that suit went even further, demanding that the school district also stop children from singing Christmas carols to the patients at area nursing homes, which they had done voluntarily for years.

In Virginia and Idaho, the ACLU filed lawsuits demanding that restrictions on abortion passed by the state legislature should be declared unconstitutional. Virginia's bill, requiring parental notification before a teenager could have an abortion, was ultimately struck down by the Supreme Court. And today the ACLU boasts in their literature that they do more litigation in support of abortion than any other organization in the country.

Where does such poison come from? The answer can be found in the group's history. The American Civil Liberties Union started during World War I as the Bureau of Conscientious Objectors. Established in May 1917 by Roger Baldwin, a self-avowed atheist and humanist, the ACLU was established to help draft dodgers learn strategies for draft evasion and to provide them with legal and financial support. Before long, Baldwin discovered that the best way to advance his radical agenda was through the courts, and thus began the tyranny of anti-American, anti-Christian, and anti-liberty litigation that continues to this day.

Baldwin grew up in the posh Boston-area community of Wellesley Hills. His parents, Frank and Lucy Baldwin, were members of a free-thinking Unitarian community. Family friends included Ralph Waldo Emerson, Booker T. Washington, and W. E. B. Dubois, as well as Supreme Court justices Oliver Wendell Holmes and Louis Brandeis. After graduating from Harvard in 1905, Baldwin set out to become a social worker. But as his political ideas became more and more radical, he decided to take on something a little more ambitious.

There's no disguising the underlying philosophy that motivated Baldwin. On January 17, 1931, the Special House Committee to

Investigate Communist Activities in the United States issued a report that said in part:

> The American Civil Liberties Union is closely affiliated with the communist movement in the United States, and fully 90 percent of its efforts are on behalf of communists who have come into conflict with the law. It claims to stand for free speech, free press, and free assembly; but it is quite apparent that the main function of the ACLU is to attempt to protect the communists in their advocacy of force and violence to overthrow the Government, replacing the American flag with a red flag and erecting a Soviet Government in place of the republican form of government guaranteed to each State by the Federal Constitution. Roger N. Baldwin, its guiding spirit, makes no attempt to hide his friendship for the communists and their principles.[12]

Was there any truth to the charges? In 1935, Baldwin wrote these words:

> I have been to Europe several times, mostly in connection with international radical activities and have traveled in the United States to areas of conflict over workers rights to strike and organize. My chief aversion is the system of greed, private profit, privilege and violence which makes up the control of the world today, and which has brought it to the tragic crisis of unprecedented hunger and unemployment. Therefore, I am for Socialism, disarmament and ultimately, for the abolishing of the State itself. I seek the social ownership of property, the abolition of the propertied class and sole control of those who produce wealth. Communism is the goal.

The language of the organization he created may be disguised a little better these days, but not much has changed in the attitudes of ACLU lawyers or their supporters since Baldwin wrote those words.

During the thirty years that Baldwin served as director of the ACLU, he was the dominant personality of the group. In fact, to this day his image and his radical ideas remain at the center of the organization's mission. Baldwin once claimed that the group was really his "one-man show." And the ACLU's first full-time attorney, Arthur Garfield Hayes, who was also the mastermind of the Scopes Monkey Trial of 1925, confessed that "the American Civil Liberties Union is Roger Baldwin." In other words, there was no distinction between Baldwin's radical atheistic beliefs and those of the organization he created.

A DANGEROUS INFLUENCE

As a young man, Roger Baldwin was strongly influenced by his grandfather and his aunt, who were both anticapitalist radicals. His grandfather, William Henry Baldwin, had been thrown out of the YMCA because of his anti-Christian rants. Throughout his life, the old man took pride in taking as many unorthodox positions as possible, and he was an outspoken critic of religion and morality. Baldwin's aunt, Ruth Standish Baldwin, was a member of the Socialist party, a staunch defender of the Bolshevik Revolution in Russia, and an activist who marched on behalf of all sorts of left-wing causes. This is where Roger Baldwin's world-view was formed.

One of the first tracts Baldwin ever wrote for the Bureau of Conscientious Objectors was found to be "unmailable" by the United States Post Office because of its "radical and subversive views." Before long, the organization's activities were attracting such negative attention from the public and the press that the FBI was compelled to raid their offices, and all the bureau's files were confiscated. Soon afterward, Baldwin was drafted for military service, but he refused to serve. He was hauled into court, where he admitted his support for socialist and anarchist causes. Charged as a draft dodger, he was sentenced to one year in federal prison.

After leaving prison, Baldwin returned to his radical pursuits but paused long enough to get married to a like-minded woman, Madeline Doty. After only a couple of months, however, Baldwin found the demands of married life too confining, so he left Doty, saying that he wanted to get away and learn to live like "the working man." The problem he soon discovered was that working people actually worked, and he wasn't ready for that. So, once again, after only a couple of months in the real world, Baldwin left. Returning first to Boston and then to New York, Baldwin transformed the old Civil Liberties Bureau into the American Civil Liberties Union.

In his book *Liberty Under the Soviets,* Baldwin hailed the Communist system for what he saw as the "far more significant freedom of workers." He was even more effusive about the freedom to practice "anti-religion" under that totalitarian regime. In the book, Baldwin admitted that he had joined the Communist party and said, "I don't regret being a part of the Communist tactic, which increased the effectiveness of a good cause. I knew what I was doing. I was not an innocent liberal. I wanted what the Communists wanted."[13] And this is the same man to whom President Jimmy Carter awarded the Presidential Medal of Freedom in 1981.

During the first sixty years of the ACLU's existence, as many as 80 percent of its board of directors and many of its rank-and-file members were active in Communist organizations; and 90 percent of the cases litigated, up until the mid-1950s, were in defense of individuals suspected of having Communist ties. In 1952, the ACLU led the fight against Senator Joseph McCarthy and the effort to expose Communists in the entertainment industry. The ACLU was either a party or a supporting organization in every major religious battle of the last fifty years: *Everson v. Board of Education, McCollum v. Board of Education, Engel v. Vitale, Murray v. Curlett, Abington v. Schempp, Stone v. Graham, Lee v. Weisman,* and *Santa Fe Independent School District v. Doe.* Through their ceaseless efforts, prayer and Bible reading have been effectively stripped from the nation's schools.

In *Roe v. Wade, Doe v. Bolton,* and *Planned Parenthood v. Casey,* the ACLU was there to help overturn the anti-abortion laws of all fifty states. In a number of widely publicized cases to grant special rights to homosexuals, the ACLU supplied the attorneys, staff personnel, and funds to enable litigants to pursue their cases to the Supreme Court. These are the values of the ACLU. They love to boast in their literature that they support "original American values" and that they're "nonpartisan" in the cases they accept. But the fact that the ACLU occasionally takes on a case in defense of a religious sect or some unorthodox minority—such as the North American Man/Boy Love Association (NAMBLA),[14] the Nazi Party of Skokie, Illinois,[15] or the Ku Klux Klan[16]—simply means that they've made a strategic decision to defend certain kinds of cases, very rarely, in order to convince mainstream America that they're really open-minded defenders of "civil liberties." But this is a lie. The record is perfectly clear.

Today the ACLU is a huge and well-funded organization of some three hundred thousand members who contend that their primary interest is upholding the Bill of Rights. The organization fields a staff of at least seventy lawyers, with as many as five thousand volunteer attorneys across the country, who handle an average of six thousand pro bono cases each year. With an annual budget in excess of $14 million, the organization is one of the most powerful lobbying and litigation enterprises in the country, and their tentacles reach into every area of modern life.[17]

According to their own published reports, the ACLU is the largest public-interest law firm in America, appearing before the Supreme Court more often than any other non-government organization. The organization has participated directly or indirectly in almost every major civil liberties case ever contested in the entire history of the courts. In recent years the organization has fought to legalize pornography, to remove moral restrictions on radio and TV obscenity, to get rid of rating codes for movies, and to remove all restrictions from homosexual bathhouses, massage parlors, and strip clubs.

The ACLU has defended the free-speech rights of NAMBLA and worked to legalize prostitution, to permit sexual solicitation in public, and to legalize homosexual sodomy. In short, there is no greater enemy of faith, family, and freedom than the ACLU. But you will never hear that from the mainstream media or from any other left-wing organization. They're all after the same goals.

The noiseless, patient work of the ACLU continues unabated. In fact, it was a little-known intramural debate between six members of the Vinson Court that, more than anything else, helped to erect the Supreme Court's "wall of separation" that has become a battering ram in the hands of the Left. In conference, and in subsequent deliberations between the members of the Court over the case of *Everson v. Board of Education* (1947), Justice Hugo Black expressed mixed feelings about denying state aid to parochial schools in the state of New Jersey, which was the substance of that case. Justice Felix Frankfurter, on the other hand, a "strict separationist" who was adamantly opposed to any connection between church and state, battled fiercely for language in the Court's majority opinion that would end, once and for all, anything that could be seen as an "impermissible establishment of religion."

During the often heated exchanges between Justices Black, Frankfurter, Robert Jackson, Wiley Rutledge, and Chief Justice Fred Vinson, Black's opinion went through at least six revisions before he finally settled on language that, to his mind, split the difference. Black upheld the state's right to pay for transportation-related expenses of Catholic schools but then gave Frankfurter exactly what he wanted. He wrote, "The First Amendment has erected a wall between church and state. That wall must be kept high and impregnable. We could not approve the slightest breach."[18] Despite that compromise, however, Frankfurter went on to write a scathing dissent, pushing the separation argument even further. But the die was already cast.

It has been reported that Leo Pfeffer, a lawyer and church-state specialist with the American Jewish Congress, actually prepared the brief from which Black appropriated that language. That is not certain, but parts of the majority opinion were taken from Charles Beard's 1944 book, *The Republic*.[19] Beard, like Justice Frankfurter, was a founding member of the ACLU in 1920, and he was no friend of the Christian religion. Here again, it was from seeds planted by the ACLU that the war against the "free exercise of religion" has burst forth in our time.[20]

THE ROOT OF THE PROBLEM

The views of the ACLU and its allies are radically different from those of the vast majority of Americans. In one of his famous fire-side chats in the years leading up to World War II, President Franklin D. Roosevelt declared, "The only sure bulwark of continuing liberty is a government strong enough to protect the interests of the people, and a people strong enough and well enough informed to maintain its sovereign control over its government." Even though Roosevelt was very liberal in his views, he really had a heart for the common man, and he realized that faith and freedom were essential to our national survival.

Today, thanks not only to the ACLU but to the legions of lawyers who have invaded the courts and the culture, such views can no longer be expressed without censure. If you doubt that, pause to remember what happened when, in a 2000 Republican debate, then Texas governor George W. Bush said that Jesus Christ was the philosopher he most admired.

Today the ACLU is stronger than ever, and new cases just keep coming. In the past five years, the Supreme Court invalidated restrictions on partial-birth abortion, in *Stenberg v. Carhart* (2000). In *Lawrence v. Texas*, which included a number of bundled cases being defended by the ACLU, the Supreme Court took sides with the homosexual agenda, handing down a contentious decision custom-designed to undermine the moral and ethical convictions of the American people.

At the same time, the Supreme Court has upheld speech restrictions on pro-lifers, as in *Hill v. Colorado* (2000), and they've upheld affirmative action based on racial discrimination, as in *Grutter v. Bollinger* (2003), involving the University of Michigan. And of particular concern today, they've ruled in favor of restrictions on the freedom to speak up about political activities or candidates prior to national elections, all under the guise of "campaign finance reform." In reality, this is nothing but an attempt by the Left to silence the political views of the Right, which is the reason that the legislation has been called the Incumbent Protection Act.

I have already mentioned the merciless attacks on Justice Roy Moore of Alabama in previous chapters. This action, pushed by the ACLU and like-minded federal courts, has been motivated by people who hold a deep hatred for freedom of religious expression. In fact, everything I've talked about in these pages, one way or the other, comes back to this issue; and nobody has described our current situation better than Justice Moore, who said:

> Any time you deny the acknowledgment of God, you are undermining the entire basis for which our country exists. Rights come from God, not from government. If government can give you rights, government can take them away from you. If God gives you rights, no man and no government can take them away from you. That was the premise of the organic law of this country, which is the Declaration of Independence. Because, if there is no God, then man's power is the controlling aspect, and therefore power will be centralized.[21]

Contrary to what the liberals claim, the Christian desire to maintain moral standards and to protect the free exercise of religion is not an attempt to force our morality down anyone else's throat. In fact, some conservative and Christian lawyers believe that Justice Moore was wrong to defy the order of a federal judge. But the free exercise of religion should not be a federal crime! Yes, the Christian majority in this country believe that Christianity has the answer to the world's dilemma. The Bible tells us that "all have sinned and fall short of the glory of God" (Romans 3:23). We're all sinners, but the Bible's answer is that Jesus Christ has paid the price for our sins. By placing our trust in Jesus Christ, each person and every nation can be set free from the grip of sin. Jesus said, "I am the way, the truth, and the life. No one comes to the Father except through Me" (John 14:6).

Christians simply want the freedom to share that message and to pursue our own lives as we see fit. This is precisely what the Founding Fathers fought and died to give us. But the Left, through the power of the Supreme Court, the federal courts, and an army of left-wing lawyers in groups such as the ACLU, People for the American Way, Americans United for the Separation of Church and State, the Freedom from Religion Foundation, and others, are determined to make sure that the free speech and equal rights of Christians are denied.

The Christian values we cherish are designed into the fabric of this nation, from the Declaration and the Constitution to the documents of the Court from as recently as the 1970s. Even the liberal justice William Brennan felt it was important to say, in his majority opinion in *McDaniel v. Paty* (1978), that "religionists no less than members of any other group enjoy the full measure of protection afforded speech, association, and political activity generally." He specifically added that the establishment clause "may not be used as a sword to justify repression of religion or its adherents from any aspect of public life." And, he said, it "does not license government to treat religion or those who teach or practice it . . . as subversive of American ideals and therefore subject to unique disabilities."

MAKING A DIFFERENCE

Misinterpretations of free speech and equal rights have left a disastrous legacy for this country. Because of the "strict separation" of church and state imposed by the Supreme Court in the *Everson* ruling, the law today implies that the rights of religious people may be tolerated only so long as they're kept out of sight: in the home, the church, or the synagogue. Most of the time, liberals completely ignore the second part of the First Amendment guarantee, which is the free exercise clause. In fact, I've come to the conclusion that, at least in the current environment, the Supreme Court will not hear a challenge based on the free exercise clause because they don't want to go there. They allow groups like the ACLU to use the establishment clause like a left-handed sledgehammer against religion, but they will not listen to an argument involving free exercise, because they don't want to deal with those issues. That's inherently unfair.

The courts have ordered that the public square must be free of Christmas carols, Nativity scenes, and other religious symbols in order not to offend the sensitivities of those who have no religious beliefs. So the minority rules the majority. National symbols, including the Ten Commandments inscribed on the wall of the Supreme Court; the words of Thomas Jefferson warning of divine judgment on any nation that fails to recognize God's holy commandments, on the walls of Jefferson Memorial; and even the court's own oath of office, "So help me God," must all be interpreted as relics of our colonial past, and of no enduring significance. In all matters, public and private, the people must be protected from religion contamination, while sexual perversions are practiced openly and fully protected by law. How far the mighty have fallen.

What we must realize, if we really want to make a difference, is that we're engaged not just in a contest of wills but in a war of worldviews. The Left has made their world-view very clear, and they're progressing with terrifying speed toward their goal of utterly deconstructing the moral framework of this nation. We, on the other hand, want to preserve the nation and its glorious heritage of faith and freedom. Our Master is the Prince of Peace, and for that reason a lot of Christians aren't inclined to take a stand and fight for what we believe. But peaceful coexistence is no longer an option. The battle is joined, and we're all in this one for the duration.

I would call on every Christian to take up spiritual arms in this great struggle, and in that regard I can offer no better counsel than the words of the apostle Paul, who reminds us that we're engaged in a confrontation of dramatically spiritual proportions:

> Put on all of God's armor so that you will be able to stand firm against all strategies and tricks of the Devil. . . . Use every piece of God's armor to resist the enemy in the time of evil, so that after the battle you will still be standing firm. Stand your ground, putting on the sturdy belt of truth and the body armor of God's righteousness. For shoes, put on the peace that comes from the Good News, so that you will be fully prepared. In every battle you will need faith as your shield to stop the fiery arrows aimed at you by Satan. Put on salvation as your helmet, and take the sword of the Spirit, which is the word of God. Pray at all times and on every occasion in the power of the Holy Spirit. Stay alert and be persistent in your prayers for all Christians everywhere. (Ephesians 6:11, 13–18 NLT)

These words, from the New Living Translation, capture the meaning of this dramatic passage with a fresh sense of urgency. The point, as Paul says in verse 12, is that "we are not fighting against people made of flesh and blood, but against the evil rulers and authorities of the unseen world, against those mighty powers of darkness who rule this world, and against wicked spirits in the heavenly realms." It's not just about courts and lawyers, or imposing our morals on somebody else—no, it's much, much bigger than that.

We're in a battle that amounts to a war of world-views. The

contest has never been harder, and the consequences have never been greater. But this is the challenge we've been given, and we have no choice but to take up our armor and fight. Christ commands it. We can do no less.

TABLE OF CASES

Abington Sch. Dist. v. Schempp, 374 U.S. 203 (1963).

County of Allegheny v. ACLU, 492 U.S. 573 (1989).

Doe v. Bolton, 410 U.S. 179 (1973).

Engel v. Vitale, 370 U.S. 421 (1962).

Everson v. Bd. of Educ., 330 U.S. 1 (1947).

Grutter v. Bollinger, 539 U.S. 309 (2003).

Hill v. Colorado, 530 U.S. 703 (2000).

Lawrence v. Texas, 539 U.S. 558 (2003).

Lee v. Weisman, 505 U.S. 577 (1992).

McCollum v. Bd. of Educ., 333 U.S. 203 (1948).

Murray v. Curlett, 374 U.S. 203 (1963).

Nat'l Socialist Party v. Skokie, 432 U.S. 43 (1977).

Planned Parenthood v. Casey, 505 U.S. 833 (1992).

Reno v. ACLU, 521 U.S. 844 (1997).

Roe v. Wade, 401 U.S. 113 (1973).

Santa Fe Ind. Sch. Dist. v. Doe, 530 U.S. 290 (2000).

Stenberg v. Carhart, 530 U.S. 914 (2000).

Stone v. Graham, 449 U.S. 39 (1980).

7

THE DIGNITY
OF HUMAN LIFE

*The Bible is a book of faith, and a book of doctrine, and a book of morals, and
a book of religion, of special revelation from God; but it is also a book which teaches
man his own individual responsibility, his own dignity, and his equality with his
fellow men.*

—DANIEL WEBSTER

Every society is the visible expression of some invisible aspiration or ideal. Greek civilization was motivated by the idea of symmetry and balance, Rome was committed to law and order, and the ancient Hebrews were devoted to justice and mercy. The fundamental ideal of the American Republic was the proposition, eloquently stated in our Declaration of Independence, that "all men are created equal, that they are endowed by their Creator with certain unalienable rights, that among these are life, liberty, and the pursuit of happiness."

Jefferson's words owe a debt to John Locke and other philosophers of the Age of Reason. But American ideals were infused with something even greater: the belief that freedom is a God-given right and a declaration of the intrinsic worth of every human life. The founders understood that human dignity is not something that can be granted by government or proscribed by law. It's an attribute of our identity as children of God.

Historian Edward J. Erler points out that the founders took the mandate of Genesis 1:26–28, in which God commanded the first generation to subdue the earth and take dominion over it, as a foundational principle. This idea of dominion applies not only to the biblical command to be fruitful and fill the earth but to our individual autonomy as well. As Erler explains:

> The right of dominion is the basis of all constitutional government and declares: as a human being, I have dominion over my total person, as well as the free exercise of that dominion, a right given to me, not by any law or government, but by the very fact that I am a human being. The primary purpose of all human law is to safeguard this right, to secure it when denied or ignored and to safeguard it when threatened. The law does not create this right, and so it has no power to interfere with it, to restrict it, or to take it away, except for the commission of some crime which is a danger to the exercise of this right in others.[1]

Accordingly, the Declaration of Independence expresses the principle of self-determination, and the Bill of Rights carefully enumerates the rights and privileges guaranteed by the Constitution, limiting only the extent to which government may interfere in the lives of citizens. The Tenth Amendment clarifies this relationship by saying that all powers not specifically granted to government by the Constitution are reserved to the states or to the people.

The amendment doesn't name the powers reserved to the people, but they're commonly understood to include such things as education, business within the state or community, work, and family issues such as marriage, divorce, inheritance, and the rearing of children.

Thomas Jefferson called this doctrine of "reserved powers" the foundation of the Constitution, and he warned that "to take a single step beyond the boundaries thus specially drawn . . . is to take possession of a boundless field of power, no longer susceptible of any definition."

AN INVASION OF PRIVACY

As indicated in chapter 5, the battles between Federalists and Antifederalists during the Constitutional Convention were primarily over this very issue. Popular fears of the predatory nature of a strong central government all but ended the framers' efforts to draft a constitution. The thirty-nine delegates who eventually signed the document did so only with the assurance that neither Congress nor the courts could violate the rights of citizens. But, as former Indianapolis mayor Stephen Goldsmith points out, this is precisely what has happened.

Thanks to ambitious social programs pushed by Congress and the courts, the federal government has invaded areas where it has no business being. "Federal judges," says Goldsmith, "run our jails, bus our children, manage our schools, determine the rights of municipal employees, detail the conditions under which art can be displayed on city property, and the list goes on. The weakening of the Tenth Amendment directly and unduly circumscribes my authority, as the mayor of a large American city, to perform my legitimate duties."[2]

Predictably, it has been the Supreme Court, through its broad interpretation of the First and Fourteenth Amendments, that has provided cover for this incursion. The First Amendment was designed as a limit on government, to restrict interference in religion, free speech, the press, peaceful assembly, or the right to seek redress for grievances. The Thirteenth, Fourteenth, and Fifteenth Amendments, ratified in the wake of the Civil War, were part of a package meant to protect the rights of slaves freed after the war and to clarify the relations of citizens in the states and in the nation as a whole. Today, however, the First and Fourteenth Amendments are commonly used to place restrictions, not on government but on the people.

For decades, politicians and jurists debated whether amendments written to limit the government could legitimately be applied to the states. Chief Justice Marshall argued in *Barron v. Baltimore* (1833) that Congress never intended for the first eight amendments to apply to the states. But it soon became apparent that the Court was already using the due process and equal protection guarantees of the Fourteenth Amendment to invade forbidden territory.

In his dissenting opinion in *Adamson v. California* (1947), Justice Black called for a doctrine of "total incorporation," meaning that all the provisions of the Bill of Rights should, thereafter, be applied equally at all levels of government. Two decades later, Professor Charles Fairman took issue with Black's decree, but by that time total incorporation had already been accomplished, bit by bit, case by case, to the point that no one could challenge the Court's right to hold states to all the provisions of the Bill of Rights.[3] Once again, by stealth and a commitment to incremental change, the Court had carried out a silent revolution.

The Supreme Court has become, in effect, a legislative body, ruling and making laws that are not within its constitutional authority to make. And nowhere has the impact of this predatory invasion been more visible than in hot-button issues such as abortion and euthanasia, the deregulation of life and death, interference in medical and health issues from AIDS to breast augmentation, biomedical research, birth control, the death penalty, family planning and adoption, homosexual marriage and so-called gay rights, and many related issues. Rather than leaving such matters to the individuals, the communities, or the legislatures to work out, as the framers manifestly intended, the Court has gone far beyond merely interpreting the law into the realm of social-policy legislation, and even advocacy of extreme liberal positions in each of these areas.

What the justices have actually done, as former attorney general Ed Meese has said, is to damage the moral foundations of American culture and to deprive citizens of the right of self-determination that was specifically guaranteed by the Constitution. To deny the people the right to make their own choices reduces the Constitution to a doctrine of moral relativism—or, in Abraham Lincoln's memorable phrase, it's like "blowing out the moral lights around us." Assessing what this invasion means today, Meese writes:

> During the past several decades an aggressively secular liberalism often driven by an expansive egalitarian impulse has threatened many of the traditional political and social values the great majority of the American people still embrace. The strong gusts of ideology have indeed threatened to blow out the moral lights around us. This has been the result of our knocking down certain institutional barriers to national political power—in particular, the abandonment of an appreciation for the necessity of the separation of powers, and for the continuing political importance of federalism.[4]

In other words, what the courts have done not only erodes the constitutional requirement of checks and balances among the branches of government but transfers the power of the states and of the people to the judiciary, effectively creating an unelected oligarchy of federal judges. "The upshot," says Robert Bork, "is that the democratic nation is helpless before an antidemocratic, indeed a despotic, judiciary."[5]

Supreme Court decisions that weaken these pillars of republican government also weaken the foundations of government and rob the people of their autonomy. To tread on the will of the people is, in short, a violation of their human dignity. Furthermore, as former attorney general Ed Meese concludes, "When we allow this principle to be transgressed, we risk severing the necessary link between the people and the polity. Indeed, we cut the moral cord that binds us together in our common belief that we have a vital role to play in deciding how we live our collective lives."[6]

LIFE-AND-DEATH MATTERS

Nothing better exposes the high stakes involved in today's culture wars than the Court's compulsion to legislate its own liberal morality from the bench rather than to leave matters of legislation to the legislators. The most polarizing issue in America today is abortion. On one side of the debate are those who hold a historic and theological view of the dignity of human life—that every life at every stage, from conception to natural death, is God-given and not subject to fads, philosophies, or judicial fiat. On the other side are those who refuse to allow the natural consequences of sexual intercourse to interfere with their freedom. One side believes that life is sacred; the other believes we invent our own morality as we go.

Never—not even during the worst days of the Civil War—have Americans been so divided, and these debates cut right to the heart of who we are as a people. What is the philosophy of life that defines us as Americans? And what are the distinctive hallmarks of our view of humanity? Pro-abortion slogans claim that pro-lifers only care about the unborn life inside the womb, and not the woman who has a problem. But this is a callous and calculated mischaracterization. Anyone who has ever seen or read about the programs of crisis pregnancy centers, or any other ministry that reaches out to women who find themselves in this situation, will appreciate the compassion that is being shown there for both the mothers and the children. All life, as I said earlier, is sacred.

Unfortunately, the Supreme Court held in the single most controversial decision in its entire history that a woman's "right to privacy" guarantees her right to abort her child under any circumstances, unless the state can show a "compelling interest" in stopping her. The Court held that, even though the state has an interest in protecting life at all stages, it is not a "compelling interest" until fetal viability (when the child can live on its own outside the womb) occurs in the third trimester of pregnancy. But this is a complex and highly contested area of debate.

It is undeniable that life begins at conception and that even in the most rudimentary stages the zygote, combining the ovum and the sperm, is fully alive and fully human. From the first hours of existence it possesses all the genes, chromosomes, and other key attributes of the person whom he or she will become. During the first four weeks of life, the spinal cord, nervous system, gastrointestinal system, and the heart and lungs are developing, and an amniotic sac envelops the body.[7] By eight weeks, facial features are forming, along with the eyes, ears, mouth, and teeth. The child's arms and legs are moving, brainwaves are present, and a heartbeat can be detected by ultrasound. New color, 3-D ultrasound technology reveals just how quickly and miraculously this process takes place; yet most abortions are done after this point, when the fetus already exhibits measurable brain waves and surprisingly mature features.

In *Roe v. Wade* (1973), Jane Roe (whose real name is Norma McCorvey) claimed to have become pregnant as a result of rape. She admitted much later that she had lied about that, but her case was just what Dallas attorney Sarah Weddington was looking for: a chance to test the one-hundred-year-old Texas law outlawing abortion. With McCorvey's affidavit, Weddington filed a class-action suit and won, but not in time to obtain an abortion for her client, who gave birth to a daughter and placed her for adoption. Step by step, McCorvey's case made its way to the Supreme Court, where Weddington felt certain the activist Warren Court would rule in her favor.

On January 22, 1973, the Court did just that, combining two separate decisions, *Roe v. Wade* and *Doe v. Bolton*. Without precedent of any sort or any foundations in law or custom, Justice Harry Blackmun persuaded a 7-2 majority of his peers to join him in reasserting a right, found nowhere in the Constitution, that had been established by fiat in the 1965 *Griswold* decision: in this case, it was a woman's "right to privacy" that would guarantee abortion-on-demand, requiring only that the woman follow the slimmest of guidelines invented by the Court.[8] During the first trimester of pregnancy, they ruled, the decision to abort would be entirely up to the woman and her doctor. In the second, the state could regulate the procedure only on the basis of health, the qualifications of the abortionist, or the type of facility. In the third trimester, the state could forbid the abortion of a viable fetus, except when the health of the mother was at risk.

With regard to the second case, *Doe v. Bolton,* the Court clarified that the health of the mother includes factors that are "physical, emotional, psychological, familial, and the woman's age." In other words, any stress on a pregnant woman may be taken as grounds to permit an abortion. Together, these decisions gave women a right to abortion up to the very moment of birth. The effect of these rulings is that the Court decided that the unborn child is not a person. If the child cannot survive outside the womb, the Court said, he or she possesses no inherent right to life, and therefore does not share in the constitutional guarantees granted to all other persons.

To say that the founders would have been shocked by Blackmun's line of reasoning would be an understatement. Yet the greatest travesty of that case, as Judge Bork has said, is that it was a wholly illegitimate action—"a combination of egalitarianism and individualism run amok . . . a fifty-one-page opinion containing not a line of legal argument." Bork writes:

> Two characteristics of those decisions are apparent. First, nothing in the written Constitution supports any one of them. They are entirely Court-made constitutional law, and, for that reason, illegitimate exercises of power. Second, all three decisions [including liberal rulings on homosexuality and pornography] press our culture in a single direction, toward the fads of radical individualism and radical egalitarianism dominant in our intellectual class.[9]

The ruling has since become a deep moral gash on the soul of the nation, but it has also made one other thing abundantly clear. As Judge Bork concludes, the decision in *Roe* reveals that "the Supreme Court is an active partisan on one side of our culture wars."

CRIMES OF COMPLICITY

Nineteen years after *Roe,* and despite several serious challenges, the Court found itself with another important opportunity to reconsider its decision. However, in that case, *Planned Parenthood v. Casey* (1992), the Court opted to travel even further down the liberal activist path by imposing another new standard to determine the validity of laws restricting abortions. As I indicated in chapter 4, this new standard said that if any state or local regulation became a "substantial obstacle in the path of a woman seeking an abortion before the fetus attains viability," the statute would be unlawful and could not stand.

Consequently, in the view of the Court, abortion is legal at any time, for virtually any reason, from conception to the moment of birth. This means also that the grisly act of partial-birth abortion—euphemistically known as a "dilation and extraction" procedure—has allowed thousands of infants, seconds away from a natural full-term birth, to be mutilated and murdered by physicians who are honor-bound to "do no harm." In a partial-birth abortion, as most people now know, the infant is delivered feet-first until the head appears, at which point the doctor pierces the skull and suctions out the brain, which of course kills the child.

Thanks to persistent pressure from Christians and others in the pro-life movement, Congress has passed laws banning partial-birth abortion on four separate occasions. The first three laws, during the Clinton years, made it through committee to the desk of the president, where Mr. Clinton promptly vetoed each of them. In each of those cases, the House of Representatives mustered the votes to override the presidential veto, but the Senate was unable to follow suit—the conservative margin was just too thin.

Subsequently, when Congress returned to the issue and passed the measure in June 2003, this time under a Republican administration, George W. Bush issued this statement from the White House: "I applaud the House for passing legislation banning partial-birth abortions. Passage of this important legislation is a shared priority that will help build a culture of life in America. I urge Congress to quickly resolve any differences and send me the final bill as soon as possible so that I can sign it into law."

Congress followed suit, and on November 5, 2003, President Bush signed the bill into law. But to no one's surprise, minutes later a federal judge in Lincoln, Nebraska, announced that he had issued a temporary restraining order blocking the Justice Department from enforcing the law. Within days, court challenges were announced in San Francisco and New York as well. Pro-abortion opponents have tried to say that partial-birth abortions are a "safe medical procedure." But you have to ask, safe for whom? Certainly not for the child. Rather, as those in the pro-life movement have said, it's "a terrible form of violence that has been directed against children who are inches from birth."[10]

This controversy, more than any other, brings home the seriousness of our understanding of human dignity and American ideals. Who are we? What do we stand for? How far are we willing to go in the name of self-indulgence? At a signing ceremony for the new abortion law held at the Reagan Office Building in Washington, President Bush told an enthusiastic crowd, "America stands for liberty, for the pursuit of happiness, and for the unalienable right of life." And he added that "the most basic duty of government is to defend the life of the innocent. Every person, however frail or vulnerable, has a place and a purpose in this world."

As obvious as those words would have sounded to Americans four decades ago, it is apparent that this is no longer the consensus view. According to a January 2003 Gallup poll, at least 70 percent of Americans would like to see partial-birth abortions banned in this country. But there's no chance the Left will be swayed by the poll numbers. Even before the legislation passed the House, pro-abortion forces were saying the new law wouldn't have a prayer in the courts. Vicki Saporta, president of the National Abortion Federation, told reporters, "This bill will never take effect. It will be declared unconstitutional."

THE EYES OF HISTORY

As a grim reminder of how many times the abortion laws have been tested and how many times pro-life forces have been trampled by the liberal courts, pause briefly to review a list of the major life-issues cases that the Supreme Court has heard:

Roe v. Wade and *Doe v. Bolton* (1973)

Bigelow v. Virginia and *Connecticut v. Menillo* (1975)

Bellotti v. Baird [I], *Planned Parenthood of Missouri v. Danforth*, and *Singleton v. Wulff* (1976)

Beal v. Doe, *Carey v. Population Services International*, *Maher v. Roe*, and *Poelker v. Doe* (1977)

Colautti v. Franklin and *Bellotti v. Baird [II]* (1979)

Harris v. McRae and *Williams v. Zbaraz* (1980)

H.L. v. Matheson (1981)

City of Akron v. Akron Center for Reproductive Health, *Planned Parenthood of Kansas City v. Ashcroft*, and *Simopoulos v. Virginia* (1983)

Diamond v. Charles and *Thornburgh v. American College of Obstetrics and Gynecology* (1986)

Webster v. Reproductive Health (1989)

Cruzan v. Missouri Department of Health, *Hodgson v. Minnesota*, and *Ohio v. Akron Center for Reproductive Health* (1990)

Rust v. Sullivan (1991)

Planned Parenthood v. Casey (1992)
Bray v. Alexandria Women's Health Clinic (1993)
NOW v. Scheidler and *Madsen v. Women's Health Center, Inc.* (1994)
Stenberg v. Carhart and *Hill v. Colorado* (2000)
Scheidler v. NOW (2003)[11]

That's thirty-three cases in thirty years, during which time the pro-abortion camp has fought a no-holds-barred war against the "right to life"—and they've won nearly every case. According to a Pew Research survey, only 19 percent of Americans believe that abortion should be legal in all cases, while a modest plurality of 34 percent say it should be legal in "most" cases. According to a survey by Zogby International, one-third of Americans aged 18 to 29 say that abortion should never be legal, compared to 23 percent of those aged 30 to 64, and 20 percent of those over 65. More than 60 percent of Americans say that if a friend or family member were contemplating an abortion, they would advise against it.

Another poll of thirty-three hundred women conducted by Princeton Survey Research Associates shows declining support for abortion. Just 30 percent of women agreed that "abortion should generally be available to those who want it," down from 34 percent two years earlier. Fully 51 percent thought either that abortion "should be against the law, except in cases of rape, incest, and to save the woman's life" or "should not be permitted at all." Moreover, only 41 percent of women said that "keeping abortion legal" should be a top priority for the women's movement.

According to the Alan Guttmacher Institute, a research organization created by Planned Parenthood, there were 1.3 million abortions in 2000, down from 1.6 million in 1990 and the lowest level since 1974—or 21.3 abortions per 1,000 women aged 15 to 44. At the same time, however, Planned Parenthood's numbers continue to rise. PPFA abortionists performed 197,070 abortions in 2000, and 213,026 in 2001. And this is at a time when the number of abortion providers in the country continues to fall. The number fell from 2,042 in 1996 to 1,819 in 2000.

A national survey by Wirthlin Worldwide posed two questions to a broad sampling of women. First, "In light of recent medical advances such as in-utero surgery and 3-D ultrasound technology, which reveals the unborn child's body and facial features in detail," the poll asked, "are you in favor of restoring legal protection for unborn children?" Respondents favored legal protections for unborn infants by a margin of 68-25. Second, the women were asked, "Would you favor judicial nominees to the U.S. Supreme Court who would uphold laws that restore legal protection for unborn children?" Two-thirds of those surveyed agreed that Supreme Court nominees ought to be committed to upholding such laws.[12]

Leaders of the abortion movement are puzzled by these numbers. Why do statistics consistently show that support for abortion-on-demand is dropping? The fact is, the average National Abortion and Reproductive Rights Action League (NARAL) member is now 55 years old, and young people are becoming pro-life in record numbers. Support for abortion among college freshmen has dropped from 65 percent to 51 percent in the last ten years. In a 1996 poll, 56 percent of young people between 18 and 29 agreed with the statement that "abortion is the same thing as murdering a child." Maybe they've realized, as Frederica Mathewes-Green points out, that "anyone under the age of 27 could easily have been killed that way." After all, she says, "A third of their generation was."[13]

But there are other factors lurking in the shadows. One of them is a matter of judicial precedent that must surely trouble those who've bet everything on the anti-life agenda. To this day, the Supreme Court bears the scars of its infamous rulings in *Dred Scott v. Sandford* (1857), which declared that a black slave could not become a citizen of the United States, and in *Plessy v. Ferguson* (1896), which established the principle of "separate but equal" status for blacks yet effectively denied them equal access to public facilities and public schools.

There are many in the pro-life movement today who believe, as I do, that *Roe v. Wade* will be overturned and that the holocaust of abortions will one day be ended. The *Roe* decision, along with the legions of women and men who have defended it with such vigor since 1973, will certainly be excoriated by the eyes of history very much as justices Roger B. Taney and Henry Brown have been for their decisions in the *Dred Scott* and *Plessy* cases. As I said at the beginning of this chapter, the dignity of life is not something that can be granted by government or proscribed by law. It's an attribute of our identity as children of God. And no court can take that away.

OF TIME AND THE RIVER

There was some good news in early 2004 that suggests the American people may be getting the picture. Certainly the statistics are promising; some people are beginning to understand the horrors of abortion and other crimes against humanity. But another inspiring story comes now from the saga of Joe Scheidler, who finally, after years of prayer and struggle, defeated the attempt of the National Organization for Women (NOW) to find pro-life demonstrators guilty of federal crimes under the Racketeer Influenced and Corrupt Organizations Act.

NOW sued Scheidler and members of the Pro-Life Action League and Operation Rescue in federal court in 1986. After an eight-year hiatus, the Supreme Court heard Scheidler's challenge but sent the case back to the district court, which found Scheidler and the other defendants guilty. Judge David Coar imposed a $250,000 judgment and barred the group from further protests. Once again, Scheidler appealed, and the case finally reached the U.S. Supreme Court in December 2003.

The Court's 8–1 opinion, read from the bench by Chief Justice Rehnquist on February 26, 2004, held that federal racketeering laws may not be used to punish pro-life demonstrators. And further, the ruling would henceforth apply to protests of all types. This was a welcome milestone for Joe Scheidler's seventeen-year campaign, but as Jay Sekulow, who served as lead counsel for Operation Rescue in that long struggle, has pointed out, the issue is still not completely resolved, and litigants in other venues, particulary the Seventh Circuit, are still trying to use this tactic to restrict the freedoms of pro-life advocates.

Victories are sweet, particularly when they're so rare and so long overdue. And while this battle may be far from over, there are hints here and there that the tide may actually be turning. We've all seen news from the Netherlands, where the culture of death is already pervasive. Doctors in that country can now decide, on their own and without any kind of consent, when it's appropriate to terminate the life of a patient. Many of us have seen the horror stories in which parents who thought their children were recovering from injuries in Dutch hospitals discovered only too late that physicians had ordered treatment halted and allowed the young people to die. And cases involving the elderly, individuals who are incapacitated, AIDS patients, and others who are merely incontinent or immobile are equally horrifying.

Americans don't want to find themselves in that situation. Most of us are outraged by the case of Terry Schiavo and the relentless efforts of her ex-husband to stop treatment and end her life in a Florida hospital. Here, as in so many cases, the courts are deeply implicated in showing callous disrespect for human life. But the next frontier in the struggle for life and human dignity is the debate currently taking place in the fields of bioethics and biomedical research. In August 2001, President Bush put a limit on federal funding for embryonic stem cell research; and in July 2002, the President's Council on Bioethics recommended a temporary ban on all forms of human cloning. These decisions have sparked an international debate on moral, religious, and political grounds, but there are still many in government and the large foundations that are eager for unrestricted experimentation to continue.

Some of these scientists believe that creating test-tube babies for embryonic stem cell research may lead to miraculous cures for all sorts of serious illnesses. Celebrities such as Christopher Reeve and Michael J. Fox are among the most outspoken advocates of these kinds of therapy. Both men suffer from chronic degenerative conditions and would gladly try anything to reverse their symptoms. But the issue of embryonic stem cell research is much bigger than gene therapy; there are serious moral questions to be addressed, and no one really knows what horrors would be unleashed if, like the sorcerer's apprentice, some unanticipated mishap were to occur in the laboratory. That's why restraint is essential.

The moral implications of genetic experimentation are enormous. Christians and Jews believe that God is the author of life. Every human life, from conception to death, possesses a soul and an immortal destiny. Creating and killing human life for convenience, for commercial reasons, or even for compassion is simply not a valid justification for tinkering with God's property or His plans for humankind.

Not everyone understands or appreciates this perspective, of course, and evidence of that can be seen in another Supreme Court case in which at least one justice showed greater respect for trees, rivers, and other inanimate objects than for human life. The case was *Sierra Club v. Morton* (1972), in which the environmentalist group wanted to stop the development of a ski lodge in the Mineral King Valley of California's Sequoia National Forest. In the first trial, the district court granted a preliminary injunction against the state and the developers. A court of appeals reversed that decision, however, holding that the Sierra Club lacked standing because it had not shown evidence of personal injury. When the case reached the Supreme Court, the majority affirmed the decision of the appellate court and allowed plans for the resort to proceed.

But Justice William O. Douglas was incensed by that opinion, and he wrote a bitter dissent, which, in light of the issues in this chapter, is both ironic and remarkably telling. In his opinion, Douglas said that standing—or the right to be heard in the case—belonged not to the Sierra Club but to the environment! If corporations could be recognized by the Court as persons for the purpose of adjudication, he said, then why shouldn't a national treasure such as the Mineral King Valley and the Sequoia National Forest be granted standing in this case? Otherwise, who will speak for the trees?

Douglas then went on to say, "The river, for example, is the living symbol of all the life it sustains or nourishes—fish, aquatic insects, water ouzels, otter, fisher, deer, elk, bear, and all other animals, including man, who are dependent on it or who enjoy it for its sight, its sound, or its life. The river as plaintiff speaks for the ecological unit of life that is part of it. . . . Those who have that intimate relation with the inanimate object about to be injured, polluted, or otherwise despoiled are its legitimate spokesmen. . . . With all respect, the problem is to make certain that the inanimate objects, which are the very core of America's beauty, have spokesmen before they are destroyed. . . . The voice of the inanimate object, therefore, should not be stilled."

All of that passion and righteous indignation over rivers, trees, and water ouzels, but no sign of compassion for the child in the womb! The irony is just overwhelming. *Sierra Club v. Morton* was heard by the Supreme Court less than a year before the decision in *Roe v. Wade* was announced, yet none of that emotion surfaced when the life and death of a child was at stake. You have to wonder what was going through the minds of those judges.

THE POWER OF IDEAS

The philosopher Richard Weaver said famously that "ideas have consequences," and it is especially true that bad ideas often have very bad consequences. In these pages we have seen how bad ideas, mistaken theories, and malicious schemes have damaged the foundations of American culture. The liberal notion that anything goes, that fundamental institutions and long-cherished beliefs can be discarded without risk, and that life-and-death decisions can be made casually or merely for personal convenience, is a dangerous enterprise with deadly serious consequences.

A moving statement from the National Pro-Life Religious Council in Washington, D.C. helps to put some of these issues into perspective. The document reads, in part:

> When the truth of the divine origin and the dignity of human life are ignored, human lives are cheapened, manipulated, violated and discarded at will. Only a few decades ago, Nazi Third Reich physicians conducted fatal medical experiments on those whom they considered to be of lesser worth than others. They justified their immoral practices with a utilitarian argument—the idea that one should aim for the greatest good for the greatest number of people. Their utilitarianism, supported by a totalitarian government, and its dire consequences stand as a warning to all governments and societies.[14]

Today many intellectuals, physicians, healthcare professionals, and people in the media are saying that advanced medical and scientific experiments in fields such as human cloning, stem cell research, and genetic therapy are the wave of the future. With these modern tools, we're told, we may be able to improve health, extend life, and bring about miraculous cures for individuals suffering from all sorts of diseases. But the truth is that the attempt to manipulate human life for medical or commercial purposes is an assault on the dignity of life, "treating human beings as commodities to be manufactured, manipulated, and marketed for the alleged good of other, more powerful human beings."[15]

Since the *Roe* decision of 1973, the activist courts have misused the idea of a "right to privacy" to legitimize behaviors that most of us find abhorrent. But that does not make these behaviors legitimate or reasonable. God is the author of life, and God's laws are never determined by majority opinion, and certainly not by the decisions of nine unelected judges. Even if every man and woman in this country were to decide one day that abortion, infanticide, euthanasia, human cloning, or genetic manipulation was completely reasonable and acceptable, that would not make any of them right.

The true measure of any society is not its wealth or power, or its achievements in science, law, literature, or the arts, but the degree to which it defends the dignity and well-being of all its people. The biblical standard, instituted by Jesus in Matthew 25:45, is that we will all be judged ultimately by the degree to which we serve "the least of these" among us. Societies throughout history that have exhibited the highest moral and cultural standards are, not coincidentally, nations like America, Great Britain, and Europe during the Age of Faith, which understood that we are all children of God. Western civilization was, from the first, a Christian culture.[16] But are we willing now to cast that legacy aside? Have we really fallen so far?

One of the most eloquent statements of our relationship with God, the Creator and Sustainer of life, was penned three thousand years ago by the psalmist, and I can think of no more fitting conclusion to this discussion than to recite David's words here:

> For you created my inmost being;
> you knit me together in my mother's womb.
> I praise you because I am fearfully and wonderfully made;
> your works are wonderful,
> I know that full well.
> My frame was not hidden from you
> when I was made in the secret place.
> When I was woven together in the depths of the earth,
> your eyes saw my unformed body.
> All the days ordained for me

were written in your book
before one of them came to be.
How precious to me are your thoughts, O God!
How vast is the sum of them! (Psalm 139:13–17 NIV)

If only all Americans could once again take those words to heart.

TABLE OF CASES

Adamson v. California, 332 U.S. 46 (1947).
Akron v. Akron Ctr. for Reproductive Health, 462 U.S. 416 (1983).
Barron v. Baltimore, 32 U.S. 243 (1833).
Beal v. Doe, 432 U.S. 438 (1977).
Bellotti v. Baird [I], 428 U.S. 132 (1976).
Bellotti v. Baird [II], 443 U.S. 622 (1979).
Bigelow v. Virginia, 421 U.S. 809 (1975).
Bray v. Alexandria Women's Health Clinic, 506 U.S. 263 (1993).
Carey v. Population Servs. Int'l, 431 U.S. 678 (1977).
Colautti v. Franklin, 439 U.S. 379 (1979).
Connecticut v. Menillo, 423 U.S. 9 (1975).
Cruzan v. Missouri Dep't of Health, 497 U.S. 261 (1990).
Diamond v. Charles, 476 U.S. 54 (1986).
Doe v. Bolton, 410 U.S. 179 (1973).
Dred Scott v. Sandford, 60 U.S. 393 (1857).
H. L. v. Matheson, 450 U.S. 398 (1981).
Harris v. McRae, 448 U.S. 297 (1980).
Hill v. Colorado, 530 U.S. 703 (2000).
Hodgson v. Minnesota, 497 U.S. 417 (1990).
Madsen v. Women's Health Ctr., 512 U.S. 753 (1994).
Maher v. Roe, 432 U.S. 464 (1977).
NOW v. Scheidler, 510 U.S. 249 (1994).
Ohio v. Akron Ctr. for Reproductive Health, 497 U.S. 502 (1990).
Planned Parenthood v. Ashcroft, 462 U.S. 476 (1983).

Planned Parenthood v. Casey, 505 U.S. 833 (1992).

Planned Parenthood v. Danforth, 428 U.S. 52 (1976).

Plessy v. Ferguson, 163 U.S. 537 (1896).

Poelker v. Doe, 432 U.S. 519 (1977).

Roe v. Wade, 410 U.S. 113 (1973).

Rust v. Sullivan, 500 U.S. 173 (1991).

Scheidler v. NOW, 537 U.S. 393 (2003).

Sierra Club v. Morton, 405 U.S. 727 (1972).

Simopoulos v. Virginia, 462 U.S. 506 (1983).

Singleton v. Wulff, 428 U.S. 106 (1976).

Stenberg v. Carhart, 530 U.S. 914 (2000).

Thornburgh v. Am. College of Obstetrics & Gynecology, 476 U.S. 747 (1986).

Webster v. Reproductive Health, 492 U.S. 490 (1989).

Williams v. Zbaraz, 448 U.S. 358 (1980).

8

HONORING OUR HERITAGE

The propitious smiles of heaven can never be expected on a nation that disregards the eternal rules of order and right, which heaven itself has ordained.

—GEORGE WASHINGTON,
FIRST INAUGURAL ADDRESS (1789)

God's plan of order is for our good. He demands obedience to moral laws and forbids destructive behaviors, not because He's a cosmic killjoy, but because He is good, and He cares for our health and well-being. In Jeremiah 29:11 we read, "For I know the thoughts that I think toward you, says the LORD, thoughts of peace and not of evil, to give you a future and a hope." Whenever I hear people complaining about all the "thou shalts" and "thou shalt nots" in the Ten Commandments, I have to wonder what they're thinking—because they're really missing the point of that incredible code. Think about it! God could just as easily have given us ten thousand commandments, but He didn't. He gave us only ten, and He did it for our own good.

Consider this: the U.S. Code, which is cited in the text of almost all Supreme Court decisions, is a compilation of federal statutes enacted by Congress and signed into law. A recent study of the code by Professor John Baker, for the Federalist Society, reveals that there are at least four thousand criminal offenses that can be punished under United States law. Federal statutory law is set forth under fifty separate headings in the U.S. Code, including everything from arson, robbery, murder, and chemical weapons offenses to bankruptcy, civil rights abuses, securities fraud, tort law judgments, and dozens more. Title 18 of the code deals with "Crimes and Criminal Procedure," but it doesn't contain a complete listing of all the punishable crimes it covers, and it doesn't even define what a crime is.

Those fifty titles of the U.S. Code take up twenty-seven thousand pages of printed text. And all these crimes that carry serious criminal penalties are jumbled together and scattered through the other forty-nine titles. Furthermore, to get judicial interpretations of the legal provisions of all those laws, you would have to go through some twenty-eight hundred volumes and more than four million pages of information to find the actual opinions rendered by the judges in each case.

Even the Hebrew law, the Halakah, contains 613 commandments.[1] By comparison, the Ten Commandments are a marvel of simplicity and restraint. Ten divine principles cover our relationship with God and our fellow man, so crisply and succinctly they can be summed up in a single sentence: "'You shall love the Lord your God with all your heart, with all your soul, with all your strength, and with all your mind,' and 'your neighbor as yourself'" (Luke 10:27). Yet there are people who have an ax to grind, apparently because a large majority of the American people believe it's important to honor these ten fundamental laws of civilization and to post them in public places, including courthouses and schoolrooms, as a reminder of the values on which this nation was founded.

I've been told that there are as many as four thousand displays of the Ten Commandments and related symbols in this country.

They're on courthouse walls, city and county seals, town squares, government buildings, and many other places, because this is the legitimate heritage of our nation. The Pilgrims and those who followed them for more than two hundred years traveled to this country in search of religious freedom—and they found it. God prospered them and they built a nation that, by any standard, is the most amazing success story in human history. The idea that later generations would try to strip away the signs of reverence to Almighty God, and to rob the American people of their Christian heritage, would be anathema to our forefathers. Yet that's exactly what's happening.

A RISING STORM

The case of Judge Roy Moore is the most recent and most widely publicized contest over these issues to reach the federal courts. The first complaint against Judge Moore was filed as far back as 1995, by—you guessed it—the ACLU, on the grounds that Judge Moore's practice of displaying the Ten Commandments and allowing prayer in his courtroom was a violation of the First Amendment. Moore disagreed strongly and told reporters, "I simply acknowledge the God upon which our Constitution and our Declaration were founded."

Moore resisted attempts to force God out of the courthouse, and poll after poll showed that the people of Alabama, along with a large majority of the entire country, agreed with him and thought it was only fitting that we should acknowledge in public places our indebtedness to the Creator. A national survey in the months after that ACLU challenge reported that 64 percent of Americans agreed that the Ten Commandments ought to remain on display. And in Alabama, more than 88 percent agreed with that view. When Moore ran for the office of chief justice of the Alabama Supreme Court, in 2000, he promised that if elected he would erect a display of the Ten Commandments in the courthouse at Montgomery.

The people of Alabama respected Roy Moore's courage and values, and they elected him to that position. Accordingly, Moore, a West Point graduate and a man of principle, kept his pledge and commissioned a granite monument to stand in the rotunda of the state courthouse. In addition to the Ten Commandments, the monument included quotes from the Declaration of Independence, the Judiciary Act of 1789 ("So Help Me God"), the National Motto ("In God We Trust"), the Pledge of Allegiance ("One Nation Under God, Indivisible, With Liberty and Justice for All"), along with quotes from George Washington, Thomas Jefferson, Supreme Court justice John Jay, James Madison, and the great English jurist Sir William Blackstone.

But once again, atheists and other anti-Christian forces went on the attack. A suit was filed by three plaintiffs who claimed that merely seeing the monument at the courthouse caused them personal injury. The first plaintiff in the suit, Stephen R. Glassroth, is a criminal defense attorney associated with the pro-marijuana group NORML. The second, Beverly J. Howard, is a criminal defense attorney and an anti-death penalty activist, while the third party, Melinda Maddox, is an environmentalist lawyer associated with the group Wild Law. The suits were supported, in turn, by the ACLU, Americans United for the Separation of Church and State, and the Southern Poverty Law Center.

Also weighing in against Moore was Judge Myron Thompson, the district court judge who was appointed to handle the case. As reported by Craige MacMillan, a columnist for the Web site WorldNetDaily, Thompson "has in the past distinguished himself as a friend of same-sex sodomy on Alabama college campuses; as a supporter of incompetents whose test results would have barred them from becoming teachers, except that his court orders intervened; and has disregarded the equal-protection clause of the Constitution by his demands for aggressive hiring quotas for blacks in faculty, administrative and supervisory positions within institutions of academia."[2] In published comments about Judge Moore's case, Judge Myron Thompson referred to the monument as "nothing less than 'an obtrusive year-round religious display.'"

THE RULE OF LAW

Not surprisingly, Moore lost his case and, a few months later, his job as chief justice. In the biting judgment read from the bench in Montgomery, Judge Thompson said Judge Moore's Christian beliefs came "uncomfortably too close to the adoption of . . . a theocracy." He added further that Moore's ideas were "incorrect and religiously offensive."[3] To say, as Moore had argued at his hearing, that the founders actually preferred Judeo-Christian beliefs to those of Muslims or Hindus or Wiccans was, in Thompson's view, simply outrageous. You have to wonder where Judge Thompson learned his American history.

Christian author and former ambassador Michael Novak offered a more informed perspective on these issues when he wrote in *National Review* that "the defense that both Jefferson and Madison gave of the right to religious liberty depends crucially on a specifically Jewish and Christian concept of God." And contrary to the claims of a supposed "pluralist" view of what the founders created, Novak said:

> Theirs is not a Hindu, Buddhist, or Muslim concept, let alone the concept of God in Aristotle or Plato, Kant or Leibniz. It is the concept of a God who reads our intentions, hearts, and consciences, not just our outward behavior. This God demands to be worshiped in spirit and in truth. . . . Jefferson and Madison both point out that the human creature owes this God a response to His initiatives, and this duty of every human individual to the Creator, they say, is precedent to any other obligation, even those of civil society. This duty is inalienable; no one can exercise it for anyone else. This duty

gives rise to our right to personal liberty of conscience, beyond the reach of the state, civil society, or any other individual.[4]

Arguments to the contrary from lawyers for the ACLU, the Southern Poverty Law Center, and Americans United for Separation of Church and State notwithstanding, this is the legitimate history that Judge Roy Moore was willing to defend. Nevertheless, after a stormy period of protest by friends and supporters of Moore, the monument was removed and placed in a storage room in the court building, out of sight, lest anyone else should be injured by the "free exercise" of religion. In the days leading up to the trial in state district court, more than ten thousand men and women traveled to Montgomery for a rally in support of Justice Moore on the courthouse portico. Among them were organizations with signed petitions from more than three hundred thousand like-minded citizens who favored Moore's right to display the Commandments.

Subsequently, about 350 people from many parts of the country took part in a "Save the Commandments Caravan," driving from Montgomery to the steps of the U.S. Supreme Court in Washington, D.C. When they arrived on Capitol Hill, the group called on lawmakers, urging them to defend our constitutional freedoms and also to protect Justice Moore's right to display the Ten Commandments. On November 3, 2003, however, Judge Moore got more disturbing news when the United States Supreme Court denied his petition for a writ of certiorari. And on November 12, a nine-member panel of the Alabama Court of the Judiciary agreed with a finding of the Judicial Inquiry Commission, which claimed that Moore had violated six tenets of the state's canons of judicial ethics.

In the panel's unanimous opinion, "Anything short of removal would only serve to set up another confrontation that would ultimately bring us back to where we are today." Thereupon, Moore was summarily removed from his elected post, and in the weeks following this bold move, his former staff and his aides were surreptitiously fired as well.

In remarks prior to being removed from office, Moore said to the people of Alabama:

> The people of this state elected me as chief justice to uphold our Constitution, which establishes our justice system on invoking the favor and guidance of Almighty God. To do my duty, I must acknowledge God. That's what this case is about. Judge Myron Thompson said . . . that the acknowledgment of the Judeo-Christian God crosses the line between the permissible and the impermissible, and that the acknowledgment of God violates the Constitution of the United States. Not only does Judge Thompson put himself above the law, but above God, as well. I have been ordered to do something I cannot do, and that is, violate my conscience.

We hear a lot of talk about "the rule of law," Moore said, but what does that really mean? If the rule of law means blindly obeying anything a federal judge tells us to do, we would still have slavery in this country. After all, that's what the *Dred Scott* decision was about. Obeying unjust edicts of unjust judges would make the Declaration of Independence a meaningless piece of paper. Furthermore, Moore said, when the law, as in the case of *Roe v. Wade,* has led to the slaughter of millions of unborn children, then bowing to the rule of law is a principle we simply cannot obey. The Declaration of Independence states, "We are endowed by our Creator with certain unalienable rights, that among these are life, liberty, and the pursuit of happiness," and that's a principle we do believe in. Then Moore added:

> Dr. Martin Luther King is proof enough that great men do follow the rule of law, and not the rule of men. I say, enough is enough. We

must dare defend our rights, which is the motto of this great state. No judge or man can dictate in whom we can believe and in whom we trust. . . . The Ninth Amendment secured our rights as a people, and the Tenth Amendment guaranteed our right as a sovereign state. . . . I will not violate my oath, I cannot forsake my conscience, I will not neglect my duty, and I will never, never deny the God upon Whom our laws and our country depend.

On hearing the news of Moore's removal from office, Alabama governor Bob Riley made a public statement, in which he said:

I have always believed that the Ten Commandments could be displayed and that acknowledgements of God and faith could properly occur within public places. That is why I displayed a copy of the Ten Commandments here in the Alabama State Capitol and that is why I have a copy of the Ten Commandments proudly displayed in my office. Like many Alabamians, I am disappointed and concerned that the federal courts continue to attempt to remove references to God and faith from public arenas. All of us must, however, respect the workings of our legal system and trust that it remains the best in the world.

Although the Supreme Court refused to take Moore's case, his attorneys predicted it wouldn't be the end of their quest for justice. With as many as two dozen Ten Commandments cases currently in litigation across the country—including more than a dozen being handled by chief counsel Jay Sekulow and his staff at the American Center for Law and Justice—it's just a matter of time until the High Court decides to take one of them.

In the meantime, Rep. Robert Aderholt (R-AL) put together a group of seventy cosponsors for the Ten Commandments Defense Act, which would deny federal judges the right to decide where the Ten Commandments can be exhibited. So far, two separate versions of that bill have passed the House, only to be knocked down by liberal Democrats in the Senate. A bill introduced by Rep. John Hostettler (R-IN) was passed by the House, as well, with the aim of prohibiting federal funds from being spent on any attempt to enforce Judge Myron Thompson's order to remove the monument.

Subsequently, the Constitution Restoration Act, sponsored by Aderholt in the House and Alabama senator Richard Shelby in the Senate, would prohibit federal courts from ruling in cases involving government officials who wish to acknowledge God "as the sovereign source of law, liberty or government."[5]

Sen. Wayne Allard (R-CO) introduced a bill that would prohibit the federal courts from ruling on issues of this sort in the future. The caveat in each of these actions, however, is that there are still enough liberal Democrats in the Senate to stop legislation of this kind. Unless there's a massive outcry from the constituents of these Democratic senators, in their own hometowns and neighborhoods, the situation is not likely to change. Furthermore, unless there's a change in the public's attitudes about judicial activism of this sort, nothing is going to change the animus of the federal courts toward free expression of religion. When the Supreme Court invented the idea of a high and impregnable "wall of separation between church and state" in the *Everson* decision, nothing like it had ever existed, but now it often seems as if nothing can stop it.

A History of Accommodation

One of the strangest ironies of the case against "Roy's rock," as it has been called, is the fact that there is an extravagant water fountain, reflecting pool, and statuary exhibit on the campus of the Montgomery courthouse. The highlight of that display is a massive granite and bronze monument in honor of, not our Christian heritage or even the patriots who fought for our freedom, but the Greek goddess Themis, identified by the architects as a symbol of justice. According to Greek mythology, Themis is an "earth goddess" and the wife of Zeus who bore his children, the Hours and the Fates. *A goddess?* you say. If that's the case, why hasn't anyone in the federal courts or the ACLU protested the "establishment of religion" in this case?

According to Auburn University professor Dr. Malcolm Cutchins, who writes a column for a local newspaper, Themis has been recognized by scholars as the goddess who "determines the destiny of all mortals and souls." She has also been described as the "mother of dreams, prophecy incarnate." The Greek goddess is supposed to offer "deep wisdom familiar with the depths of earth and the heights of sky, a guide into the soul." Is this a pagan shrine? A graven image to false gods? I'm hard-pressed to see it any other way. But in light of all this, I might ask, what do Judge Myron Thompson and the Judicial Inquiry Commission have to say about the monument of Themis? And more importantly, what do the citizens of Alabama have to say about it?

It's perfectly clear that there's a double standard here. Liberal judges pretend to be open-minded about religion and traditional moral values, but there's no denying that they're hostile to any public expression of Christian faith. It wasn't always this way, as the record of the courts makes perfectly clear. For the first hundred years of the American judicial system, from the establishment of the Supreme Court in 1790 until the end of the nineteenth century, very few religious liberty cases ever came to the Court. In *Terrett v. Taylor* (1815), the Supreme Court settled a land dispute between two congregations. In *Reynolds v. United States* (1878), *Clawson v. United States* (1885), *Davis v. Beason* (1890), and several others of a similar nature, the Court upheld laws prohibiting polygamy, usually with regard to Mormon practices. But no one would have thought to challenge the long-established symbols of religious reverence in those days.

In fact, several cases during that period provided the Court with opportunities to affirm the common understanding of the American people that Christian precepts were foundational to law and governance in all aspects of our daily life. In *Vidal v. Girard's Executors* (1844), Justice Joseph Story said, "Christianity is not to be maliciously and openly reviled and blasphemed against, to the annoyance of believers or the injury of the public." Further, in the unanimous opinion of the Court, Story posed the rhetorical question, "Where can the purest principles of morality be learned so clearly or so perfectly as from the New Testament?" Anyone in the Court, including the parties to the suit in question, would have agreed on the answer.

The first chief justice, John Jay, said, "Providence has given to our people the choice of their rulers, and it is the duty as well as the privilege and interest of our Christian nation to select and prefer Christians for their rulers," and for decades this view was accepted as common wisdom. In the case of *People v. Ruggles* (1811), the Supreme Court of Judicature of New York convicted a man of vulgar and blasphemous oaths against Christ and the church. In its ruling, the court said, "The morality of the country is deeply ingrafted [sic] upon Christianity, and not upon the doctrines or worship of those imposters. . . . [In] people whose manners are refined, and whose morals have been elevated and inspired with a more enlarged benevolence, [it is] by means of the Christian religion."

Even closer to the issue at hand, the majority opinion held that "offenses against religion and morality strike at the root of moral obligation, and weaken the security of the social ties. . . . This [First Amendment] declaration . . . never meant to withdraw religion in general, and with it the sanctions of moral and social obligation from all consideration and notice of the law." They concluded, "Whatever strikes at the root of Christianity tends manifestly to the dissolution of civil government . . . because it tends to corrupt the morals of the people, and to destroy good order."

Four decades later, in March 1854, the House Judiciary Committee concluded a yearlong study of issues related to the "separation of church and state" with this powerful statement:

Had the people, during the Revolution, had any suspicion of any attempt to war against Christianity, that Revolution would have been strangled in its cradle. . . . At the time of the adoption of the Constitution and the amendments, the universal sentiment was that Christianity should be encouraged, not any one sect. . . . In this age there can be no substitute for Christianity. . . . That was the religion of the founders of the republic and they expected it to remain the religion of their descendants. . . . The great vital and conservative element in our system is the belief of our people in the pure doctrines and divine truths of the gospel of Jesus Christ.

One of the most famous statements in support of our religious heritage comes from the majority opinion in the case of *Church of the Holy Trinity v. United States* (1892). In this instance, the Supreme Court itself had chosen to review thousands of documents to determine from history what sort of polity the founders had set out to create; and in their summation of the process the justices concluded, "From the discovery of this continent to the present hour, there is a single voice making this affirmation. . . . We find everywhere a clear recognition of the same truth. . . . These, and many other matters which might be noticed, add a volume of unofficial declarations to the mass of organic utterances that this is a Christian nation."

Still later, Justice George Sutherland (who was, incidentally, one of the "Four Horsemen" of the Court who resisted the excesses of Franklin Roosevelt's New Deal) wrote the majority opinion in the case of *United States v. Macintosh* (1931), in which the Court declared, "We are a Christian people . . . according to one another the equal right of religious freedom, and acknowledging with reverence the duty of obedience to God."

Perhaps even more remarkable were the words of Chief Justice Hughes in his dissent, in which he said, "When one's belief collides with the power of the state, the latter is supreme within its sphere and submission or punishment follows. But, in the forum of conscience, duty to a moral power higher than the state has always been maintained. . . . The essence of religion is belief in a relation to God involving duties superior to those arising from any human relation." In this, Hughes affirmed the belief of Christians that the ordinances of God take precedence over the laws of man.

THE END OF AN ERA

For the first 150 years of the Court, such views were common: America was a God-fearing nation. It was not until 1947, in *Everson v. Board of Education,* when the Supreme Court erected a previously nonexistent "wall of separation" between church and state, that the tide began to turn against the prevailing Christian beliefs of the founders. The Court cited no precedents for that bizarre ruling. Rather, the *Everson* ruling was a frontal assault on our Christian heritage, an attempt to strip religious principles and symbols from the public square, and a villainy that haunts us to this day.

Today, rather than the favored place Christian values have held since the founding of our nation, freedom of expression is buried in government codes along with sexual orientation, national origin, gender, and race. Title VII of the Civil Rights Act of 1964, with amendments added in 1991, prohibits employment discrimination based on race, color, religion, sex, and national origin. Regarding accommodation for religion in the workplace, the statute says, "The term 'religion' includes all aspects of religious observance and practice, as well as belief, unless an employer demonstrates that he is unable to reasonably accommodate to an employee's or prospective employee's religious observance or practice without undue hardship on the conduct of the employer's business." The statute adds, however, that religious organizations can recruit and hire employees of their own faith in preference to those of other faiths and creeds.

Outside of such protections, there is constant litigation from the ACLU and other liberal groups to strip every reference to God or

Jesus Christ or symbols such as the cross and Nativity scenes from public view. Among these, the case of Michael Newdow is simply the most conspicuous. The first test of the official American motto "In God We Trust" on paper currency and coins was the case of *Aronow v. United States* (1970). In that challenge, the United States Court of Appeals for the Ninth Circuit ruled against the plaintiffs, saying, "It is quite obvious that the national motto and the slogan on coinage and currency, 'In God We Trust,' has nothing whatsoever to do with the establishment of religion." Even during that troubled and confrontational decade, the Ninth Circuit Court felt compelled to say that use of the motto "is of a patriotic or ceremonial character and bears no true resemblance to a governmental sponsorship of a religious exercise."

A second challenge, *Madalyn Murray O'Hair v. W. Michael Blumenthal, Secretary of the Treasury, et al.* (1978), was heard in the U.S. District Court for the Western District of Texas, pursuing a very similar argument as that of the *Aronow* challenge. This time the district court said, based on the ruling of the Ninth Circuit, that "the primary purpose of the slogan was secular; it served a secular ceremonial purpose in the obviously secular function of providing a medium of exchange. As such it is . . . clear that the use of the motto on the currency or otherwise does not have a primary effect of advancing religion."

Michael Newdow's case, *Newdow v. United States Congress* (2002), was heard by a very different Ninth Circuit Court of Appeals in a very different environment. The Ninth Circuit court has issued some of the most outrageous rulings on record and has been over-turned by the U.S. Supreme Court more often than any other federal court. In 1997, twenty-seven of the Ninth Circuit's twenty-eight rulings appealed to the U.S. Supreme Court were reversed, two-thirds of those by a unanimous vote.

In one case, the Ninth Circuit reversed the conviction of an armed bank robber because he never intentionally displayed the gun.

In another, the court ruled unanimously that citizens are not authorized to possess guns under the Second Amendment; only the military may possess weapons. And in the case of *Doe v. Tenet,* the court ruled that a pair of former intelligence agents could sue the CIA, which Supreme Court precedent had already forbidden in the case of *Totten v. United States,* on the grounds that such a suit "would inevitably lead to the disclosure of matters which the law itself regards as confidential."

The most notorious ruling of the Ninth Circuit Court of Appeals, however, was the 2–1 decision declaring that the phrase "under God" in the Pledge of Allegiance violates the First Amendment protections against an unlawful establishment of religion. The U.S. Supreme Court heard oral arguments on the case on March 24, 2004, and advocates on both sides of the issue are now weighing how best to respond to the Court's decision, which was simply to deny Newdow's standing—his right to bring suit in the first place. But whatever happens as new challenges to the Pledge or other Christian symbols are brought to this Court, pursuing always the same objective, you can be assured the action will make major headlines and could lead to major demonstrations of public outrage.

History of the Pledge

To put all of this in context, however, let's start by remembering where the Pledge and the religious references came from. The Pledge of Allegiance was written by Francis Bellamy, an ordained Baptist minister affiliated with several very liberal organizations in his home state of Massachusetts. He was a founding member of the Society of Christian Socialists, as well as a member of the National Education Association, and first cousin of author Edward Bellamy, who wrote the utopian novels *Looking Backward* (1888) and *Equality* (1897).

Bellamy wrote the Pledge for a Columbus Day program honoring the 400th anniversary of the arrival of Christopher Columbus in the New World. It originally said, "I pledge allegiance to my flag and the Republic for which it stands, one nation, indivisible, with liberty and justice for all." The purpose of the Pledge, Bellamy said, was to help Americanize immigrant children, and the idea was well enough received by community and government officials that President Benjamin Harrison issued a proclamation in 1892 endorsing the Pledge. Thereafter, public schools around the country began reciting the words at the beginning of each school day.

The Pledge attracted widespread attention only after it was published in the magazine *The Youth's Companion,* which was a popular publication with a large circulation at the time. Bellamy was hired as an editor after he was forced to leave the Baptist church he pastored due to the socialist content of his sermons. Twenty years after the Pledge was in common usage, members of the American Legion and Daughters of the American Revolution revised Bellamy's words from "my flag" to "the flag of the United States of America," for the National Flag Conference of 1923.

In 1954, during the Eisenhower administration, Congress was persuaded, in part by the request of a group of Catholic businessmen, to add the words, "under God." There was little dissent to the change; in fact, there was a general sense of gratitude in most places when the addition was announced in local newspapers. This was certainly the case in my hometown. That same year President Eisenhower said, "Our government makes no sense unless it is founded on a deeply felt religious faith, and I don't care what it is." Francis Bellamy and his socialist colleagues were predictably annoyed by the change, but most Americans thought of the Pledge as both a patriotic oath and a prayer for God's continued superintending mercy—particularly in those early days of the cold war when we faced a relentlessly atheistic Communist adversary—and for the past fifty years it has been recited by millions of Americans in that spirit.

More recently, however, the Pledge has come under attack once again. To respond to this challenge, Sen. Tim Hutchinson (R-AR), introduced Senate Bill 2690 on September 27, 2002, titled the Pledge of Allegiance Reaffirmation Act, in support of the national motto, "In God We Trust," as well as the Pledge of Allegiance in its entirety, including the phrase "one nation under God." The Senate passed the bill on June 27 of that year by a vote of 99–0. Subsequently, the bill was approved by the House Judiciary Committee on September 10, 2002, by a voice vote.

In the House of Representatives, the principal defenders of the Pledge have been Missouri Republican Todd Akin and North Carolina Democrat Mike McIntyre, who introduced the Pledge Protection Act of 2003, to put that body on record with specific regard to the decision of the Ninth Circuit Court. The Pledge Protection Act, said the congressmen, was written to use the powers granted to Congress by Article III of the Constitution to restrict outrageous rulings of this kind by the federal courts.

In his press announcement, Representative Akin said, "While the Supreme Court is granted certain areas of jurisdictions by the Constitution with 'such exceptions, and under such regulations as the Congress shall make,' the lower federal courts derive their jurisdiction entirely from the Congress. As a consequence, the Congress has the power to add to or remove from the jurisdiction of the lower courts virtually any issue. The exercise of this power by Congress is settled legal doctrine and has been used more than two hundred times."

The congressman made the point even more explicitly, saying, "Within the Declaration of Independence is found a simple formula: There is a God. God grants rights. The primary role of government is to protect those rights. The Ninth's decision to declare 'under God' unconstitutional strikes at the very foundation of our rights and liberties. And as Thomas Jefferson, the author of that Declaration, put it: 'Can the liberties of a nation be secure when we have removed a conviction that these liberties are the gift of God?'" So far the Republican Congress has been holding the line.

But how long will the liberal courts continue to protect these important symbols of our heritage? We may find out very soon.

A LANDMARK DECISION

According to the annual Gallup Poll of Religion in America, 96 percent of all Americans believe in God, and 81 percent of those over age eighteen identify themselves as Christians. In addition, more than a quarter of Americans say they've had an evangelical conversion experience. For those like Michael Newdow who want to give a small minority of atheists and agnostics the right to overrule the interests of the vast majority, the federal courts is the obvious way to go. Where else could they have such a dramatic impact with so little effort? And where else—particularly considering the record of the Ninth Circuit in San Francisco—could they find such willing collaborators in that task?

Atheists have said that use of the phrase "under God" is without precedent in America's public life and that the phrase is a wholly arbitrary "establishment of religion," but that's simply not the case. When George Washington received word that the new Declaration of Independence had actually been signed in Philadelphia, he was serving as commander-in-chief of the army of the Continental Congress. He promptly wrote a military order to be read to the troops with the following directions:

> The several brigades are to be drawn up this evening on their respective parades at six o'clock, when the Declaration of Congress, showing the grounds and reasons of this measure, is to be read with an audible voice. The General hopes that this important event will serve as a fresh incentive to every officer and soldier to act with fidelity and courage, as knowing that now the peace and safety of this country depends, *under God,* solely on the success of our arms[6] (emphasis added).

The document signed that day was the declaration of a new democratic nation, and in his announcement, General Washington wanted his soldiers to appreciate the gravity of the situation, as well as the degree to which their future hopes were in the hands of their God and Maker.

One hundred years later, in the thick of another terrible war, Abraham Lincoln used that same term, "under God," in the famous peroration of the Gettysburg Address, in which he called for a new dedication to the cause of freedom. He said, "It is rather for us to be here dedicated to the great task remaining before us—that from these honored dead we take increased devotion to that cause for which they gave the last full measure of devotion—that we here highly resolve that these dead shall not have died in vain, that this nation *under God* shall have a new birth of freedom . . ." (emphasis added).

Even with our nation's long and illustrious history of faith—we're still recognized as the most religious nation on earth, despite the secularization of the last forty years—there's no guarantee that the Supreme Court will take a stand that favors the accommodation of religion. One way or the other, the *Newdow* case will have a major impact on law and custom, influencing how federal courts rule on this and related issues for decades to come.

In the days leading up to the March 2004 hearing of oral arguments, Newdow called for Justice Scalia to recuse himself from the case. At a Religious Freedom Day celebration in Fredricksburg, Virginia, shortly after the Ninth Circuit's ruling, Scalia had said, "Although the Constitution says the government cannot 'establish' or promote religion, the framers did not intend for God to be stripped from public life." Michael Newdow claimed that Scalia's remark was evidence of prejudice against his case. After considering the request for recusal, Scalia agreed not to participate in the case, even though there was no policy or precedent to prevent him from doing so if he wished.

Throughout the arguments by Newdow on one side, and

Solicitor General Ted Olson and Elk Grove School District attorney Terrence Cassidy on the other, the Court peppered the lawyers with questions. Questions from Chief Justice Rehnquist and Justice O'Connor were especially pointed, while those of Justice Kennedy seemed to reflect his agonizing uncertainty over this issue. But in comments to the media after the hearing, Michael Newdow was jubilant, saying he expected to get a vote of 8–0 from the Court, in support of his case. That turned out to be a silly prediction.

Among the hundreds of people who gathered outside the Supreme Court that day, the vast majority disagreed strongly with Newdow's views. That morning, prior to the justices taking their places, Pledge supporters gathered to pray together. They sang "America the Beautiful" and filled the concourse in front of the building with signs and banners that said, "In God We Trust," "Keep USA One Nation Under God," and "God Bless America." Opponents of the Pledge held their own rally, with signs such as "Public Schools Should Teach Not Preach," but they were vastly outnumbered.

Solicitor General Olson, whose presence clearly indicated the level of interest of the Bush White House, argued that the phrase "under God" is not a prayer but a historical reference—what some in the government have referred to as "ceremonial deism." Olson said that the Pledge is not what this Court says the establishment clause protects against. Rather, he said, it was one of various "civic and ceremonial acknowledgments of the indisputable historical fact that caused the framers of our Constitution and the signers of the Declaration of Independence to say that they had the right to revolt and start a new country." The framers believed that "God gave them the right to declare their independence when the king has not been living up to the unalienable principles given to them by God."

In his response, Newdow ridiculed Olson's argument and said that the interpretation of "one nation under God" is that "government is saying there's a God." And at one point he claimed that passage of the revised text of the Pledge by Congress in 1954 was a divisive issue. At that point, the chief justice asked how the vote had gone, and Newdow confessed that it was unanimous in favor of adding the words "under God." Justice Rehnquist responded, "Well, that doesn't sound very divisive." To which Newdow replied, "That's only because an atheist can't be elected to Congress." At that, the gallery immediately burst into applause, and the chief justice threatened to clear the courtroom if there was any more clapping.

An Associated Press poll released on the day of the hearing reported that 87 percent of respondents thought that "under God" ought to remain in the Pledge. At a time when the nation is increasingly divided, most Americans understand that the Pledge of Allegiance is a source of unity. Geoffrey Holland, an American History teacher at San Benito High School in Hollister, California, may have said it best when he told a local reporter that the pledge is important to his students because it brings people together.

"It's a common bond that everyone shares," said Holland. "Some kids take algebra, and some take geometry, but reciting the pledge is something that makes everyone equal and puts them on the same playing field."[7] Especially in a part of the country where there is a tremendous diversity of races and family background, restoring the meaning of *e pluribus unum,* that we are one nation who come from many places and backgrounds, is not a bad thing. And the assurance of God's continued blessing makes the situation so much better.

A NEVER-ENDING STRUGGLE

The answer to all the speculation about this case finally came on June 14, 2004, when the Supreme Court announced that the justices had overturned the ruling of the Ninth Circuit Court of Appeals. All eight justices (voting without Justice Scalia) concluded that the Ninth Circuit's holding was wrong. Five justices said that Michael Newdow lacked standing. Three justices concluded that Newdow had standing but that the phrase "under God" in the Pledge does not violate the establishment clause of the First Amendment.

In the majority opinion, delivered by Justice Stevens, Justices Ginsburg, Breyer, and Souter overturned the Ninth Circuit Court's ruling, finding Newdow had no standing to sue because he was neither the child's legal guardian nor had any authority to make educational or legal decisions for her. In the majority opinion, Justice Stevens quoted Judge Robert Bork, saying that the standing requirement is born partly of "an idea, which is more than an intuition but less than a rigorous and explicit theory, about the constitutional and prudential limits to the powers of an *unelected, unrepresentative judiciary* in our kind of government" (emphasis added).[8]

Chief Justice Rehnquist and Justices O'Connor and Thomas concurred in that judgment, but they addressed the issue of the constitutionality of the Pledge under the establishment clause. They adopted the Ninth Circuit Court's reasoning that Newdow had standing to sue but ruled in our favor on the merits, finding that use of the words "under God" in the Pledge of Allegiance did not violate the establishment clause. In her concurrence, Justice O'Connor stated, "Certain ceremonial references to God and religion in our Nation are the inevitable consequence of the religious history that gave birth to our founding principles of liberty. It would be ironic indeed if this Court were to wield our constitutional commitment to religious freedom so as to sever our ties to the traditions developed to honor it."[9]

The various statements of the justices, indeed, pay lip service to religious liberty; yet from one week to the next it's impossible to know what to expect from this Court. As *Boston Globe* columnist Jeff Jacoby pointed out in the wake of a group of hearings in December 2003:

Lawsuits are filed each December to block the placement of a crèche or a menorah on public property. Children have been barred from reading the Bible in class—even on their own time. A U.S. Court of Appeals decided that teachers may not lead students in the Pledge of Allegiance, since it contains the phrase "under God." The state of Washington revoked a student's college grant when he decided to major in theology. More than ever, it seems, the First Amendment's command forbidding "an establishment of religion" is being enforced as a ban on *any* religious expression in the public square.[10]

When Jacoby asked Democratic candidates for the presidency in January 2004 where they stood on issues of church and state, General Wesley Clark described the separation of church and state as essential "both to protect religious faith and diversity of faith." Rep. Dennis Kucinich (D-OH) said, "they have not gone far enough," and "by removing the trappings of religion" from all government facilities, "we actually increase the freedom of everyone to freely and openly practice the beliefs of their choice." The logic of such statements doesn't hold up to scrutiny, of course. But even Reverend Al Sharpton essentially agreed, saying, "Our public places should not be used to put forth any particular religious viewpoint or message."

Candidate John Edwards, who was eventually selected as Senator John Kerry's running mate for vice president, said that he had "no comment on whether the courts in general have been too hostile toward religion," but then he went on to say that "it is right not to have teachers leading prayers in public classrooms." In the months following Jacoby's two-part series, each of these candidates dropped out of the race, leaving Senator Kerry and Senator Edwards as the contenders to President Bush and Vice President Cheney in November's elections. But of that original field of hopefuls, only one Democrat spoke respectfully of our religious heritage and the role of faith in contemporary society.

Senator Joe Lieberman of Connecticut stood alone as the only

Democrat who would go on record in support of freedom of religious expression in the public square, and he didn't run from the issue during his short-lived bid for the presidency. When asked for his views on the subject, Lieberman said, "I strongly believe in the separation of church and state and the right of every American to worship or not worship as they see fit. But I don't believe that the First Amendment was ever intended to remove from the public square all displays and expressions of faith or prohibit the inclusion of the words 'under God' in the Pledge of Allegiance, as some courts have found and some groups advocate. When I am president," the candidate said, "I will work to preserve the balance we have observed throughout our history of protecting individual freedoms and embracing the constructive role that faith in general continues to play in our public life."

As laudable as those comments were at the time, they simply didn't play to the senator's liberal base, for whom matters of faith are thought to be either intensely private or inappropriate. A far more typical view of the Democratic Left is that of Nicholas Kristof, a columnist for the *New York Times,* who rarely misses an opportunity to take a shot at those who dare to speak with respect for the nation's religious history.

In an opinion editorial dispatched from Iran, where he had gone to review the sad state of liberty in that troubled land, Kristof used the occasion to equate the intolerance of the ayatollahs and mullahs who act as dictators in Iran with the desire of law-abiding Christians for religious freedom in America. In his hopelessly shallow comparison of the breakdown of culture in the two nations, Kristof concluded the column by saying:

There's a useful lesson here for George Bush's America as well as for the ayatollahs' Iran: when a religion is imposed on people, when a government tries too ostentatiously to put itself "under God," the effect is often not to prop up religious faith but to undermine it. Nothing is more lethal to religious faith than having self-righteous, intolerant politicians (who wince at nose studs) drag God into politics.[11]

The assumptions inherent in that statement are so specious and naive they hardly merit a response; anyone with a lick of common sense can see through them. Comparing the bloody tyrants of Islam to the benevolent founders of America is a shocking calumny. It's only since the Supreme Court and federal courts began turning their backs on religious freedom and dishonoring our heritage of faith that American culture has fallen into decline. The purpose of President Bush's faith-based initiatives, in fact, is to restore the moral fiber of the nation by putting the restorative properties of faith to work where they can do the most good. That's what being "salt and light" in the culture is all about—preserving the good and exposing the bad.

As we've seen on almost every page of this book, there is no disguising the good that Christian culture has done, particularly in giving birth to a nation that is regarded around the world as a land of liberty and unparalleled opportunity. As I said earlier, the French statesman Alexis de Tocqueville relayed this important message to his countrymen when he said that America is "the place where the Christian religion has kept the greatest power over men's souls; and nothing better demonstrates how useful and natural it is to man, since the country where it now has the widest sway is both the most enlightened and the freest."

But whether we're defending against the attacks of journalists, left-wing politicians, radical atheists, or federal judges with an ax to grind, Christians must realize that we're engaged in a contest of wills that we simply cannot afford to lose. "For our struggle is not against flesh and blood, but against the rulers, against the authorities, against the powers of this dark world, and against the spiritual forces of evil in the heavenly realms" (Ephesians 6:12 NIV). Paul's words are as true today as they were two thousand years ago, and we need to realize that we're in it for the duration.

TABLE OF CASES

PART THREE

A PRESCRIPTION
FOR CHANGE

9

OUR BLACK-ROBED MASTERS

It is the people, and not the judges, who are entitled to say what their constitution means, for the constitution is theirs; it belongs to them and not to their servants in office—any other theory is incompatible with the foundation principles of our government.

—THEODORE ROOSEVELT (1912)

Once considered "the least dangerous branch" of government, today's Supreme Court wields almost unlimited power over the affairs of the nation. Consequently, the attitudes and opinions of nine justices of the Supreme Court can affect everything we do: how we live, how we raise our children, how we worship, even what we think and believe. These justices' beliefs, responses to controversial social issues, and influences on their own thinking have a critical influence on how decisions are rendered and how the laws are interpreted and enforced. And for the past five decades, the Court has been moving in a frightening direction. Fortunately, there are still a few justices on the bench who care about constitutional principles, but too often those brave men are outnumbered by the majority on the Left who see the world through very different lenses.

Thanks to fifty years of judicial activism, a lot of people believe that the Supreme Court is the custodian of the Constitution and that whatever a majority of black-robed justices declare is the law of the land. But this is a false and misleading idea. It's also a dangerous misunderstanding of the fundamental structures of government. This misconception has been encouraged by the Court, of course, but placing the Republic under a left-wing tribunal puts the sovereignty and integrity of the American people in great peril. As social critic Richard Lessner has written:

> The notion of judicial supremacy, that the court has the final say on the meaning of the law and Constitution, is nowhere to be found in the thoughts of the Framers or the text of the Founding document. It is a power the courts have arrogated to themselves over time with little resistance from the legislative or executive branches of government. Federalist 78 by Alexander Hamilton contains not so much as a hint that the courts constitute the supreme branch of government or that judicial rulings irrevocably settle issues in dispute. Such a notion of unaccountable, unanswerable, unfettered judicial power does violence to the whole notion of separated powers.[1]

The Supreme Court was never meant to be the sole or final arbiter of the law, but merely the arm of government instituted to settle controversies of great substance within the framework of the Constitution. By the same measure, the framers intended for the federal courts to be held in check both by the Supreme Court and by the even greater authority of the executive and legislative branches. As Alexander Hamilton explained in Federalist 81, "There is not a syllable in the plan under consideration which directly empowers the national courts to construe the laws according to the spirit of the Constitution, or which gives them any greater latitude in this respect than may be claimed by the courts of every state."

The clear mandate of the Constitution is that Congress is the body responsible for establishing, framing, and amending laws, which they are to do in response to the wishes of the people and the requirements of the executive branch. It is, thus, the people, by means of their representatives in Congress, who have ultimate authority over the courts—and not the other way around. "Not only can the people amend the Constitution," writes Richard Lessner, "but the Congress also can limit the courts' jurisdiction under the Constitution's 'exceptions clause' in Article III, Section 2, putting specific matters beyond the reach of grasping judges."[2] And, in any case, the authority of the government was designed to be "distributed" among the three branches. It is certainly not the exclusive property of an out-of-control judiciary.

THE GERM OF DISSOLUTION

Thomas Jefferson, who endured many clashes with the courts, understood the risks of judicial overreach as well as anyone. In a letter to a citizen who shared his concerns, Jefferson said, "It has long, however, been my opinion, and I have never shrunk from its expression . . . that the germ of dissolution of our federal government is in the constitution of the federal judiciary . . . working like gravity by night and by day, gaining a little today and a little tomorrow, and advancing its noiseless step like a thief, over the field of jurisdiction, until all shall be usurped." I can think of no better description of the sort of judicial usurpation that confronts us today.

As we've seen throughout these pages, examples of heavy-handed judicial activism are not hard to find. In *Lawrence v. Texas* (2003), the Supreme Court overruled its own prior decision in *Bowers v. Hardwick* (1986) and not only struck down a 145-year-old Texas statute prohibiting homosexual sodomy, but at the same time the Court overturned comparable laws in thirteen other states. Then, when presented with an emergency appeal to respond to the 180-day stay order issued by the Massachusetts Supreme Court, in a case that allowed homosexual marriage in that state, the Supreme Court of the United States refused to intervene, thus giving tacit approval for the Massachusetts ruling to stand and condoning homosexual marriages not only in that state but, by implication, in every state.

The Court's record is all too clear. In *Santa Fe Indep. Sch. Dist. v. Doe* (2000), the Court struck down student-led prayer at public-school sporting events. In *Stenberg v. Carhart* (2000), the Court overturned Nebraska's ban on partial-birth abortions. In the majority opinion in that case, Justice Stephen Breyer was apparently alarmed that "all those who perform abortion procedures using that method must fear prosecution, conviction, and imprisonment." In other words, doctors who break the law by killing an infant at the moment of birth and then sucking out the baby's brain would have to deal with the legal repercussions. Unlike Justice Breyer and company, most Americans don't have a problem understanding the logic of that.[3]

As ardent defenders of a woman's right to kill her unborn child, Breyer and his liberal colleagues were incensed. For that reason, he wrote a tendentious opinion, saying that the Nebraska law places "an undue burden upon a woman's right to make an abortion decision." In an emotional dissent, Justice Scalia pointed out the illogical assumptions of Justice Breyer's reasoning, saying, "The notion that the Constitution of the United States . . . prohibits the States from simply banning this visibly brutal means of eliminating our half-born posterity is quite simply absurd."

The attitude of today's Supreme Court is deeply troubling. But, as George Will pointed out in a recent column dealing with the implications of *Brown v. Board of Education* (1954) fifty years later, that highly controversial decision (which ordered an end to segregated public schools in every state) may have helped to achieve the constitutional goals of liberty and equality for all Americans, but there were unseen and unanticipated consequences. "*Brown v. Board of Education,*" Will writes, ". . . also encouraged the abandonment of constitutional reasoning—of constitutional law. It invested the judiciary with a prestige that begot arrogance. And it seemed to legitimize a legislative mentality among judges wielding an anti-constitutional premise. The premise is that 'unjust' and 'unconstitutional' are synonyms."[4]

This insight helps to explain a lot of the arrogance we've seen during the past four or five decades. Because the Court has been right in taking bold and controversial stands in a few landmark cases, like *Brown,* they've come to believe they're infallible and beyond the need for accountability. In rebuffing the people of Nebraska by judicial fiat, Justice Breyer made no apology for abandoning any reference to constitutional law. And, once again, the consequences of the Court's action had far-reaching implications, voiding federal and state laws because, in Justice Breyer's estimation, "a law designed to further the State's interest in fetal life which imposes an undue burden on the woman's decision before viability is unconstitutional."[5]

A CALL FOR REFORM

The American people have said repeatedly, as every major survey has reported, that we want the practice of partial-birth abortion outlawed once and for all. Still, the courts refuse to allow any challenge to be sustained—no doubt for fear that it will be the first step in a general assault on all forms of abortion. But not everyone is sitting on their hands waiting for the courts to wise up. In an effort to counter the Supreme Court's resistance to the will of the people, the U.S. House of Representatives and the Senate both passed bills banning the practice—on four separate occasions. The politicians went to the mat for the people. They did their part, but Bill Clinton vetoed three of those bills. Then, when Congress passed a fourth ban on the procedure, President George W. Bush signed it, on November 5, 2003, only to have the law suspended the next day by an unelected federal judge in Nebraska. Thus the courts continue to desecrate the Constitution and silence the voice of the people.

To date, at least thirty-one states have passed laws banning the partial-birth procedure, only to have them suspended by unelected federal judges. On September 5, 1999, the Missouri legislature passed a ban on partial-birth abortions, only to see it vetoed by then governor Mel Carnahan, a liberal Democrat. Not to be denied, however, more than fifteen thousand men, women, and children gathered on the grounds of the state capitol, where they knelt in prayer as legislators voted to override the governor's veto. But, once again, an unelected federal judge suspended the law, and Missouri's life-saving efforts remain in limbo.

In September 2000, Missouri legislators passed a bill entitled A Woman's Right to Know, designed to ensure that those seeking abortions would be informed of the medical risks and the realities involved, as well as their options. But Governor Holden vetoed the bill. Once again, legislators overrode the governor's veto, and a district judge overruled them.

Elsewhere, the citizens of Arizona passed Proposition 106 in March 1997 to recognize English as the state's official language, but federal judges of the Ninth Circuit Court overruled them. In March 1996, citizens of the state of Washington voted against physician-assisted suicide, but federal judges of the Ninth Circuit overruled them. The very next month, the citizens of New York voted against physician-assisted suicide, but federal judges of the Second Circuit ruled against them. In May 1995, Washington voters wanted term limits for politicians, but in the case of *Term Limits v. Thornton,* the Superior Court took the opposite view. And the list goes on.

Citizens of Arkansas passed a term-limits bill, but federal judges overruled them. In 1995, Californians passed Proposition 187 to stop state-funded taxpayer services to illegal aliens, but federal judges overruled them. In a 1995 statewide referendum in Colorado, voters passed Amendment 2, which said that while homosexuals are already entitled to full and equal protection under the law, they are not entitled to "special status" under the law. However, a federal district judge denied the will of the people and overturned the election results. That decision was challenged but was later upheld by the United States Supreme Court, which, in the case of *Romer v. Evans,* went a step further by accusing the voters of Colorado of animosity toward homosexuals.

In still other acts of judicial overreaching, a federal judge overruled California's Proposition 209—a hard-fought case that ended affirmative action at the University of California—while in San Antonio, Texas, a federal judge ordered that election ballots completed by the county's military personnel had to be thrown out. Why? Because the military is generally conservative, and this liberal judge was intent on blocking the duly elected Republican sheriff and county commissioner from taking their seats.

THE BREAKDOWN

How do these blatant acts of judicial overreaching happen? In large part, they happen because Congress and the president have so far refused to use their authority to reign in the courts. William J. Quirk and R. Randall Birdwell, authors of the book *Judicial Dictatorship,* take this view a step further, saying that the reason the other branches of government don't stop the courts is for fear of the people and the press, who have bought into the idea that the Supreme Court is "supreme."[6]

Some commentators have suggested that one reason politicians don't complain is that they prefer for these unelected judges to take the blame for divisive legislation. Whatever is actually at the root of such behavior, the doctrine of judicial supremacy simply does not exist. The Constitution gives Congress the power to create the federal courts or to abolish them if they so desire. The framers gave the legislature the power to limit the Supreme Court to "cases affecting ambassadors, other public ministers, and consuls, and those in which a state shall be a party." But so far Congress has not been willing to take any such actions. Legislators are good about complaining when their authority is stepped on by the courts, but they have assiduously avoided using their legitimate powers in defense of the "common good."

The result is that the Court has gotten more and more aggressive over time, entering areas of social legislation where they have no business or authority. And now, especially disturbing, is the fact that the decisions of some justices refer to "international law" and thus threaten to surrender American jurisprudence to the rulings of courts in countries whose customs, beliefs, history, and traditions have no relevance or authority in this country. If this is not over-reaching, I don't know what is. And if the trend continues, there really will be a culture war in America.

Anyone looking at the nature of recent federal court rulings would have to wonder if these men and women even inhabit the same planet with the rest of us. These judges have defended almost unrestricted access to pornography, defended the rights of anarchists and protesters to burn the American flag, defended the right to partial-birth abortions, and have given schools the right to forbid voluntary, student-led prayers at public-school football games, which is certainly not a constitutional right. Furthermore, they have ruled that atheists have a right not to be offended by the Ten Commandments and that homosexuals have a right to sodomy, and the future of the words "under God" in the Pledge of Allegiance are anything but safe from their grasp. Who knows what's next on their hit list?

There are only a few possible explanations for such irrational conduct. One may be that the judges enjoy such elevated status, so far above the common man in their knowledge, wisdom, and level of enlightenment, that they feel they've been granted a "divine right" to shape our laws and social policy as they wish. In this case, the Constitution and judicial precedent are merely inconveniences for them, to be used or not used as our black-robed rulers see fit.

Another reason could be that these judges actually despise this country and all it stands for; therefore, they believe that the best way to undermine and humiliate America is to break down its laws, morals, beliefs, and standards, and to bring about as much cultural anarchy and chaos as possible, so that the nation will eventually destroy itself and make way for a "new order of the ages."

A third reason may be that the liberal view of the Constitution as a "living, breathing document" makes Supreme Court justices not simply judges but framers of an all new "Constitution in the making," a document that is evolving, always changing, and always subject to the latest vogue of elite doctrine. And a fourth possibility is that the justices don't recognize or understand the dramatic consequences that may result from their actions. Maybe it's one of these possibilities—framed as forms of oligarchy, nihilism, relativism, or ignorance—or, more likely, it's a combination of all of them. But whatever is behind the breakdown of American justice, it's wrong, and it has to stop.

What Are We Thinking?

In response to the Court's sodomy ruling in *Lawrence v. Texas,* conservatives in many places are now pushing for a constitutional amendment to define marriage very specifically as a covenant between "a man and a woman." One of my deepest concerns is that Christians and other conservatives keep trying to figure out what we can do to force the courts to abide by the Constitution. But when these same justices persist in believing that their own words and opinions are, in fact, the essence of a "living, breathing Constitution," it is nearly impossible to hold them to the language of a document written by a group of dead, white European males in the eighteenth century.

No reasonable person would vote for the vast majority of leftist social policies supported by the courts today. Federal judges have turned the nation upside down in the name of social justice.

Whatever legitimate risks there may be in a government "of the people, by the people, and for the people," the American people would never have passed laws that have led to the slaughter of more than forty million unborn children. Yet these are the values of today's federal courts.

Federal judges may be granted life tenure, but the Constitution specifies, as we have already seen, that their term in office is based strictly on the condition of "good behaviour." A presidential appointment does not entitle federal judges to act as tyrants and dictators for life. The reason the American people abide by the Court's rulings in the first place is because we believe in the authority of the Constitution that these same federal judges are sworn to uphold. When will we realize that a large majority of the men and women on the federal bench have failed any reasonable standard of good behavior and are making judgments that are so outlandish we're no longer responsible for paying attention to them? When will we begin to hold the federal courts and the Supreme Court of the United States accountable for their *bad* behavior?

It's high time Congress and the president stood up to the bullying of the courts. Abraham Lincoln certainly understood that United States presidents are entitled to make constitutional judgments independent of the courts. In his first inaugural address, Lincoln said that rulings of the Supreme Court should be considered binding on the parties to the particular case, and as such they deserve "very high respect and consideration in all parallel cases by all other departments of the government." But it goes no further than that. If the president or the legislature were forced to defer to the Supreme Court's decisions in every case, Lincoln said, "the people will have ceased to be their own rulers, having, to that extent, practically resigned their government into the hands of that eminent tribunal."

As I said earlier, the authority of the United States government was designed to be distributed among three branches. It was not vested in an unaccountable judicial aristocracy. We were not meant to be under the thumb of a judicial oligarchy, or an out-of-control Congress for that matter. When confronted by an act of Congress he could not obey, Thomas Jefferson simply refused to enforce it, as was the case with the Sedition Acts. Andrew Jackson vetoed the reauthorization of the Second Bank of the United States because he believed it was unconstitutional. He said, "Each public officer who takes an oath to support the Constitution swears that he will support it as he understands it, and not as it is understood by others."

The problem today is that too many Americans have accepted the view that we are indentured servants of the courts. Too many of us have decided to bow rather than to fight the loss of our sovereignty. But it is perfectly clear that the world-view of the Supreme Court is no longer the world-view of the American people. As the red and blue maps in the 2000 election demonstrated so clearly, we live in a divided nation, with roughly half of the voting public taking sides with those on the Left, who are behind the slide into moral relativism and social anarchy, and the other half fighting to hold onto standards that have been been tried and proven over time but are deemed by the cultural elites to be against the law.

WHERE ARE WE GOING?

In this environment, the justices of the United States Supreme Court have become what journalist and author Max Boot calls "the high priests of our civic religion."[7] But this is precisely what the founders wanted to avoid. They saw the potential for unelected judges to exceed their authority, but they believed that a system of checks and balances would be enough to restrain the courts from doing very great harm. Unfortunately, the founders had not foreseen what would happen when the cultural Left, abetted by an activist liberal media, began the insidious process of transforming these "high priests" and their unelected allies in the federal court system into an army of unaccountable oligarchs. But that's precisely what we have today.

In his introductory essay to Max Boot's book *Out of Order,* Judge Robert Bork writes that the federal courts have pushed the idea of an independent judiciary far beyond anything the Constitution allows. Judicial independence, he says, was designed to prevent political pressures from affecting the interpretation of the law. Today, however, *judicial independence* is simply a buzzword meaning that neither Congress nor the American people are allowed to interfere with the social and political judgments of the courts. But this is a big mistake. Bork writes:

> Judicial independence was never intended to make courts what they have become, unaccountable and uncheckable partisans in our culture wars. As for the system of checks and balances, there is no check upon the federal courts provided by the Constitution precisely because it was assumed, as Alexander Hamilton, James Madison, and others put it, that there was no need for such a check. The courts were to interpret, not create the law. Placing the federal courts under democratic restraints would in no sense violate the original understanding of their place in our government.[8]

Unfortunately, whenever the subject of democratic restraints or accountability comes up, judges and lawyers—along with their professional associations and the elite law schools—react with shock and alarm. Even the slightest hint that the federal courts ought to be more responsible to the republican principles of government is interpreted as an assault on judicial independence. But as Judge Bork argues, "Suggestions for the serious reformation of the judicial system ought not be treated with the combination of alarm and scorn that is their usual lot. People forget that such proposals have been consistently offered throughout our history and that they were put forward by some of our most revered public figures."[9]

In fact, if some of those historic proposals had actually been carried out, many of today's problems might have been avoided. Thomas Jefferson, for example, proposed reigning in the courts by impeaching and convicting judges who exceeded their authority. He also proposed that Supreme Court decisions dealing with constitutional issues should only be binding on the judicial branch itself. As I've said, Andrew Jackson and Abraham Lincoln ignored court orders they found to be objectionable, and the feisty Wisconsin congressman Robert LaFollette proposed in the 1890s that decisions of the Supreme Court that went too far into policymaking and legislation should be overturned by a two-thirds vote of the Senate. These men would have found the notions exalted by today's liberals, that the Supreme Court and the federal courts are some kind of sacred institution, to be utterly laughable.

When I interviewed Judge Bork about his new book, *Coercing Virtue*,[10] on my television program, *The 700 Club*, I asked him what he thought the courts were trying to do with their radical social agenda. I asked him, "Who's driving this train?" He replied that the train is being driven by the so-called intellectual elite, made up of the cultural Left and the mainstream media. "They're not very elite," he said, "but I can't think of a better name other than the 'chattering class' or the 'Olympians' or something of that sort. I'm talking about university professors, law school professors, journalists (print and electronic), Hollywood celebrities, much of the clergy, church bureaucracy, foundation staffs, and so forth. These are people who shape opinions, people who are verbalists, and they are well to the left of the American public.

"The most distinguishing feature," Judge Bork told me, "is that they are much less religious. In fact, they have a real animosity toward religion—more than the American public in general. They are doing their best to drive public religion out of the public square and they've just about succeeded." I wasn't surprised by his answer, I'm sad to say, since I've been seeing the same thing for years, and I have often said so on the broadcast. But I followed up by asking the judge what he thought the next step would be if these so-called elites actually get their way. "If they get rid of religion," I said, "they're sort of idealistic. What is it they're trying to do?"

Judge Bork said, "Well, they're trying to have their own version of utopia, manifested largely through the courts. They have a value system that, when you put it up for election, when someone confesses to it as a candidate, he loses. They can't get the more extreme items through the legislatures. So the courts, being part of the intellectual class, and responding to that class, have by and large joined that side of the 'culture war.' Not all judges, of course, but enough of them to make theirs the winning side in the courts."

I couldn't help thinking that many of these judges seem to be trying to rival God Himself, acting out roles as the benefactors and healers of society, repairing all our social ills, and building a better world. If that's what they think, it would be the ultimate form of blasphemy.

Then I asked Judge Bork to describe what he perceived to be the primary goals of these socialist utopians, and he said, "It would be strict separation of the church and state, which is contrary to the Constitution's original meaning. It would be abortion-on-demand. It would mean the normalization of homosexuality, and a whole list of cultural aims that the majority of Americans don't agree with."

WHO'S RUNNING THE SHOW?

A *utopia,* as the word connotes in its original form, is a grand and idealistic scheme of some sort, a perfect world or society. That's the dictionary definition, but the original Greek words (*ou topos*) mean "no place," which is a fitting description of most of the Left's ideas. But if they're really intent on pushing their unrealistic plans through the courts or the Congress, you have to wonder how they expect to make their radical agenda work in the real world. So I asked Judge

Bork about that. I said, "How do they keep the trains running? How do they balance the budget? How do they do all the mundane things of government? They don't seem to have much interest in that."

And he told me, "Well they don't balance the budget, certainly, and I don't think they have much to do with the trains. I think right now, the Left in America, the liberal Left, is less concerned with economic issues than with lifestyle issues. And they're determined to have a very permissive morality, particularly in matters of sexuality. And they're determined to have very permissive laws about that achieved through the courts."

Most responsible Americans are concerned about the left-wing agenda they see behind the move to normalize homosexuality. Hollywood and the mass media are huge boosters of this sort of thing, of course. We would expect that, but the Court's advocacy of such behaviors is more troubling. The Court's *Lawrence* decision may be the most notorious example, but it's only the latest in a long string of abuses. I wanted Judge Bork to comment on that as well, so I asked him, "Where does the Supreme Court come off saying that homosexuality is a constitutional right?" What surprised me most of all in that decision, I told him, was the fact that a Roman Catholic justice, Anthony Kennedy, had written the decision. How could that be?

Judge Bork responded, "One of the really terribly disturbing features of the Supreme Court, and this is true of the courts of all Western nations, is that they are making up constitutional rights that are nowhere in the Constitution. There is nothing in the Constitution one way or another about homosexual sodomy, yet the Supreme Court finds it's a constitutional right. There's nothing in the Constitution one way or another about abortion . . . but the Supreme Court made up a right to abortion. Now, that's the most disturbing thing. They are constantly making up the Constitution as they go along, and they're making it up according to the agenda of the Left-liberals. The ACLU might as well be writing the Constitution these days."

In his book *Coercing Virtue,* Bork goes into detail about some of the more dangerous trends in the justice system, including the use of precedents from foreign courts—in Europe, Africa, and beyond—as well as the practice of granting legal standing to litigants who would not have been allowed to bring suits in any previous era. So I said, "You've pointed out that the courts today give standing that was never given before. They find aggrieved persons that really have no legitimate claim in a particular case, but the justices let them intervene, and they hear their point of view. What's going on there?"

"Yes, that's troubling," Bork said, "because in order to have standing to sue you usually have to suffer some injury either to your person or your wallet or something of that sort. The mere fact that you're offended, or that you don't like something the government is doing, is not grounds to sue—except in one case. The Supreme Court made one exception, and that is for people who are offended by *religion.* They may sue without showing any particular harm to themselves other than the fact that they are offended by looking at something." This is of course the motivation for the *Lemon* test and all the others, invented out of whole cloth by the Court.

"You also refer in your book to something called 'the American disease,'" I said. "And some people have stood in some horror to see a democratic nation like the United States being seized by what amounts to a judicial coup d'état. And yet, you say this disease is spreading. As a matter of fact, we're seeing judges making reference to cases from Zimbabwe or from the European Court of civil rights."

"That's right," he said. "That phrase actually came from the Canadians. When they framed their constitution in 1982, they said they didn't want to undergo 'the American disease.' But of course their court is at least as activist as ours, and they should have discovered that it's not just an American disease; it's a judicial disease. Everywhere courts have been given the power to override legislatures, they've begun to make up the Constitution to fit their Left-liberal desires. That's because the culture war runs across all

Western nations, and the forces in that war are the same every-where."

THE MOST SERIOUS THREAT

I think most Christians understand that perspective. The culture war really is universal in scope. It may seem more pronounced in the United States simply because we've had such a high standard of public virtue until recently. As I mentioned in previous chapters, it wasn't until the *Everson* decision of 1947 that the courts began their assault on the free exercise of religion. And then it wasn't until the school-prayer and Bible-reading cases of the 1960s that judges were able to begin forcing God out of our public institutions. Nevertheless, because the culture war is ultimately a spiritual contest between those who love God and those who want to eradicate all evidence of religion from society, it's a bigger problem than most of us realize.

As Judge Bork and I came to the end of our conversation, I mentioned our special weeklong broadcasts on *The 700 Club*, called Operation Supreme Court Freedom, in which we were asking people to pray, to appeal to the Supreme Judge of all the earth, that He might overrule some of these unjust judges. None of the sitting justices of the Supreme Court resigned that week, and we didn't expect them to. But we did discover that millions of people who had paid little attention to the courts were suddenly aware of the urgency of the situation, and they were concerned about what's happening. So as I spoke briefly about that with Judge Bork, I asked him if he thought there's anything we can do to turn things around.

"In your book," I said, "you pointed out several things that could be done to change things, but for each one of them you said it wouldn't work. What we're seeing is obviously a usurpation of power that doesn't appear in the Constitution. So how do we get rid of these guys?"

Bork's reply was simple but disturbing. "I don't know if it can be done," he said. "The only way to do it would be through political means. That is, having a president who understands who he's nominating and a Senate that's willing to confirm people who stick to the Constitution. The Democratic Party has displayed complete hostility to the idea of judges who stick to the actual Constitution. They view the Supreme Court as a political prize and a political weapon, and they want to control it. And hence you see these filibusters against President Bush's nominees to the federal courts. The Left wants Left-liberal justices or none, and that's a problem."

I certainly appreciate the wisdom and courage of this great man, and I understand that by any standard of history or common sense, Judge Bork was absolutely right in his assessments. But I also understood that God doesn't depend on history or common sense to work His will. I'm not overstating the case when I say that the challenge before us today—an out-of-control federal judiciary abetted by legions of left-wing culture warriors—is the most serious threat America has faced in nearly four hundred years of history.

If the courts succeed in unraveling our great Constitution, which has protected our heritage of faith, family, and freedom for so long, there will be nothing but God's sovereign grace to prevent the utter collapse of everything we hold dear. And unless something changes soon, that would seem to be our fate.

But I am not willing to accept that judgment. Furthermore, I don't believe that's what God has in mind for our nation. There is every reason to believe that this situation can be turned around, that the courts can be reprimanded, brought back into line, and forced to become more accountable. I believe also that, in God's own time, the moral foundations of our nation can be restored. But it won't happen overnight, and it won't happen without a fight.

Before we can enlist in that fight, we need to know our adversaries. We need to know where they're coming from and what they're up to. And that will be the subject of the next chapter.

Table of Cases

Bowers v. Hardwick, 478 U.S. 186 (1986).

Brown v. Bd. of Educ., 347 U.S. 483 (1954).

Goodridge v. Dept. of Pub. Health, 440 Mass. 309 (2004).

Lawrence v. Texas, 539 U.S. 558 (2003).

Planned Parenthood v. Casey, 505 U.S. 833 (1992).

Santa Fe Indep. Sch. Dist. v. Doe, 530 U.S. 290 (2000).

Stenberg v. Carhart, 530 U.S. 914 (2000).

Term Limits v. Thornton, 514 U.S. 779 (1995).

10

A NATION AT WAR

The destiny of mankind is not decided by material computation. When great causes are on the move in the world . . . we learn that we are spirits, not animals, and that something is going on in space and time, and beyond space and time, which whether we like it or not, spells duty.

—WINSTON CHURCHILL
"BROADCAST TO AMERICA," 1941

rticle II, Section 2 of the United States Constitution gives the president, with the advice and consent of the Senate, authority to appoint judges of the Supreme Court and inferior courts. In ceremonies at the White House, on May 9, 2001, President George W. Bush introduced eleven nominees to the federal courts. Four of those individuals were currently serving as federal district judges, each confirmed by unanimous votes. Two were judges on state supreme courts. Four had served as law clerks in the U.S. Supreme Court, another served as associate counsel to President Bush, and the eleventh was currently serving in the position for which he was nominated, having been put there as a recess appointment by President Clinton.

In recognizing this distinguished group, the president expressed his belief that a chief executive has very few responsibilities of greater importance than nominating men and women to the federal courts. "When a president chooses a judge," said Mr. Bush, "he is placing in human hands the authority and majesty of the law. He owes it to the Constitution and to the country to choose with care. I have done so." The high caliber of this group of nominees, President Bush added, was an indication of his judicial philosophy. "These first nominations are also an opportunity to outline the standards by which I will choose all federal judges. The American people expect judges of the highest caliber, and my nominees will meet that test. A judge, by the most basic measure, has an obligation shared by the president and members of Congress. All of us are constitutional officers, sworn to serve within the limits of our Constitution and laws. When we observe those limits, we exercise our rightful power. When we exceed those limits, we abuse our powers."

"Every judge I appoint," Bush continued, "will be a person who clearly understands the role of a judge is to interpret the law, not to legislate from the bench. To paraphrase the third occupant of this house, James Madison, the courts exist to exercise not the will of men, but the judgment of law. My judicial nominees will know the difference. Understanding this will make them more effective in the defense of rights guaranteed under the Constitution, the enforcement of our laws, and more effective in assuming that justice is done to the guilty and for the innocent."[1] A good judge exercises his authority with discernment, courage, and humility. And these are matters, not just of philosophy, Bush said, but of character.

FROM THE OTHER SIDE

For Washington liberals and left-wing activists everywhere, these were fighting words, and they were ready to do just that. Representatives of the ACLU, People for the American Way, the National Abortion Rights Action League, the National Organization for Women, NAACP, and others, including the Democrat-controlled labor unions, expressed outrage that this president would challenge the Left's practice of legislating from the bench. Just ten days earlier, Sen. Richard Durbin (D-IL) had revealed his party's view of what judges do, saying that, "Most of us in the Senate will come and go, and they will still be sitting on the bench with gavel in hand, in their black robes, meting out justice according to their own values."[2]

Senator Durbin's comments were not accidental or misspoken. Judges who render decisions based on settled law and constitutional principles have a narrow range of options from which to choose. Court procedures are clearly prescribed. Those who follow constitutional principles understand that judicial interpretation is bound by precedents, and there are also social, cultural, and moral reasons for abiding by historic standards of jurisprudence. Judges who rule "according to their own values," on the other hand, believe they can do whatever they like under the cloak of their high office, transforming not only the Constitution but the entire fabric of American culture to their own liking—which is precisely what liberal judges have been doing for years.

So this is the battle we're engaged in today. It's a contest of wills, with enormous risks and consequences. President Bush wants reliable conservative judges on the bench, and his adversaries want to make sure that doesn't happen. So far the Left has managed to have it their way most of the time, obstructing the president's highly qualified nominees, and even forcing the president to compromise on the men and women he appoints. Tactics used by Senate Democrats are clearly unconstitutional, but they've managed to get away with it, thanks in large part to the complicity of the media and the apathy of the public. All of this has helped create a battlefield mentality in which name-calling and invective are the rule of the day.

At a January 27, 2003, press conference hosted by Washington liberals, the director of the NAACP's Washington office, Hillary

Shelton, accused Bush's nominees of harboring "a secret agenda" to eliminate federal protections against "all forms of discrimination." He said, "Today's judicial nominees—like Priscilla Owens, Jeffrey Sutton, Carolyn Kuhl, Terrence Boyle, and Miguel Estrada—are proven political ideologues with a right-wing extremist agenda to reverse hard-fought civil rights advances." In other words, these men and women have shown that they would rather abide by the law than create, out of whole cloth, the kinds of race-based quotas the NAACP prefers.

The fact that there were women, blacks, and Hispanics among the judicial nominees was of no importance to this group. What frightened Shelton and his allies was that these judges would do precisely what the Constitution requires: judge fairly and without prejudice. They would, in fact, offer federal protection against "all forms of discrimination." The real problem was that what these liberals actually wanted was federally mandated discrimination based on race, gender, sexual orientation, and support for abortion-on-demand.

Kate Michelman, president of the National Abortion Rights Action League, said, "The Bush administration is packing the federal bench with right-wing ideologues willing to ignore thirty years of precedent to undo freedom of choice. This strategy goes beyond the most visibly egregious nominees, such as Charles Pickering and Priscilla Owens. Not surprisingly, not a single one of the president's appellate court nominees has demonstrated any hint of support for freedom of choice." In other words, choosing impartial judges is not enough: nominees have to pass a litmus test on abortion and other left-wing issues to be approved.

A few weeks after that press event, another volley was fired when Edward Lazarus, a former law clerk to liberal Supreme Court justice William Brennan and now a West Coast law professor, penned a blunt editorial in the *Washington Post*, in which he pointed out something that most of us have known for a long time: we are a nation at war, battling over two very different views of reality. The battle over federal judges is just one arena, but it's at the very center of the controversy. Unfortunately, Lazarus said, whenever Democrats attack conservative nominees to the federal bench, they pretend politics isn't an issue. They say their real concern is credentials or qualifications, when, in fact, all these judges have outstanding credentials. What the Democrats don't like is the nominees' politics, and it's a sham to pretend otherwise.

The heart of today's culture war is a fundamental dispute over our most basic values. Rather than denying what they're up to, Lazarus wrote, in the future Democrats ought to go ahead and attack the president's nominees based not on qualifications but on "overtly ideological grounds." Why? Because, he said, the values and beliefs of conservatives are simply wrong. Liberals should do whatever it takes to block conservatives from serving on the bench, and thereby "force the administration into a compromise on judicial nominations."[3]

THE FRONTAL ATTACK

To the dismay of many on the Left, Edward Lazarus let the cat out of the bag. Here was a respected left-wing lawyer confessing in a national newspaper what everyone knew but few would admit. In a point-by-point reply to that editorial, published the next day, the director of constitutional studies at Washington's Cato Institute, Roger Pilon, wrote that Lazarus was not only wrong but surprisingly unprincipled in advocating such tactics. The Senate's duty, he said, is not to demand litmus tests but to "stand on principle." Other than that, he said, there were just two basic problems with the logic of the Lazarus editorial: it was unethical and it was manifestly unconstitutional. Pilon wrote:

> In fact, the dirty little secret about the modern liberal's approach to constitutional interpretation is that it makes a mockery of the document. Ignoring the text, it finds sweeping power for the political branches, especially the federal government, to promote "social

change," failing which the job falls to the judiciary. Stated simply, the ends justify the means, whatever the Constitution may say. Constitutional interpretation thus becomes a handmaiden to the liberal's conception of "progress."[4]

The roots of this liberal view of justice, Pilon pointed out, can be seen in Franklin Roosevelt's 1937 court-packing scheme. If Congress fails to deliver the goods that "progressive" forces have in mind, then handpicked federal judges will do the job for them. With liberals on the federal bench, authority to accomplish their purposes can be found in the "emanations" and "penumbras" of the "living Constitution." But this is not how the system is supposed to work. Lawmaking is the responsibility of Congress, and the efforts of Democrats to manipulate that process is a disservice not only to the Republic but to the generations of Americans who used the system fairly, as it was meant to be used. "Abolitionists, suffragists, and others fought long to secure the equal protection promised by the Constitution," wrote Pilon. "Modern liberals sully that history by asking judges to ignore the promise. They make a mockery of equal protection."

The debate over such issues, and the name-calling between the Left and the Right in all these controversies, aren't going to change anytime soon. But recent battles over the Ten Commandments, the Pledge of Allegiance, partial-birth abortion, genetic experimentation, free exercise of religion, and same-sex marriage ought to make a couple of things abundantly clear. First, we're a nation at war, and no one can pretend to be neutral in this contest. The stakes are too high for that, and all of us will be affected by the outcome. Your children and mine will be touched by what happens in the next few years, so nobody can afford to act as if they're disengaged.

Second, we need to realize that the Left will stop at nothing to get what they want. If the American people reject the Left's social agenda at the polls, then liberals will try to manipulate the Supreme Court or the federal courts to do their bidding. Failing that, they'll use other more insidious tactics until they get their way. The two sides in this clash represent two diametrically opposite points of view, and it's clear where they stand. Those on the Right tend to believe in absolute and eternal standards of right and wrong. We believe that history and tradition are important guideposts because they show us what works and what doesn't. We believe we can learn from the past, and we believe it's wrong to dismiss the great legacy passed down to us by our fathers and mothers.

Those on the Left, however, believe that everything is relative and nothing is absolute. They believe we invent our reality as we go. History is merely a record of exploitation and abuse, they say, and the judgmentalism of religion and traditional social mores must be rejected in order to accomplish their sexual, social, and political agenda. Thanks to the court packing that took place during the Clinton years, today's federal courts are already lined up on that side of the debate, and efforts by the Bush White House to change the balance by appointing principled, conservative judges have been largely unsuccessful.

To complicate matters even further, blunders in the selection of Supreme Court justices by the administrations of Presidents Reagan and Bush Sr., led to a 6-3 liberal majority in the Supreme Court, and the prospects of changing that balance are not very good at the moment. Anyone who remembers even a little of what happened during confirmation hearings for Judges Robert Bork and Clarence Thomas will recall the lengths to which the Left was prepared to go in order to discredit conservative nominees. Those tactics were irresponsible and disturbing to most Americans; but, more and more, that's how the war is being waged.

Who Picks Judges?

A glance at who and what is involved in making judicial selections may provide a better picture of what's at stake. According to a presidential commission on the selection of federal judges headed by former attorney general Nicholas Katzenbach, the size of the federal judiciary is increasing at an alarming pace. In the first 160 years of the courts, the number of district and appellate judges went from zero to 277. By 1994, however, the total had grown to 828. That's a stunning increase, but that number was expected to exceed 1,300 by 2000; 2,350 by 2010; and more than 4,100 federal judges by the year 2020. And based on current trends, those numbers may increase substantially.

What we need to think about is, where will all those judges come from? Who's going to train them? Who will appoint them to serve on the courts? And what will be the impact of all those decisions on the future of the Republic? We need to be concerned about the explosion in litigation: as I reported in chapter 6, we're already the most litigious society in history. But the fact that most of these judges will have been trained in left-wing law schools ought to concern us even more. Imagine what sorts of social and political beliefs they'll be upholding.

During his two terms in office, Bill Clinton appointed 374 judges to the federal bench, of which all but one were confirmed by the Senate. Most of those people are still on the bench, still living by the terms of the liberal litmus tests they were given prior to appointment. According to a report prepared by Dr. Virginia Armstrong for Eagle Forum, judges appointed by former president Clinton are on record opposing efforts to ban partial-birth abortions, opposing health regulations for abortion clinics, refusing to allow city and county seals to contain crosses or other religious symbols, banning prayers at school board meetings, and refusing to uphold restrictions on homosexual scout leaders for Boy Scouts. Some even ruled against curfews for teens in areas where 85 percent of juvenile crimes could have been reduced by curfews.

On the other hand, Clinton's appointees have supported the right of minors to seek abortions without parental consent, the right of prison inmates to possess pornographic and sexually explicit materials, and the right of college professors to access pornography on state-owned computers. They've upheld the claims of criminal defendants in appellate courts more than twice as often as other judges. And in the controversial election battles in December 2000, Clinton-appointed federal judges defended the right of Florida's Democrat-controlled state supreme court to rewrite election laws, ex post facto, in order to swing the election to the Democratic candidate.

The United States Supreme Court is shockingly out of touch with the views of most Americans. With a 6–3 liberal majority, this Court has effectively silenced conservative opinion in critical social issues. Consider, for example, the decision upholding race-based admissions at the University of Michigan law school, striking down the sodomy laws of Texas, or the challenge by the Virginia Military Institute in district court forbidding the school's ancient tradition of mealtime prayers—such things clearly reveal the bias of this Court.

During CBN's Operation Supreme Court Freedom, my goal was to focus the nation's attention on these imbalances, and particularly to call for Christians all over the country to pray for changes in the Supreme Court. The record on the Court's most predictable liberals, Justices Stephen Breyer and Ruth Bader Ginsburg, is perfectly clear. Both judges were appointed by Bill Clinton, and they have consistently supported far-Left positions on social issues. John Paul Stevens, who has been on the Court since 1975, is also one of the most consistent liberals. Like Sandra Day O'Connor, Stevens was a Republican nominee who turned out to be anything but a defender of conservative ideas.

Voting in the majority with Justices Kennedy, Souter, O'Connor, Ginsburg, and Breyer, Justice Stevens was in favor of striking down sodomy laws in the *Lawrence* decision. The efforts of Justices Scalia, Thomas, and Rehnquist to focus on the rights of states to determine their own laws, under the Tenth Amendment, was disregarded. In the majority opinion, Justice Kennedy flippantly dismissed the moral purpose and the long history of sodomy laws, saying that Texas had "no legitimate interest" in preventing homosexual behavior. To buttress their case, the majority cited not constitutional law but the European Convention on Human Rights and the Wolfenden Report on homosexuality from Great Britain and the United Nations.

WHERE DO THEY COME FROM?

The Supreme Court is often characterized today by its 5–4 decisions. In narrowly divided cases where one vote makes all the difference, the Left usually prevails; and at the center of the struggle are the two justices who often seem to float with the winds of controversy. Justice Anthony Kennedy, a 1988 appointee of the Reagan White House, votes with the majority more often than any other justice, followed by Justices O'Connor and Souter. David Souter, who was appointed by George H. W. Bush, has been a major disappointment for conservatives, and he almost always marches in lockstep with the Clinton appointees, Ginsburg and Breyer. And these two vote together on hot-button moral issues more than 80 percent of the time.

So where do such people come from? Ruth Bader Ginsburg earned a bachelor's degree at Cornell, attended Harvard Law School, and completed her law degree at Columbia. She became a law professor at Rutgers University in 1969, and three years later was selected to be the first tenured female professor at Columbia Law School. In 1971, she helped found the Women's Rights Project of the ACLU, then served as the ACLU's general counsel from 1973 to 1980. She was on the ACLU's national board of directors from 1974 to 1980, and her decisions consistently mirror the left-wing, anti-religious positions of that organization.

Subsequently, Ginsberg was appointed to the United States Court of Appeals for the District of Columbia, and was nominated to the Supreme Court by Bill Clinton. With surprisingly little protest from conservatives in the House and Senate—or from Christian activists for that matter—Justice Ginsburg took her seat on the Court in August 1993, where she has defended every left-wing cause to come before the Court. She was for *Lawrence* in 2003, against the Boy Scouts in *Boy Scouts of America v. Dale* (2000),[5] against protecting children from pornography in *Ashcroft v. Free Speech Coalition* (2002),[6] against requiring parental consent for abortions in *Lambert v. Wicklund* (1997),[7] and against allowing Bible clubs to meet in public schools in *Good News Clubs v. Milford Central Schools* (2001).[8]

In a report she coauthored for the U.S. Commission on Civil Rights in 1977, Ginsburg and ACLU colleague Brenda Feigen-Fasteau identified eight hundred federal laws that would have to be changed in order to satisfy women's rights activists. As expressed in that report, "Sex Bias in the U.S. Code," and her other papers and court rulings, Ginsburg believes that the traditional family concept of husband as breadwinner and wife as homemaker must be eliminated, the government must provide comprehensive childcare, women must be drafted and assigned to combat duty as often as men, affirmative action must be used to equalize the numbers of men and women in the armed forces, prostitution should be legalized, and the age of consent for sexual activity should be lowered to age twelve. By any standard, these are not mainstream views. Yet this nominee raised hardly an eyebrow during her Senate confirmation.

Ginsburg's ally on the court, Justice Stephen Breyer, earned bachelor's degrees from Stanford and Oxford and a law degree from Harvard before being selected as a law clerk by former Supreme Court justice Arthur Goldberg in 1964. He was an assistant special prosecutor in the Watergate scandal before returning to teach at Harvard and the Kennedy School during the 1970s. He spent fourteen years on the United States Court of Appeals for the First Circuit before being named to the Supreme Court by Bill Clinton in 1994. On major social issues, Breyer's record is virtually identical to that of Justice Ginsburg, except that he supported the Good News Club's position on the grounds that, so long as groups such as the 4-H Club and Boy Scouts were already using school facilities, the Bible club could hardly be denied.

Justice David Hackett Souter, who was a bit of a mystery in his 1990 Senate confirmation, has been called "the stealth justice." During the vetting process, former chief of staff John Sununu had called Souter a "home run" for conservatives, but Souter was nothing of the kind. Instead of the quiet conservative he was presumed to be when George H. W. Bush nominated him in 1990, Souter has been a steady vote for the liberal phalanx. A graduate of Harvard Law School and a Rhodes scholar, he served as attorney general, chief judge of the superior court, and state supreme court justice in New Hampshire before being named to the High Court. During his freshman term, Souter voted with the moderate Sandra Day O'Connor at least twenty-four times, but he soon found his voice and has voted with the Left ever since.

Souter voted for *Lawrence,* against the Boy Scouts and the Child Pornography Protection Act, and he spoke very strongly against the Good News Clubs. In his dissent, joined by Justice Ginsburg, Souter said the majority had glossed over the real purpose of the Bible clubs, which was "religious conversion." Anyone could see that club leaders specifically invited children to be "saved," he scowled. "The majority avoids this reality only by resorting to the bland and general characterization of Good News' activity," he said, by calling it simply the "teaching of morals and character."[9]

A New World Order

Misconstruing the Constitution in order to legislate left-wing social policies is dangerous business, but that's exactly what's happening in the Supreme Court at this hour. To compound the damage, liberal justices are looking for ways to subordinate the Constitution of the

United States to the policies and laws of other nations. In a speech before the liberal lawyers' group, the American Constitution Society (ACS), Justice Ginsburg said that she and her liberal colleagues are hoping to incorporate more and more foreign precedents into American law, particularly in cases involving contentious social issues.

ACS members, who had previously invited speakers such as Senators Hillary Clinton, John Edwards, Tom Harkin, Edward Kennedy, and Barney Frank, as well as Jesse Jackson, Jr., Michael Dukakis, and Janet Reno, were no doubt thrilled by what Justice Ginsburg had to say. "Our island or lone-ranger mentality is beginning to change," she told them. And she added that she and other liberals on the Supreme Court "are becoming more open to comparative and international law perspectives."

In the *Lawrence* case, as in *Atkins v. Virginia* (2002),[10] which dealt with capital punishment for mentally retarded criminals, as well as in the Michigan Law School's affirmative action case, concurring opinions had been included for the obvious purpose of drawing attention to issues of international law. In *Grutter v. Bollinger,* in which the University of Michigan's methodology for determining racial quotas for undergraduate admissions was invalidated, Justice Ginsburg made a point of writing (in the first sentence of her concurring opinion) that the Supreme Court's decision "accords with the international understanding of the office of affirmative action."[11]

During a junket by five members of the Court to an international conference on the new European Constitution, in the summer of 2003, Justices Ginsburg, O'Connor, and Breyer stopped off to compare notes on terrorism and the death penalty with French president Jacques Chirac. French courts outlawed capital punishment in 1981, and these American justices were inclined to do the same. In addition to the French connection, the liberal members of the Court have also met with Chinese judges, both in

Washington and in China. And Justice O'Connor is active in a reform project sponsored by the very liberal American Bar Association in Eastern Europe.

George Washington, who knew a thing or two about foreign laws and legal precedents, warned in his Farewell Address to be wary of "foreign alliances, attachments, and intrigues" that would threaten America's hard-won freedoms and would subject this nation to governments that are "hostile to republican liberty." Unfortunately, America is being drawn deeper and deeper into a globalist intrigue that may do precisely that. Participation in and funding of the United Nations is a serious threat I've written about on numerous occasions. The eagerness of Congress to sign treaties that are inimical to our interests, and the policy of sending American soldiers to serve under foreign flags as part of a so-called international peace-keeping force, are signs that America's national interests are already being subverted by "entangling alliances."

Despite protests from many quarters, there is constant pressure from the Left to sacrifice American autonomy to some nebulous new world order. Appearing on the ABC news program *This Week* with George Stephanopoulos, Justices Stephen Breyer and Sandra Day O'Connor wondered aloud whether the United States Constitution, with its eighteenth-century moral values and emphasis on judicial restraint, could even survive in the new globalist age. The European Court of Human Rights, Breyer pointed out, ruled that homosexuals have a fundamental right to privacy, which makes the debates in this country over "gay rights" and "same-sex marriage" seem primitive and unrealistic by comparison.

"We see all the time, Justice O'Connor and I, and the others, how the world really—it's trite but it's true—is growing together," Breyer told that network's nationwide audience. "Through commerce and through globalization, through the spread of democratic institutions, through immigration to America, it's becoming more and more one world of many different kinds of people. And how they're going to live together across the world will be the challenge, and whether our Constitution and how it fits into the governing documents of other nations, I think will be a challenge for the next generation."

Most Americans would find such perspectives shocking. Supreme Court justices, after all, are sworn to uphold the existing United States Constitution and can be impeached for failing to do so. Yet these justices have said they doubt whether the Constitution is even valid anymore. Justice O'Connor, who obviously shares Breyer's views, expressed her sense that international influences would soon become a bigger factor in the way American courts deal with difficult social issues. When asked if she could imagine a time when the Constitution would no longer be the defining instrument of law, she said, "Well, you always have the power of entering into treaties with other nations, which also become part of the law of the land, but I can't see the day when we won't have a constitution in our nation."

VOICES OF REALITY

Thank goodness for that. But it didn't escape notice that she said "a constitution," and not necessarily "the Constitution" as we know it. *Washington Post* columnist Charles Krauthammer, like many court watchers, has expressed disappointment at the behaviors of those, like O'Connor and Breyer, who would gladly submerge American constitutional law in a sea of internationalist blather. In a much-quoted column, Krauthammer quipped, "The Constitution is whatever Justice Sandra Day O'Connor says it is. On any given Monday."[12] Does anyone really know what Sandra O'Connor believes? Does she?

Krauthammer pointed out that, in *Bowers v. Hardwick* (1986),[13] Justice O'Connor had agreed that state laws forbidding homosexual sodomy were constitutional. In the *Lawrence* decision, however, she apparently changed her mind. Nothing in the Constitution had changed during the last twenty years. But, inexplicably, O'Connor's interpretation of the Constitution had. Such shifts of thinking are not exactly confidence-building for the American people. But such changes also have deep roots, and I think that is perhaps the greatest concern.

Justice Anthony Kennedy, who came to the Court in 1988, was, like Sandra O'Connor, one of the great disappointments of the Reagan years. Seen at one time as a steady conservative voice, Kennedy is now one of the most unpredictable votes on the Court. Completing his bachelor's degrees at Stanford and the London School of Economics, he went on to earn his law degree at Harvard. He began his career in private practice in San Francisco and then joined the law faculty at the McGeorge School of Law in his hometown of Sacramento. He served on a number of federal panels, was appointed to the Ninth Circuit, and was then named to the U.S. Supreme Court.

In his majority opinion in the *Lawrence* case, Kennedy took a hard stand for cultural relativism, saying, "As the Constitution endures, persons in every generation can invoke its principles in their own search for greater freedom." Here again were shades of the "mystery of life" clause of the *Casey* decision. It was the same skewed notion of morality that had surfaced in Kennedy's majority opinion in *Romer v. Evans* (1996). In that decision, the Court overruled Colorado's Amendment 2, which had been passed by a statewide referendum, denying "special rights" for homosexuals.[14] But the will of the people was no impediment for Kennedy. As Justice Scalia pointed out in his powerful dissent in *Lawrence,* this Court has already taken sides in the culture wars.

Among the five justices who joined the majority in *Lawrence,* perhaps the most predictable was David Souter. From the first, Souter has been an advocate for shifting moral standards. In a long-winded and perplexing dissent in *United States v. American Library Association* (2003),[15] Souter attacked the efforts of Congress to protect children from Internet pornography in public libraries, comparing the Child Internet Protection Act to the McCarthy hearings of the 1950s. Pornography filters, he said, would block access to pornography for adults as well as children, and he concluded, "There is no good reason, then, to treat blocking of adult enquiry as anything different from the censorship it presumptively is."

In *United States v. Drayton* (2002),[16] Souter disagreed with the Court's decision that police searching for drugs or evidence of crimes do not have to inform public-transportation passengers of their legal rights. In *Bd. of Ed. of Kiryas Joel v. Grumet* (1994),[17] Souter delivered the Court's opinion that New York lawmakers violated the separation of church and state when they created a public-school district for a community of Hasidic Jews. In his scathing dissent, Justice Scalia referred to Souter by name, saying the Court's opinion was astounding, reflecting the most "facile" reasoning. "It is presumptuous for this court to impose—out of nowhere—an unheard-of prohibition against proceeding in this manner upon the legislature of New York State."

In response, Souter said, "Justice Scalia's dissent is certainly the work of a gladiator, but he thrusts at lions of his own imagining." Then he added, "the license he takes in suggesting that the Court holds the Satmar sect to be New York's established church is only one symptom of his inability to accept the fact that this court has long held that the First Amendment reaches more than classic, 18th century establishments." Here, as elsewhere, Souter expressed contempt for conventional morality and, in particular, for the protection of religious freedoms.

CIVIL RIGHTS AND WRONGS

The gradual softening of morality in America, and the constant drumbeat of homosexual activists for more and more "rights," is having an effect on the nation, and nowhere is this more visible than in the attitudes and opinions of Supreme Court justices. In one case, a homosexual law clerk played a role in shaping the opinions of former justice Harry Blackmun, who was appointed by President Nixon in 1970. Blackmun had joined Justice Rehnquist in dissenting to the Court's denial of certiorari in *Ratchford v. Gay Lib* (1978), thereby giving its permission to a group of homosexual students to hold club meetings on the campus of the University of Missouri. In the dissent, Rehnquist said, "From the point of view of the University . . . the question is more akin to whether those suffering from measles have a constitutional right, in violation of quarantine regulations, to associate together and with others who do not presently have measles."[18]

The real danger of permitting gay students free access on the college campus, Rehnquist said, "may be particularly acute in the university setting where many students are still coping with sexual problems which accompany late adolescence and early adulthood." But sometime later, Justice Blackmun discovered that one of his own law clerks was a homosexual. "For Blackmun, it was tantamount to finding out that he had a gay son. It changed what he thought it meant to be gay. It changed the eyes with which he read the Constitution."[19]

"There's no question," as authors Joyce Murdoch and Deb Price observe with disturbing candor, "the justices are affected by the evolving understanding of homosexuality in America. The Constitution doesn't mention homosexuality, heterosexuality, marriage, or even privacy. There are only grand promises, to which the justices bring their own views. This is a court that doesn't want to be out front. But it also doesn't want to be embarrassed, and *Bowers* was an embarrassment."[20] Reading those words, one can only wonder if this isn't the social dynamic behind the Court's ruling in *Lawrence* and the Court's increasing interest in "hate crimes" legislation.

In the same vein, Murdoch's coauthor, Deb Price, penned a newspaper article in which she speculated that Justice Frank

Murphy, who served on the Court under Chief Justice Harlan Stone during the 1940s, may have been a homosexual. And others, such as William O. Douglas, maintained close friendships with homosexuals, including a longtime correspondence with a lesbian couple who ran a Western dude ranch. Justice Ruth Bader Ginsburg made a point of giving a distinctive "wedding" gift to a lesbian couple for their "union ceremony," and Justice Souter, she says, has been especially helpful to homosexual law clerks at the Court.[21]

The writer says, further, that a large number of the law clerks who come from elite East Coast law schools are homosexuals, and these people use their influence with the justices to help change the Court's thinking about "gay rights" and related issues. Justice Lewis Powell, who was the deciding vote in the case of *Bowers v. Hardwick* (1986), reportedly said at one time that he had never known anyone who was homosexual. However, according to Price, Powell had a steady stream of gay clerks in his offices, most of whom kept their sexuality to themselves.[22]

But not everyone is thrilled with this wave of homosexual-friendly justices. While homosexual activists are celebrating the decision of the Massachusetts Supreme Court creating an unprecedented right to marry, a number of polls and surveys reveal that most Americans still believe homosexuality is a sin. Among them, a poll by the Pew Research Center found that 55 percent of Americans believe it's a sin to engage in homosexual behavior. Among those with a high degree of religious commitment or church attendance, that number tops 76 percent.

THE DISORDERED COURT

Once again, this is evidence of two very different world-views fighting for supremacy in the American culture. The Christian world-view is centered on a belief in a transcendent moral code and absolute standards of right and wrong. Underlying this view is a four-thousand-year-old heritage of Judeo-Christian biblical morality. The other view, however, is based on the belief that we invent our morality as we go. God help those who have no more than that to live by.

Republican congressman Walter Jones, of North Carolina, is a cosponsor of the Federal Marriage Amendment (FMA), which has been a hot topic of debate in the House and Senate, and in the nation's living rooms and boardrooms as well. "If we fail to act," Jones told a reporter, "the will of the people may again be tossed aside by a nonelected judge who places his personal ideology and politics before the law." Apparently a lot of Americans agree with that assessment, and many feel that the avalanche of same-sex marriages on the East and West Coasts may be the spark that will make the FMA a reality.

When the Court struck down Texas sodomy laws, most conservatives feared the decision would lead to a string of defeats for traditional morality. But since the crusade for same-sex marriages began, there has been a visible shift in public attitudes about homosexuality and gay rights. A 2003 Gallup poll showed that support for "civil unions" dropped after the Supreme Court's sodomy ruling. A couple of months earlier, the public had been evenly split on the issue. But after *Lawrence,* just 40 percent of those surveyed still favored such unions.

At the same time, the percentage who say "homosexual relations between consenting adults should be legal" dropped from 60 percent to 48 percent. And the number who say that homosexuality is "an acceptable alternative lifestyle" went from 54 percent to 46 percent. And there are other factors that don't necessarily show up in the polls and surveys, such as the news we've seen from places like Canada, where civil unions and gay marriage are already a matter of fact. In that country, anyone who objects to homosexuality on religious grounds may be charged with a hate crime and subjected to fines, imprisonment, and other types of punishment.

As just a sample, the Human Rights Commission of the province of Saskatchewan, Canada, ruled that a newspaper advertisement that quoted biblical passages opposing homosexuality was a "human rights offense." The newspaper and the man who bought the ad were both forced to pay their three homosexual accusers $1,500 each. Meanwhile, in the western province of British Columbia, the Supreme Court upheld a high school teacher's suspension without pay because he wrote a letter to the editor of a local newspaper saying that no one is born homosexual.

As disturbing as this is, these are not isolated problems. Wherever homosexuals have been given recognition and open acceptance, severe measures are being taken against anyone who would stand by biblical beliefs about homosexual behavior. In England, the Right Reverend Dr. Peter Forster, Anglican bishop of Chester, was investigated under hate crimes laws and reprimanded by the local chief constable for saying that some people can overcome their homosexual inclinations and "reorientate" themselves. In January 2004, a Swedish pastor was prosecuted for "hate speech" because of a sermon he had given that incorporated biblical references to homosexuality.

In Belgium, Cardinal Gustaaf Joos was sued for remarks about homosexuality published in a local magazine. In Spain, Cardinal Antonio Maria Rouco Varela is now facing a lawsuit for speaking against homosexuality in a homily at the Cathedral of Madrid. And in Ireland, with a long history of Christianity, Catholic priests and bishops have been warned that distribution of a Vatican publication on recognition of same-sex relationships would result in prosecution under "incitement to hatred" laws passed by the national legislature. Every one of these warnings is a wake-up call for America. This is precisely where we're headed if we continue down this road toward lawlessness and immorality. But that seems to be precisely where a majority of the members of today's Supreme Court want to take us.

Nineteenth-century moral philosopher Lord Acton was a great admirer of America, and he once observed that the primary reason for this country's success in the world was the belief of America's leaders that "a nation can never abandon its fate to an authority it cannot control." This was certainly the motivation for George Washington's warnings about "entangling alliances" and the reason that, until this century, most Americans have been wary of the idea of submitting our future well-being to the United Nations or any other international body.

In light of all we've seen in these pages, you have to wonder whether Lord Acton's dictum still has meaning. When justices of the United States Supreme Court are willing to subject this great Republic to the whims of international law, you have to wonder what's going on. It's true, we're not the country we were fifty years ago, before the cultural elites began their rampage through the courts. Faith and tradition have been undermined at every turn, and the increase in crime and violence, even among young children, tells us that the system is broken. But if our national sovereignty is compromised, you can be certain that even greater disasters are just ahead.

THE LAST LINE OF DEFENSE

Despite the constant drumbeat from the Left, three conservatives on the Supreme Court have done their best to stand on principle, defending what Justice Scalia has called a "textualist" view of the Constitution. This is simply the belief that the Constitution means what it says and says what it means. American jurisprudence demands that this document must be obeyed: it is the source of all our laws and has served us faithfully for more than two hundred years. America is the longest-surviving constitutional republic in the entire history of mankind; yet liberals in the courts and other elite institutions reject the textualist view, because it restricts their freedom to make up laws on the fly. Chief Justice Rehnquist and Justices Scalia and Thomas have been strong defenders of the Constitution, but how much longer can they hold on?

Ultimately, the answer to that question comes down to the matter of character, where this discussion began: our character and theirs. Chief Justice Rehnquist, a Milwaukee native, served in the army air corps in World War II. He earned his law degree at Stanford and an M.A. from Harvard. He served as a law clerk for Justice Robert Jackson before going into private practice in Phoenix. He served as an assistant attorney general in that state, from 1969 to 1971, and was named to the Supreme Court by Richard Nixon in 1972. He was promoted to chief justice by President Reagan, succeeding Warren Burger in 1986. Despite mounting pressures, the chief has held onto his principles and remains a model of strong character.

Justice Antonin Scalia was born in Trenton, New Jersey, and earned bachelor's degrees from Georgetown University and the University of Fribourg, Switzerland, and a law degree from Harvard. He was in private practice in Cleveland, Ohio, in the early 1960s, then served on the law faculties of the University of Virginia, the University of Chicago, Georgetown, and Stanford. He held various federal posts during the 1970s, including assistant attorney general, before being named first to the United States Court of Appeals for the District of Columbia and then the Supreme Court, nominated by President Reagan in 1986. Not only one of the brightest justices to ever serve on the Court, Justice Scalia is also one of the bravest and most tenacious. He is also a man of character.

By comparison, Clarence Thomas may have had the longest and hardest journey to the Court. Born in the tiny community of Pin Point, Georgia, he attended Conception Seminary before going on to earn a bachelor's degree from Holy Cross College and a juris doctorate from Yale Law in 1974. Thomas served as an assistant attorney general in Missouri from 1974 to 1977, and as legislative assistant to Senator John Danforth from 1979 to 1981. From 1981 to 1982, he was assistant secretary for civil rights in the Department of Education, and from 1982 to 1990 he was chairman of the Equal

Employment Opportunity Commission. Nominated to the Supreme Court by the first President Bush, he took his seat in October 1991, after what must have been the most hostile and contentious Senate hearing in American history. Only a man of resolute character could have survived the torture that Senate liberals inflicted on him.

At this moment, these three justices, joined occasionally by one or two in the middle, are the last line of defense against the tyranny of the Left. They seldom win the hard cases, and they often end up writing bitter dissents, pointing out the hypocrisy of the liberal idea of justice. But this can't go on indefinitely; even strong men grow weary if they fear that help will never come. So what can we do? There are a number of things, and I'll cover them in greater depth in the concluding pages of this book. But, for now, know that prayer is still our greatest resource, followed by political action, voicing our opinions to our congressmen and senators, and then uniting with others of like mind who want to restore the balance of power to the people.

In a perceptive analysis of this situation, columnist Thomas Sowell acknowledged that the American people hold a wide variety of opinions on quotas, abortion, pornography, and other controversial issues. This is why we hold elections. But there are people who have no patience for the democratic process, and they're committed to rewriting the laws by controlling what happens in the courts. This is where you and I can make a real difference by exercising our constitutional rights while there's still time.

"At the heart of the Constitution," writes Thomas Sowell, "is a separation of powers, which limits each branch of government and allows other branches of government to stop it from over-stepping its bounds. Without that, we are at the mercy of whoever happens to be the most ruthless in grabbing power. That is why impeachment has to be a remedy. . . . Nothing is more dangerous," he adds, "than the idea that some public officials are above the law. If they are, then we don't have law—and we won't have freedom much longer either."[23]

The loss of our freedom is a reality we cannot afford to risk, and in the next two chapters, I will deal with this idea in greater depth, taking a look at the battle before us and how, with God's help, we may yet be able to turn things around.

TABLE OF CASES

Ashcroft v. Free Speech Coalition, 535 U.S. 234 (2002).

Atkins v. Virginia, 536 U.S. 304 (2002).

Bd. of Ed. of Kiryas Joel v. Grumet, 512 U.S. 687 (1994).

Bowers v. Hardwick, 478 U.S. 186 (1986).

Boy Scouts of America v. Dale, 530 U.S. 640 (2000).

Good News Club v. Milford Central Schools, 533 U.S. 98 (2001).

Grutter v. Bollinger, 539 U.S. 306 (2003).

Lambert v. Wicklund, 520 U.S. 292 (1997).

Lawrence v. Texas, 539 U.S. 558 (2003).

Mellen v. Bunting, 327 F.3d 355 (4th Cir. 2003).

Ratchford v. Gay Lib, 434 U.S. 1080 (1978).

Romer v. Evans, 517 U.S. 620 (1996).

United States v. American Library Association, 539 U.S. 194 (2003).

United States v. Drayton, 536 U.S. 194 (2002).

11

TO RESTORE JUSTICE

Without God, there is no virtue, because there's no prompting of the conscience. Without God, we're mired in the material, that flat world that tells us only what the senses perceive. Without God, there is a coarsening of the society. And without God, democracy will not and cannot long endure.

—PRESIDENT RONALD REAGAN
NATIONAL PRAYER BREAKFAST (1984)

I have in my library a set of volumes on the messages of America's presidents. They contain a veto message written by President James Monroe in which he vetoed the Cumberland Road Bill, which had been passed by Congress in 1822, on the grounds that the Constitution does not give the federal government the right to authorize funds for local highway projects. Monroe didn't say he would refer the matter to the Supreme Court. After all, he had sworn an oath to protect and defend the Constitution, just as every congressman and Supreme Court justice had done. All federal officials are sworn to uphold the Constitution, so Monroe didn't need the Court's permission to do his job.

But in 2002 we had a situation involving the McCain-Feingold Bill, which proposed a bizarre set of restrictions on campaign financing. President Bush said he disagreed with the legislation but would sign it and leave it for the Supreme Court to resolve. He was sure the Court would overturn the law, but then, to everyone's amazement, the Court affirmed the matter just as it had been written by Congress, and the Bipartisan Campaign Reform Act became law. One part of the law prohibited minors from contributing to political campaigns or supporting candidates they favor. Jay Sekulow argued for the ACLJ that this provision is an invasion of civil rights, and the Supreme Court agreed with his logic. This was the only section of campaign finance that the Court deemed unconstitutional.

To the amazement of the dumbstruck Republicans who had played politics hoping the Supreme Court would bail them out, the Court uncharacteristically affirmed the law and let it stand. If the president and members of Congress had had the wisdom and courage of President James Monroe, that terrible piece of legislation would never have been passed into law. But in the matter of campaign finance, the Court was unusually deferential to the elected bodies. Usually it does not hesitate to strike down those pieces of legislation which are essential to the moral well-being of our nation.

An unimaginable tragedy occurred on September 11, 2001. It woke our people up to the threat of Islamic terror in this country. On that day, millions of people discovered that they are patriots, that they love their country, and that they want to take action to protect this nation from crazed foreign zealots. But will it take something of equal proportions to make the American people decide to take action against the tyranny within our own borders? Will it take another *Lawrence* decision, or a decision authorizing unrestricted homosexual marriage, or a decision that the Ten Commandments or other references to God must be removed from public places to get our attention? What will it take to make enough Americans willing to rise up and say, "This far and no more"? Will it take some terrible tragedy, comparable to 9/11, before the American people are willing to become mobilized?

Recently the ACLU threatened to sue the County of Los Angeles, California, if it did not remove a small cross from the official county seal. The ACLU claimed the county seal was an unconstitutional establishment of religion, and three compliant members of the county board agreed that the Christian symbol might tend to make Hindus and Muslims feel unwelcome. So by a 3–2 majority, they voted to cave in to the ACLU's demand. A Christian legal defense group filed a challenge to block this action, but the commissioners didn't take them up on the offer.

It looked as if another piece of our Christian history was going to be scrubbed away before our eyes, until a group of angry citizens decided that enough is enough and launched a petition drive to override the board. With the support of nationally syndicated radio host, Dennis Prager, who helped publicize the issue, a citizen, John Hernandez, along with a group of conscientious Los Angelinos, gathered the 341,000 petition signatures needed to overturn the votes of that three-person majority, and if necessary to bring the Thomas More Law Center into the battle to save the county seal. It was true democracy in action and a lesson for liberals everywhere.

A TIMELESS CHALLENGE

I suppose my real fear is that life is too good in America. We're doing very nicely, thank you. We have money in our pockets, and the unemployment problem is getting better every day. Most people are quite comfortable, and it's hard to imagine anything short of divine intervention that can cause Americans to stand up and say no. And all the while, the gradual transformation of our culture, coming primarily through the courts, is boiling us alive, like frogs in a kettle.

There's a passage in the book of Ezekiel, in the Old Testament, that ought to trouble those who are inclined to be passive about these troubling times. The passage describes a time of great evil and wickedness among the people of Jerusalem. God sends a heavenly messenger into the streets of that city and instructs him to "go through the midst of the city, through the midst of Jerusalem, and put a mark on the foreheads of the men who sigh and cry over all the abominations that are done within it." Then the Lord tells another heavenly being to follow the messenger through the streets and to slay everyone who does not have the mark, which indicates that they are deeply troubled by the sins of the people. God says, "Do not come near anyone on whom is the mark." Yet He tells the messenger to "begin at My sanctuary" (Ezekiel 9:4–6).

This is not just a powerful statement of what God thinks of evil but a warning to all of us about what God expects us to think and do about the evil in our midst. We need to show that we care. In this passage, God tells the angel to judge the sins of the people and to begin at the house of God. This is reminiscent of what Peter says in the New Testament: "the time has come for judgment to begin at the house of God; and if it begins with us first, what will be the end of those who do not obey the gospel of God?" (1 Peter 4:17). One way or another, the earth will be judged, and God is looking to see who cares. He's asking, who's sighing and moaning? Who's doing something to make a difference?

We are living in a dramatic time in history. I can't remember any period in my lifetime when there have been so many important challenges to our spiritual, political, and emotional well-being. Hollywood, the mass media, the universities, the public schools, and virtually every other cultural institution seem to be against us. A large majority of the American people today no longer recognize the important role that Christianity played in the founding of this nation. But things simply cannot continue as they are. Either they will get better or they will get immeasurably worse, and in either case those of us who believe in the founding vision of this nation cannot afford to be passive any longer.

There is a chance, of course, that if George W. Bush is reelected, and if conservatives can gain a few more seats in the House and

Senate, we may be able to accomplish some of our more important goals. For one thing, I feel certain that two and perhaps three of the current justices of the Supreme Court are ready (even eager) to retire, and they're just waiting for the next election cycle to make their announcement. If Democrats take the White House, however, we know what will happen. The men and women chosen to fill those vacancies will not share our Christian values, more than likely, and they will work to continue the dismantling of Christian culture in this nation.

If Republicans manage to hold onto the White House and gain a couple of seats in the Senate, there's a chance things may go in a very different direction. But even in that situation it's important for Christians and like-minded conservatives of all persuasions to stay engaged. Prayer, as I said earlier, ought to be our first priority. But we can't stop there. Jesus said, "I must work the works of Him who sent Me while it is day; the night is coming when no one can work" (John 9:4), and we can do no less. Regardless how daunting it may seem at times, and no matter how difficult it may be to stand our ground in the face of all the secularizing forces arrayed against us, we must stay the course and fight for what we believe to be right and just.

It seems to me that what's arising in American society today is an all-out assault on Christianity. There's no question that the Christian faith is under attack. Political correctness, at its core, limits anyone from criticizing anyone else for being a sinner, for not following God's Word, for needing a Savior. There is no sin. Nothing is ever right or wrong, good or evil, because that's what political correctness is really all about. No culture can ever be abhorrent or repulsive, and there can be no norms. So anyone who says, as Jesus did, that "I am the way, the truth, and the life" is not politically correct. Anyone who says that American culture is superior to other cultures is deemed a chauvinist and a fascist.

We did a story on *The 700 Club* about how public-school textbooks are written. One of the history textbook writers we interviewed was from California. His premise in his textbook is that American civilization actually grew out of African, West Indian, and Native American cultures and that contemporary society is a conglomeration of these non-European cultures. There wasn't anything in his version of history about the British or European origins of Western culture, and not a word about Christianity.

This is a complete fraud, an all-out assault on everything this country has stood for, for nearly four hundred years. But this deception is being included in textbooks our children are expected to read in the public schools. This is only one of the egregious examples of the kinds of falsehoods that are being taught to public-school students as the "facts of history."

According to the American Center for Law and Justice, there are as many as four thousand seals and emblems in this country that include Christian symbols, and the ACLU is out to change or destroy every one of them. The case in Los Angeles is just one example, and this is taking place in a city named for "The Angels," and a state with cities and towns named for saints—from San Francisco to San Diego—and even a state capital, Sacramento, which is named for the holy sacraments. But the greatest horror is not that the ACLU would threaten to sue—after all, we know what they stand for. The horror is that elected officials caved in immediately, without considering what the people of California had to say in the matter.

THE HEAT OF BATTLE

In his book *Persecution: How Liberals Are Waging War Against Christianity*, columnist David Limbaugh describes in great detail the battle against Christianity being waged by secular liberals. Wherever they can find a loophole—a compliant judge, school administrator, or public official—atheist liberals are working by night and by day to eradicate every vestige of faith from the public square. Some of the incidents described in that book are truly shocking.[1] In one case, a teacher at a Houston middle school saw two young women carrying Bibles. She was so incensed, she hauled the students off to the principal's office and called their mothers. When the mother of one girl arrived, the teacher waved the offensive Bible in her face and yelled, "This is garbage!" and threw it into the trash can.

In another incident at the same school, teachers confiscated book covers that featured the Ten Commandments and threw them in the trash cans, saying that the Ten Commandments were "hate speech" deemed offensive to other students. And who will forget the case, in May 1995, when U.S. district court judge Samuel Kent, of the Southern District of Texas, said that any student who so much as uttered the word "Jesus" during high school graduation ceremonies would be held in contempt of court?

Kent went on to say, "Make no mistake, the Court is going to have a United States marshal in attendance at the graduation. If any student offends this Court, that student will be arrested and will face up to six months incarceration in the Galveston County Jail for contempt of Court. . . . Anyone who violates these orders, no kidding, is going to wish that he or she had died as a child when this Court gets through with it." Talk about hate speech: this is clearly a man who was boiling with bitterness.

In my book *The Turning Tide,* I also described many other cases of this type.[2] In one of them, the Supreme Court upheld a ruling that prohibited a fifth-grade teacher in Denver from simply having a copy of the Bible on his desk, even though there were books on other religions and on Greek mythology on a nearby bookshelf. In Michigan, a five-year-old girl was forbidden to bow her head and say a silent prayer over her lunch because, as her teacher said, it was "against the law." The child went home in tears.

At Moorehead State University, students painting a mural weren't allowed to include an image of a fish because it was "a forbidden religious symbol." And in Vancouver, a third-grade teacher tore up a youngster's drawing that spoofed a popular television commercial because the caption said, "If Bo don't know Jesus, Bo don't know Didley!"

In Grand Rapids, a district judge ordered a picture of Jesus, which had hung on the wall outside the principal's office for more than thirty years, removed, because it supposedly violated the "separation of church and state." In Louisiana, the ACLU sued a local school board for removing from its library shelves a book on voodoo rituals and spells that contained explicit descriptions of murder and sexual rituals. And in Nazareth, Texas, the ACLU brought a complaint against the local post office because during the Christmas season their local postmark included a Nativity scene.

Meanwhile, in Florida, an ACLU affiliate filed a case on behalf of American Atheists demanding that a statue of Jesus be removed from a federal park. The fact that the park was located three miles offshore, and under twenty feet of water, was apparently of no concern. They claimed that any evidence of Christian faith had to be removed. And in Stockton, California, third-graders preparing to sing Christmas songs at their school's "Winter Festival" were forbidden to use the words "Lord," "Savior," or "King" in their carols and were told to simply remain silent during those parts of the songs.

According to another report, a group of Christian students at a public high school were suspended for "possession of Christian material." They could carry a copy of the *Communist Manifesto* or *Playboy* magazine in their backpacks, and that would have been all right; but if they were discovered carrying a Bible or a Christian magazine, that would mean a trip to the principal's office, a serious reprimand, and possible expulsion.

The animus toward Christ and His church is perfectly clear. Secular liberals and atheists, abetted by their friends in the ACLU and other like-minded organizations, are intent on eradicating every vestige of Christianity from American society. In that regard, I saw a woman on a television news program when the case involving the Los Angeles County seal first broke, saying that the Constitution forbids Christian symbols in public places. But this is simply not true; the Constitution says nothing of the kind. In the final analysis, what we're facing is an all-out assault on our beliefs. But we've been warned that such things would come to pass.

An Oligarchy at Work

At the end of the 2003–2004 term, the Supreme Court announced a spate of controversial decisions in which we could see, once again, the silent, patient labors of a judicial oligarchy at work. In the case of *Rasul v. Bush* (2004),[3] the Court held that federal courts must review the status of military detainees at Guantanamo and other holding centers, under habeas corpus laws reserved for American citizens, to determine whether they are actually enemy combatants. In the case of *Hamdi v. Rumsfeld* (2004), the justices ruled that U.S. citizens detained as enemy combatants have the Sixth Amendment right to representation by counsel. In other words, prisoners of war suddenly have the same rights as loyal Americans, with the opportunity to hire slick lawyers to convince a liberal judge of their innocence, or at least of their status as "victims."

As several news reports have already shown, detainees who've been freed from military confinement in recent months are already returning to their old al-Qaeda units, rejoining the fight against coalition forces in Afghanistan and Iraq. Thanks to liberal judges who, in many cases, are not only outspoken opponents of President Bush and the war on terrorism but are on record against capital punishment, enemy soldiers now have the "right of discovery," which means they have access to confidential military records that could compromise future military operations and threaten the lives of loyal American soldiers in the future.

In another eleventh-hour decision, in *Sosa v. Alvarez-Machain*

(2004),[4] the Supreme Court overturned a ruling from the Ninth Circuit that had granted standing to a foreign businessman to sue in this country under the Alien Tort Statute (ATS). But then, having reached a just decision, they proceeded to send the case back to the San Francisco court with instructions to "try again." In his hard-hitting concurrence in that case, Justice Scalia forced the Court and a watching world to recognize what's really at stake in such cases. He wrote:

> We Americans have a method for making the laws that are over us. We elect representatives to two Houses of Congress, each of which must enact the new law and present it for the approval of a President, whom we also elect. For over two decades now, unelected federal judges have been usurping this lawmaking power by converting what they regard as norms of international law into American law. Today's opinion approves that process in principle, though urging the lower courts to be more restrained.

Once again, Justice Scalia said, we're seeing evidence of a judicial branch that feels empowered to barge into every controversy and make decisions that are not theirs to make. "This Court," he said, "seems incapable of admitting that some matters—any matters—are none of its business. . . . In today's latest victory for its *Never Say Never Jurisprudence,* the Court ignores its own conclusion that the ATS provides only jurisdiction, wags a finger at the lower courts for going too far, and then—repeating the same formula the ambitious lower courts themselves have used—invites them to try again" (emphasis added).

The most offensive of the Court's eleventh-hour rulings, however, was issued in the case of *Ashcroft v. ACLU* (2003),[5] which dealt with the constitutionality of the Child Online Protection Act (COPA), which had been passed by Congress to protect minors from pornography on the Internet. That law required Web publishers to limit access to obscene images by requiring identification numbers or credit cards for verification of a user's age. The ACLU challenged COPA's reliance on "community standards," and on two occasions the Third Circuit held COPA unconstitutional. But, given a chance to do the right thing, the Supreme Court refused to overturn the appeals court decision declaring COPA unconstitutional and instead sent the case back for trial.

The American Center for Law and Justice filed an amicus brief in December 2003 on behalf of thirteen members of Congress, including one of the cosponsors of COPA in the House, Rep. Ernest Istook (R-OK). The brief focused on the government's compelling interest in safeguarding minors from the dangers of pornography on the Internet. However, in its 5–4 decision, handed down on June 29, 2004, the Supreme Court simply sent the case back to the Third Circuit Court for another trial. Is there any doubt what the justices were saying? "The procedures were wrong, so go back and get it right this time!" Once again, the Court had a chance to declare a law defending the morals of America's children constitutional, but instead it dodged the issue and left intact an injunction that actually prevented the COPA law from taking effect.

THE TYRANNY OF THE FEW

Recently, when reading Psalm 2, I noticed something very interesting. It says, "The kings of the earth set themselves, and the rulers take counsel together, against the LORD and against His Anointed, saying, 'Let us break Their bonds in pieces and cast away Their cords from us'" (Psalm 2:2–3). As I reflected on the meaning of the passage, I wondered, *How did that apply in the days of David when it was written?* And I decided that it couldn't have applied at that time, because the kings of the earth weren't plotting against Jehovah God or against His Anointed Son. The Messiah, Jesus, hadn't been revealed. He wouldn't even be born until one thousand years later.

But I realized that when the kings of the earth say, "Let us break Their bonds in pieces and cast away Their cords," this is precisely what we're seeing today. The secular rulers of our day want nothing more than to be rid of the moral restrictions of Christianity. That's why they hate the Ten Commandments and want to remove them from the schools, the courts, and every other public place. They want nothing to do with God or Jesus Christ, and they're determined to eradicate every last trace of Christian morality. They want to break the bonds of religion and instill a new secular ideology that is the exact opposite of the truth the Bible teaches.

If you look at the things that are being done today by the ACLU and the liberal courts, there's no doubt what's at the heart of their agenda. They want to get rid of every type of sexual restraint, every limit on pornography and indecency, and to forbid any criticism or restraint on homosexuality. They want the freedom to abort the evidence of their sexual sin when it results in the creation of human life; and they want to make sure that Sundays are not viewed as sacred days of worship but are just like every other day.

They want to get rid of holidays that remind people of our moral traditions, and thus we have "Winter Recess," or as we saw in one state, "Sparkle Days," instead of Christmas, and "spring break" or "Mayfest" instead of Easter. The American people would never do such things on their own, and our legislatures would never pass such laws. But thanks to the federal courts, a few activist judges can do the bidding of the atheists, effectively changing the entire context of American culture with little or no resistance.

Jay Sekulow and attorneys at the American Center for Law and Justice were legal counsel a few years ago in a very contentious case in Alabama, in which an assistant principal filed a complaint against the DeKalb County School Board for allowing student-led prayer in the schools. With the help of the ACLU and other anti-Christian groups, the case made its way to the U.S. District Court for the Middle District of Alabama, where Judge Ira DeMent issued a sweeping ruling restricting prayer and other religious activities and threatening to bring serious action against violators. He even ordered the school board to hire full-time professional "monitors" to make sure that no religious activities took place on school property.

The judge's permanent injunction order forbade "vocal prayer; Bible and religious devotional or scriptural readings; distribution of religious materials, texts, or announcements; and discussions of a devotional inspirational nature, regardless of whether the activity is initiated, led by, or engaged in by students." Even in the event of a local or national crisis, such as the Columbine tragedy or the 9/11 terrorist attacks, DeMent said, DeKalb County students could not pray for any reason. Furthermore, there was to be a "teacher reeducation program," like something out of the Soviet Gulags, to make sure that educators were suitably reindoctrinated against any tendency to permit the free exercise of religion on school grounds.

The official anti-religion monitors would be authorized, under DeMent's order, to enter any classroom or public-school property, school assemblies, sporting events, commencement exercises, or any other school-sponsored event for the purpose of observing and reporting on compliance with the court's demands. It was as if Big Brother had descended on the public schools. And all this was to be done at taxpayer expense, at the court's command.

Former Alabama governor Fob James, who is a devoted Christian, was so incensed by the case that he wrote an incredible thirty-four-page letter to Judge DeMent. In it, he recited almost the entire history of American jurisprudence involving the establishment and free exercise of religion, with dozens of historical examples, citations from the founders, and powerful footnotes. Basically, he told Judge DeMent that he had violated every principle of constitutional law with his extreme anti-Christian ruling.

In the letter, Governor James reminded the judge that "George Washington spoke of a time when 'cunning, ambitious, and unprincipled men will be enabled to subvert the power of the people, and to usurp for themselves the reins of government,'" and Washington warned further that "'change by usurpation' was the 'customary weapon by which free governments are destroyed.'" In opposition to this, Justice William Brennan told us that in our society, "obviously we Americans must accept that . . . upon judges, and particularly Justices of the Supreme Court, rests a great share of the delicate responsibility of deciding what must be preserved and what must be changed."[6]

This was a view that would put the Supreme Court above the Constitution. But Governor James asked, "Was George Washington an American?" If so, then someone needed to explain the discrepancy between the revisionist views of Justice Brennan and those of George Washington and the framers. Then James went on to say:

Late in his career on the Supreme Court, Justice William Douglas said publicly what had been known for decades in the higher echelons of the legal community: that "due process" was the "wildcard to be put to such use as the judges choose." This meant that when the Supreme Court wanted to implement a particular social or political policy for the nation, the justices would first pick a case involving the issue in question, and then simply say that "due process" required the policy they favored. Then the Court would give their ideological reasons for the policy in a written Opinion. Finally they would insist that their Opinion, containing their ideological reasons for the policy, was now the law of the land and must be obeyed by the rest of society, at least until they changed their mind and made different policy in a new case. This is the sum and substance of modern American "jurisprudence."[7]

Governor James had put his finger, brilliantly, on the real issue. And then he concluded his letter by challenging Judge DeMent's reasoning in the case and quoted from the Old Testament book of

Second Samuel, in which King David revealed the words God had spoken to him, saying:

> He who rules over men must be just,
> Ruling in the fear of God.
> And he shall be like the light of the morning when the sun rises,
> A morning without clouds,
> Like the tender grass springing out of the earth,
> By clear shining after rain. (2 Samuel 23:3–4)

One can only wonder what the impact of that incredible missive must have been. For nearly three years, and at great expense of money and effort, the case was fought all the way to the United States Supreme Court, where it was eventually remanded back to the district court for action, precisely as Jay Sekulow and his colleagues had requested. Eventually most of the draconian measures of that terrible injunction were stripped from the ruling. The Court of Appeals held that Judge DeMent's injunction could "neither prohibit genuinely student-initiated religious speech, nor apply restrictions on the time, place, and manner of that speech which exceeded those placed on students' secular speech."[8]

REVEALING THE BIG LIE

In the end, the students' right to pray was vindicated, but not without a fight. And that brings up some very important points that we need to recognize. We need to know that, first of all, there are people in this nation who will go to any lengths to strip God and the Bible from our public life. Second, we need to know that it's only when we stand and fight that we have any chance of overcoming our adversaries and blocking their evil advances. Most of the time, the attempt to eradicate evidence of faith is unfounded and illegal, but unless it is challenged, our adversaries will carry the day.

But there's something else we need to know. When liberal judges or justices of the Supreme Court talk about "the Constitution," they're not talking about the same thing that you and I have in mind. They don't mean that incredible document drafted by James Madison and the other members of the Constitutional Convention in 1789. What they have in mind are all the decisions that have accumulated since 1790, when the Supreme Court heard its first case. In other words, they're thinking about all the judgments that have been added to the Constitution, and about how they've used and abused that document since the time of the founding.

As I pointed out in chapter 4, as early as *McCulloch v. Maryland* (1819), the Court held that the Constitution "confides to this court the ultimate power of deciding all questions arising under the constitution and laws of the United States. The laws of the United States, then, made in pursuance of the constitution, are to form the supreme law of the land."[9] Truth be told, the courts, as Fob James said, tend to feel that judicial precedent and due process may be used to enact practically any policy a majority of judges agrees on. There can be no greater danger to freedom and the sovereignty of the people than that mistaken belief. When conservatives say we want to stop this kind of overreaching by the courts, liberal judges cry out in alarm that we're attacking their right of "judicial independence." But this is a battle we simply must fight.

As an indication of the scope of the problem, the American Center for Law and Justice received more than 102,000 appeals for help in 1998 alone, from individuals all across the country being threatened because of their religious beliefs. Teachers were shutting down Bible clubs, tearing up papers and artwork with religious symbols, and demeaning the faith of students and teachers alike. The ACLJ was able to take perhaps a thousand of those cases, and then they began actively suing the organizations that were violating the rights of Christians. Those who weren't sued were notified that they were in violation of the Supreme Court's ruling in the *Westside*

Community Schools v. Mergens decision, which Jay Sekulow argued and won in 1990. And suddenly things began to change.

Notable cases were won, and with the victories came an assessment of damages or attorneys' fees, which could amount to as much as $700,000. The schools were covered by insurance, and the insurance companies began to advise their clients to stop persecuting Christians. Had there not been a vigorous legal arm willing to stand up for the rights of Christians, the anti-Christian educational steamroller would have continued. But because of active, innovative, and skillful legal counsel, the number of cases filed against Christians has declined dramatically.

Up to the time of the founding of the American Center for Law and Justice, the ACLU had a field day trampling on our religious freedoms. Now at least there is a champion ready to take them on and fight them, case by case. But the vendetta of the ACLU to remove every vestige of religion from the public life of America continues unabated.

The Left operates through terror and intimidation. They use the big lie, saying that religion is forbidden in this country and that the courts have ruled that religion is a private matter. But the only way they can win is to make people believe this lie. Joseph Goebbels, who was Adolf Hitler's propaganda minister during World War II, knew that the only way to make the German people line up behind Hitler's diabolical schemes was to convince enough of them to follow a lie. In a very telling diary entry, Goebbels wrote, "The lie can be maintained only for such time as the State can shield the people from the political, economic and/or military consequences of the lie. It thus becomes vitally important for the State to use all of its powers to repress dissent, for truth is the mortal enemy of the lie, and thus by extension, the truth becomes the greatest enemy of the State." And, I might add, truth is always the enemy of the lie.

As Christians, we have a powerful weapon on our side: it's called truth, and it's found in the Word of God and in our wonderful heritage of faith passed down to us through the last two thousand years. The kings of the earth may set themselves up, as David said in the psalm cited earlier, but God is not mocked, and He is in no way threatened by their villainy. In subsequent verses in Psalm 2, David writes, "He who sits in the heavens shall laugh; the Lord shall hold them in derision. Then He shall speak to them in His wrath, and distress them in His deep displeasure" (vv. 4–5). One day, God will deal with the liars and profaners in a very personal way; but in the meantime, He looks to us to confront evil and work for justice.

What strikes me about the abuses we've talked about in these pages is the audacity of those black-robed judges who would dare to rule that our Christian beliefs are unconstitutional when practically *everything* they do is unconstitutional. Declaring prayer and Bible reading unconstitutional? Declaring a moment of silence during a school assembly unconstitutional? Saying that high school athletes and their friends and parents can't pray for safety before a football game? Who do they think they are?! By what right do these nonelected judges propose outlawing beliefs and practices that our Founding Fathers fought and died to preserve?

Nowhere is this arrogance more apparent than in the Court's decision in *Stone v. Graham* (1980), in which they declared, "If the posted copies of the Ten Commandments are to have any effect at all, it will be to induce the schoolchildren to read, meditate upon, perhaps to venerate and obey, the Commandments. However desirable this might be as a matter of private devotion, it is not a permissible state objective under the Establishment Clause."[10] In other words, teaching children to obey their parents, not to steal, not to murder, and not to lie under oath has no public value. This is preposterous. The very idea that this would be an "impermissible" act just beggars the imagination.

Yet it stands to reason that if the courts want to exalt their own authority above every other institution, then it's inevitable that they would, as George Washington warned, "subvert the power of the people, and . . . usurp for themselves the reins of government." If God and the Bible stand in their way, then religion must be subdued. If the Ten Commandments, which call for allegiance to a higher power, are honored by children in the public schools, then the Commandments must be condemned and removed.

In her remarkable book *One Nation, Two Cultures,* author and scholar Gertrude Himmelfarb writes that laws created by men are taking the place of the laws created by God. "Just as the state often acts as the surrogate for a dysfunctional family," she says, "so the law is the surrogate for a dysfunctional culture." But, as Himmelfarb is quick to point out, it's the judges themselves who are responsible for most of the dysfunction in contemporary American life, through their casual disregard for morality, faith, and the historic values of the people. "As the law has become more intrusive, so has the judiciary," she writes.

Himmelfarb concludes with this stirring admonition: "The law, we are discovering, is too serious a matter to be left to lawyers or even judges."[11] How right she is. And I can think of no better motivation for becoming active in this struggle and taking back our liberties than the need to restore justice in the land and to give our allegiance, once more, to the great Lawgiver and Father of mankind. That's where it has to begin.

TABLE OF CASES

Bd. of Educ of Westside Cmty. Sch. v. Mergens, 496 U.S. 266 (1990).
Chandler v. James, 985 F. Supp. 1062 (M.D. Ala. 1997), reversed by 180 F.3d 1254 (11th Cir. 1999).
McCulloch v. Maryland, 17 U.S. 316 (1819).
Stone v. Graham, 449 U.S. 39 (1980).

12
THE PATH TO VICTORY

You come against me with sword and spear and javelin, but I come against you in the name of the LORD Almighty, the God of the armies of Israel, whom you have defied. This day the LORD will hand you over to me, and I'll strike you down.

—1 SAMUEL 17:45–46 NIV

Some struggles are protracted and bloody. Some involve great personal sacrifice. But at other times the forces arrayed against a seemingly impregnable stronghold reach what has been called a "tipping point," and victory comes effortlessly as the stronghold collapses.

In 1917, the empire of Russia was one of the most powerful nations on earth. It had a large army, as well as seemingly bountiful agricultural and mineral wealth. The Russian government of the tsar should have been impervious to any attempt to overthrow it, but such was not the case.[1]

By 1917, the tsar had long since ceased caring for the needs of his people. The ruling elites had focused their attention on their personal lives of luxury and privilege. The Russian army had been repeatedly weakened by losses during World War I in the struggle against Germany. The troops were poorly led, underpaid, demoralized, and mutinous.

The tipping point came as the once great Russian Empire began disintegrating.

To the amazement of the world, a small band of seventeen thousand Bolsheviks proclaiming a vision of a collectivist workers' paradise overthrew the tsarist government, confiscated the estates of the rich nobles, and, in the space of a few short years, brought upon the Russian people the totalitarian regime of the Union of Soviet Socialist Republics.

The tsarist giant fell before the onslaught of a determined few. But what about the giant of the federal judiciary that has unlawfully seized control of vital aspects of the life of the United States of America? What can be done to bring it under control?

The federal government of the United States has grown to hitherto unimagined proportions, taking from this great economy $2.3 trillion or more each year to pay for its ever-increasing demands. This frighteningly huge giant has three parts, two of which are in large measure subservient to the wishes of the people. All of the members of the House of Representatives and one-third of the Senate are subject to a popular vote every two years. We may not always concur with every vote our congressmen and senators might make, but one thing is certain: if they cavalierly disregard the wishes of their constituents, they will not remain long in office.

Members of Congress are pressured by the White House, by their colleagues, by lobbyists for special interest groups, by city and state officials, by federal bureaucrats, by members of a host of civic groups, by large contributors, by ordinary citizens, and, of course, by what is called the "chattering class" in the print and broadcast media. This is democracy in action, and rough and crude as it may be, we would want it no other way.

THE DEMOCRATIC PROCESS

Every four years the president, our chief executive, must stand before the American people to give account of his tenure in office. Polls taken every week or two announce whether qualified voters approve or disapprove of his handling of the economy or one or more aspects of foreign policy. The president may be the most powerful man on earth, but his power is severely curtailed by the Congress, and particularly by the opinions of the American people.

Just consider what happened to Ronald Reagan, an enormously popular president who won a second term over his hapless opponent, Walter Mondale, in one of the biggest electoral triumphs of all time. Reagan was one of the most popular presidents of the last century; yet the attempt by his subordinates to free American hostages held by radical Muslims in Lebanon, and the attempt to circumvent the Boland Amendment in order to assist the so-called Contras fighting the Communist Sandinista regime in Nicaragua, led to the Arms for Hostage and Iran-Contra scandals, an incessant media outcry, protracted congressional hearings, the convictions of two key White House aides, and a nationally televised apology to the American people by the president.

Despite President Ronald Reagan's enormous accomplishments and great popularity, just two attempts to accomplish worthy goals by unworthy means severely marred his second term and vitiated the ability of his administration during those years to accomplish anything of significance.

Our Constitution limits power, circumscribes power, and places institutional restraints on power. I have already cited the words of James Madison, who said in Federalist 41, "If men were angels, no government would be necessary." Madison and the framers of the Constitution were keenly aware that men are not angels. They believed the biblical doctrine of original sin, and they went to great lengths to be sure that sinful men, once elected to office, could never exercise the absolute power that so easily corrupts.

America is a constitutional republic made up of sovereign states. It was not, and never has been, a pure democracy. Only those powers specifically enumerated by the Constitution were granted to the federal government. All the rest were reserved to the states or to the people. The states were ceding a portion of their power to a central government, but they were unwilling to do so without a firm contract spelling out what they were giving up and what they were *not* giving up. That solemn contract is contained in the Bill of Rights, specifically the Ninth and Tenth Amendments to the Constitution, which state the following:

Amendment 9: The enumeration in the Constitution of certain rights shall not be construed to *deny or disparage others retained by the people* (emphasis added).

Amendment 10: The powers not delegated to the United States by the Constitution, nor prohibited by it to the states, *are reserved to the states respectively, or to the people* (emphasis added).

As we have seen in the early chapters of this book, the foremost concern of the founding states was not reserved rights but interference by the central government in their religious affairs. That is why the First Amendment clearly binds the federal Congress with these words: "*Congress shall make no law* respecting an establishment of religion or prohibiting the free exercise thereof" (emphasis added). Hollywood producers and newspapers make a big deal of the First Amendment clause forbidding Congress from passing laws "abridging the freedom of speech, or of the press." But both of these groups steadfastly refuse to acknowledge that the free exercise of religion is the *first and foremost* First Amendment right. In fact, in recent surveys, a substantial majority of respondents failed to identify "religious freedom" as the first protected right of the Bill of Rights.

But the Constitution places bounds and limits around the central government. It also places severe limits around the relations of the respective arms of the federal government with each other. Only the people's Congress has the power to tax and spend. Tax bills must originate in the body that is most closely accountable to the people, the House of Representatives. It may sound ridiculous, but the president of the United States does not have the power to use public money to purchase a light bulb for the White House unless there is a valid congressional appropriation covering White House upkeep and maintenance.

All legislative bodies under the pressure of the moment may hastily pass ill-considered legislation. The framers of the Constitution wisely provided for such an eventuality. To be valid, a bill passed by Congress must be signed by the president. If the president finds legislation to be ill considered, he vetoes it. At that point, the supporters of the legislation require not a simple majority but a two-thirds vote for passage.

The federal giant is large beyond comprehension, but this nation of more than 290 million inhabitants rests in the assurance that the giant is tamed because of a document that was crafted by men whose political philosophy had been framed by biblical truth supplemented by the great philosophers of the Enlightenment. They were not utopian dreamers, they were not anarchists, they were not socialists, and they were not tyrants. They were patriots who loved freedom and believed in God. In the founding of a great nation, they understood the intricate working of God's will, man's free will, and the rule of law.

But did these wise founders leave our nation a way to keep in check the third part of the giant when it attempts, as it has, to break free of constitutional restraint, assume powers never given it, and begin in the name of law to destroy the fundamental law under which it was created? The answer is a resounding YES! The federal judiciary has no power under the Constitution to enforce any of its rulings. It has no army, no police force, and no independent source of funds. It has only what the people's legislature and the people's executive care to give it.

ANARCHY AND LAW

Someone might say that to refuse a federal court order is anarchy. Indeed, it is anarchy to disobey a court order if that order is lawful— if it comports with the legitimate judicial powers granted by the Constitution. However, if federal judges are clearly and blatantly making decrees that violate their own oath to uphold and defend the Constitution, why cannot the other more powerful branches of government simply ignore them?

What's to prevent a president of the United States from boldly declaring, "I have taken an oath that is as valid as that taken by members of the Court. The Court's ruling violates the United States Constitution. The Court has no constitutional authority to require enforcement of such a ruling; therefore, I order the Justice Department, the FBI, and the federal marshals not to enforce it."? As President Andrew Jackson once said of Justice John Marshall's extravagant decree, "Marshall has made his ruling; now let him enforce it."

To do so would require a president strong enough and popular enough to go over the heads of the liberal intelligentsia and gain the support of the people. Such support could not come overnight, of course, or as the result of a single case. But, in the cause of justice, such an action could be accomplished by a carefully planned public relations campaign spanning several years. The president has the power under the United States Constitution to say no to the Court. But does any president have the courage to do so?

The United States Congress is granted clear and specific authority under the Constitution over the federal courts, which are, other than the Supreme Court, to be the creation of Congress. Article III of the Constitution expressly states that the "judicial power of the

United States shall be vested in one Supreme Court, and in such *inferior courts as the Congress may from time to time ordain and establish.*" Further, the Supreme Court shall have "appellate jurisdiction, *both as to law and fact, with such exceptions and under such regulations as the Congress shall make*" (emphasis added).

Congress can act on a number of fronts to curb the runaway judiciary; but remember, this is not easy. Supreme Court liberals are philosophically part of an establishment elite that comprise most of the national news media, prominent academics, leaders of major foundations, elite law schools, liberal think tanks, well-funded radical legal and lobbying groups, radical feminist and homosexual activists, atheists, agnostics, left-wing clergy, internationalists, and, of course, a sizeable number of Democratic Party office holders.

But given a congressional majority willing to act, the Constitution offers a number of measures that can be put in place to rein in the runaway judiciary.

First, the Congress, by a simple majority vote, can deny the Supreme Court appellate jurisdiction over a single piece of legislation or over a class of legislation. I have seen this technique in action. In a farm aid bill favored by Senate Minority Leader Tom Daschle, a simple clause was added stating that the federal courts were denied jurisdiction over the matter contained in the bill. No lengthy debate. No court challenge. And since the sponsor was a liberal Democrat, no press outcry either.

Second, the Congress can pass legislation that has been proposed in the current Congress stating that Supreme Court decisions are *not* the "supreme law of the land," but are only "supreme law" as a guide for decisions by the federal district and circuit courts, not the general population. Since the Supreme Court's arrogant assertion on this issue contradicts the clear language of the Constitution, a congressional resolution on this issue should not be difficult.

Third, the Congress can pass tort reform legislation that restricts damage awards to actual monetary loss, severely restricts punitive damages, and abolishes class-action lawsuits and so-called forum shopping. Congress could also limit attorney fees in federal cases and apply federal standards in those state cases involving interstate commerce.

More than anything, Congress could include in reform legislation a provision that the losing party in a civil lawsuit should pay the legal expenses of the winner. As things stand now, a lawyer is free to bring a frivolous lawsuit, inflict great financial burden on an innocent defendant, and then face little or no financial retribution if he and his client lose the case. Under the British rule that transfers all costs of litigation back to the party losing the action, which I advocate here, a lawyer and his client will be forced to consider carefully the risks of bringing an unfair legal action. No longer would the plaintiff be able to inflict unwarranted pain without consequent penalty.

Tort reform would dramatically reduce the number of cases brought to court and, in the process, diminish the spreading web of judicial interference in the lives and business of ordinary citizens.

Fourth, the House of Representatives can bring an impeachment action against one or more judges for violating their oath to defend the Constitution. In my opinion, destroying the moral standards of an entire society is a much graver offense than stealing money or violating drug laws. However, absent sustained national outrage and evidence of an indictable crime, the prospects of successful impeachment are slim.

Fifth, the number nine is hardly a sacred number to be preserved at all costs. Congress, assuming a presidential signature, has the power under the Constitution to increase the number of judges to any number it wishes—say, to eleven. Two added judges could conceivably tip the margin in favor of judicial restraint. But this scenario implies a president who wants strict constructionist judges and a Senate willing to confirm them.

It also implies that there would not be the incredible public uproar that accompanied President Franklin Roosevelt's court-packing scheme. In the late 1930s, Roosevelt had enormous personal popularity. He had a compliant Congress led by Democrats ready to do his bidding, and the nation faced an economic emergency of great magnitude. Even with all that, the law-abiding American people would not allow tampering with the Court. Do conditions exist in our bitterly divided nation that would permit a plan such as that proposed by Roosevelt to succeed in the twenty-first century? I seriously doubt it.

Sixth, the social turmoil that the Supreme Court of the United States has brought about in this nation has been caused primarily by the rulings of the Court through federalized actions that the First, Ninth, and Tenth Amendments specifically reserve to the states. The people and their representatives need to make the case, once again, for abiding by these constitutional amendments and reserving the powers delegated to the people for the people.

LIMITING JUDICIAL AUTHORITY

The issues of the origin of human life, medical treatment, the termination of pregnancy, what constitutes medicine, and what constitutes murder are not, and should never be, matters for the central government to decide. Without question, such issues belong to what is called the "police power" of the states. They should be regulated, permitted, or criminalized by actions of state legislatures and state executives, not by the federal Supreme Court. *Roe v. Wade* has been called "Blackmun's Abortion" not only because of its poor reasoning from nonexistent authority, but because of the violence that ruling did to the constitutional principle of federalism. Even judicial liberals, such as Harvard law professor Alan Dershowitz, who personally favors abortion, admit that *Roe v. Wade* was unconstitutional and ought to be reversed by the Court.

In like manner, the next most contentious action of the Court has been visible in decisions such as *Cantwell v. Connecticut* (1940) and

Everson v. Board of Education (1947), which by judicial fiat wrapped the long arm of the federal courts around the religious practices and educational policies of the states. The tools used for this power grab were the due process and equal protection clauses of the Fourteenth Amendment. As one sitting justice said to me, no rational reading of the text of the First Amendment, which begins, "Congress shall make no law," could ever lead to the conclusion that it was subsumed by the Fourteenth Amendment as a restriction on state action.

The historical record clearly shows that Senator James G. Blaine of Maine offered the Blaine Amendment (1875) to make the post-Civil War Fourteenth Amendment apply the First Amendment restrictions to the states. The Blaine Amendment was defeated by Congress at the federal level; yet the Supreme Court has gone the Congress one better, and in the *Cantwell* and *Everson* decisions of the 1940s started the process that has resulted in the systematic stripping of our national affirmation of faith from the public arena.

As we've seen throughout these pages, great mischief has been done by the Supreme Court over many years in the guise of enforcing the First and Fourteenth Amendments. As early as 1873, in the so-called Slaughterhouse Cases, the Court began exploring ways to make all the provisions of the Bill of Rights apply to the states. By the early twentieth century, the Court incorporated provisions of the Bill of Rights in certain cases and rejected them in others. The common view of the Court today, as seen in cases such as *Duncan v. Louisiana* (1968), is that some rights, such as trial by jury, may be applied to the states under the due process clause, while others, such as "the right to a jury trial in a civil case involving more than twenty dollars," may not. Even the liberal Justice Felix Frankfurter, in his last published work, in the *Harvard Law Review,* wrote that he found it impossible to believe that those who drafted and ratified the Fourteenth Amendment ever meant to make it apply the Bill of Rights in such ways.[2]

It is clear that the framers of the Constitution placed a limitation on the power of Congress to establish a national religion or by law to prohibit the free exercise of religion. But the Constitution created no such limitations on the Court, simply because it was, and still is, inconceivable that a court designed to decide cases between individuals or corporate litigants would ever have morphed into an unelected legislature, controlling Congress, the president, and the states. Obviously, in case after case, the federal judiciary restricts the free exercise of religion in a fashion totally forbidden to any arm of the federal government.

I've mentioned the magnificent temple of the Supreme Court in a few places in this text, but I have not previously addressed the fact that this "temple of justice" may well be part of the problem. The beautiful building that stands majestically at the corner of First and Maryland streets in Washington, D.C., directly across from the Capitol, is an awesome and imposing structure. From its inception, the building was designed to overwhelm and inspire, and by form alone to add authority and luster to the rulings of the Court.

I recall reading at some point about the reactions of Justice Stephen Breyer, a former Harvard law professor and for many years a judge of the United States Court of Appeals for the First Circuit, in Boston, on his first day in office at the Supreme Court. He was overwhelmed by the majesty of the place, and also by the role he would be expected to assume in it. To step into those hallowed halls is an unforgettable experience, and even those few men and women deemed worthy to wear the robes of the nation's highest tribunal cannot help but feel it as well.

In fulfilling his last great commission, architect Cass Gilbert, who had previously designed the Woolworth Building and the George Washington Bridge in New York City, set out to create a monument for all time. He and his associates studied the great temples and cathedrals of Europe. They visited the shrines of Greece and Rome, and focused especially on the historic Church of La Madeleine in Paris, erected to honor the glory of Napoleon

Bonaparte. From those models Gilbert took the best and most inspiring elements, and he incorporated them into the structure of the Supreme Court. Cost was not an object. He had been authorized to create a home for the judicial branch of the American government, and he was clearly up to the task. But, oddly enough, when that building was at last completed and opened to the public in 1935, it surpassed even the designer's wildest dreams.

Visitors who climb the vast marble steps to that cathedral of justice today cannot help but be captured by the awe and majesty of the place. The giant frieze that spans the entire width of the portico, high above those eight massive Corinthian columns, memorializes the history of justice and the great lawgivers of the ages. Moses stands in the midst of them, along with Solon of ancient Greece, and Confucius, and even in the corners we see the rabbit and tortoise of Chinese legend. The massive bronze doors through which each visitor must pass are inlaid with eight magnificent bronze panels depicting great men and epochs in the history of law, from Hammurabi to John Marshall and Justice Story. And the interior is even more lavish.

It is, indeed, a splendid creation and an edifice worthy of a great nation. But what, we must now ask, is the impact of this great physical structure on justice and the rule of law? Since 1935, the justices of this Court have taken the law into their own hands as no tribunal before them would ever have dreamed of doing. Since the offices of the Court were transferred from the basement of the Capitol—and from the "potato hole" where they were housed for decades—there has been a shift not only in the dignity of the Court but in the type of justice our unelected judges have dispensed.[3]

Very much as the dapper Charles Evans Hughes, the first chief justice to occupy this daunting structure, would have wanted, the glory attached to the temple, as if by some sinister magic, has now transferred to its occupants. It's not merely the edifice that is glorified in the public imagination but the justices who occupy it. This may have been to the Court's good fortune, but should this be a matter of concern? Is this unseemly metamorphosis something that politicians and constitutional scholars should address? At the very least, it seems to me, the glorification of the Court is a danger that ought to be recognized and addressed.

WHO STANDS FOR TRUTH?

As it has usurped powers that it was not intended to have, requiring expertise and staff support that it does not possess, the Court has literally brought chaos and violent division into this great land. Jesus said that a "house divided against itself will not stand" (Matthew 12:25). If America ever falls, the principal blame will be placed at the steps of that marble temple in Washington, D.C. So what should be done? Could there be a congressional resolution stating that the Fourteenth Amendment was not intended to apply the First Amendment restrictions to the states? After almost fifty years, does there exist sufficient will in America for such a change? Sadly, I doubt it.

The issue is perhaps too complex to generate political will unless a constitutional amendment clarifying the issue is drafted, passed, and ratified. However, if such an action is undertaken, there will likely be a cry of outrage from some in the African-American community who believe that states' rights is just another name for Jim-Crow laws and segregation. So how do we rectify the incredible blunders of an activist Court while we still preserve the racial progress made under the successive pieces of civil rights legislation passed by Congress? Given the political composition of this nation and the pressures on Congress today, the resolution of the problem will not be easy. There must first be a national outcry and a resolute will to change the system.

Like the giant who faced a little shepherd boy on the Judean hills three thousand years ago, what faces people of faith today seems huge. But, like Goliath, it can be brought down. In truth, the best recourse is for the Supreme Court to reverse itself and acknowledge that it erred in declaring "a wall of separation between church and state" and mandating the baffling three-part *Lemon* test for governmental support of spiritual values. The Court could acknowledge that its decrees since 1947 do not comport with the great history of the United States or its institutions, practices, and customs since 1607. The court in 2003, in declaring homosexuality a constitutionally protected right, did not hesitate to overthrow the carefully worded decision of *Bowers v. Hardwick* (1986), which upheld Georgia's sodomy law. If *Bowers* could have been overturned that easily, why not *Roe v. Wade* or *Everson v. Board of Education?*

Of course, the Court can do this! But what will it take for that to happen? There are now on the Court three judges (Rehnquist, Scalia, and Thomas) firmly committed to historic interpretation and the rule of law. There are four (Souter, Ginsburg, Breyer, and Stevens) who believe in the sociological treatment of a pliable, "living" Constitution. These four are unalterably opposed to the Judeo-Christian roots of our nation and, without exception, have been opposed to any public affirmation of faith in any case brought before them.

The one exception may be the phrase "under God" in the Pledge of Allegiance. If in some future action, which can be expected in the next year or two, the justices should actually vote that down, their own hypocrisy will be revealed. The Court opens its own sessions with the words "God save the United States of America and this honorable Court!" Even the former ACLU general counsel, Justice Ginsburg, alluded to this fact during oral arguments in the Pledge of Allegiance case.[4]

On the fence in most issues is Justice Anthony Kennedy, who blasted the constitutionality of a graduation prayer by a rabbi in the case of *Lee v. Weisman* (1992) but who, in the case of *Lawrence v. Texas* (2003), broke into prose that bordered on the ecstatic while creating a constitutional right for adults to practice homosexual sodomy. Justice Kennedy voted in favor of the rights of public-school students to participate in Bible clubs and against laws which created so-called moveable bubble zones to protect abortion clinics from nonviolent protests.[5] But what does he really believe? Under no circumstances could Justice Kennedy ever be counted on for a sweeping overhaul of the erroneous past decisions of the Supreme Court.

Nor can Sandra Day O'Connor be relied on for any sweeping decisions. Her thinking seems locked in an incremental mode—sometimes favoring religion, sometimes not; sometimes favoring free speech, sometimes not; normally favoring broad-based abortion rights, but occasionally permitting some incremental restrictions. We cannot rest our hopes for restoring judicial restraint on someone who wavers to that degree.

It goes without saying that in order for the Court to reform itself, America must have a new majority on the Court. Between now and 2008, there will undoubtedly be two or three Supreme Court vacancies. George W. Bush has shown himself totally committed to placing strict constructionists of the highest caliber on the federal courts. If Mr. Bush is elected to a second term, he will have the opportunity to appoint justices of high principles and integrity to the Supreme Court. The radical left is fighting Bush today with such passionate intensity because they realize that, in a second Bush term, Republicans will not only control the White House and the executive branch of government, but the House and Senate as well. He would thus be able to make conservatives the majority on the High Court bench. The Left is apoplectic at the prospect of losing their hold on government power. But this could very well happen, God willing.

Bush wants to appoint an able Hispanic jurist and an African-American woman to the Court. This accounts for the bitter filibuster tactics that have been employed by the Democratic minority in the Senate, orchestrated by Ralph Neas, who is head of Hollywood producer Norman Lear's People for the American Way, against such eminent legal scholars as Judge Miguel Estrada and

Janice R. Brown, the popular associate justice from the California Supreme Court.

Not only does President Bush need to win a second term to be able to make sound judicial appointments, but the Republicans must also hold their Senate majority and pick up three or more additional seats out of the five vacancies occurring in Southern states—as the result of the retirement of Democratic senators. Even without many new senators, however, the Republican majority must rewrite Senate rules to curtail the historically unprecedented filibusters that have been used by Democratic senators for the past couple of years to block Bush's judicial nominees to various circuit courts. The actions of Senators Daschle, Kennedy, and their confederates represent a dangerous manipulation of congressional procedures that threatens the very foundations of American government.

The Constitution makes clear that the task of selecting and appointing federal judges rests with the president of the United States. Nominations are to be made with the "advice and consent of the Senate." This means simply that a nominee deserves an "up or down vote" of the members of the Senate for confirmation. If there are insufficient votes for confirmation, the nominee is withdrawn. If there is a simple majority, the nominee is confirmed. Fairness demands a hearing, vigorous debate, *then a vote*. That's the democratic way.

But, as I've said, the radical Left hates democracy, because when the majority of Senate members vote, the Left always loses. So rather than permit a vote on highly qualified judicial nominees, Senate Democrats are employing the tactic of their Democratic predecessors who fought against civil rights legislation in the 1960s—the filibuster—during which no vote can be taken. The word *filibuster* was originally a Dutch term applied to pirates who unlawfully seized vessels on the high seas. Today the term is used fittingly to describe the act of taking the Senate majority hostage, and it has been distorted once again by the radical Left to require not just a simple majority of fifty-one votes, but a sixty-vote supermajority for confirmation of presidential nominees to the Court.

THE DESTINY OF THE NATION

Until the November 2004 presidential election and the forming of a new Congress in 2005, the slim Republican majority in the Senate can do nothing to break this disgraceful logjam. But with a new Congress, indeed, something good may be possible.

Established parliamentary practice in the House and Senate forbids one legislative body from putting in place rules of procedure which will be binding on its successor. In other words, procedures adopted by the 108th Congress cannot bind the 109th. In the new Senate in 2005, a simple majority of senators can amend Rule 23 (the filibuster rule) to its own liking. And in a procedure to adopt new rules, the filibuster does not apply.

Article I, Section 4 of the Constitution says explicitly, "Each house [of Congress] may determine the rules of its proceedings." In other words, a change in the Senate rules made by a majority of senators when a quorum is present cannot be appealed to any other authority. The Senate can eliminate the filibuster altogether, or, as has been suggested in the case of the confirmation of judges, in a series of votes, reduce the number needed to close debate from sixty-one to fifty-one. At fifty-one votes, cloture would be invoked to stop debate and a vote taken to confirm or deny the nomination.[6]

In my opinion, the destiny of the United States of America may very well depend on the 2004 presidential election. We are faced not only with the external threats posed now by radical Islam, but we are faced with the gradual elimination of our fundamental rights and beliefs at the hands of a runaway federal judiciary. If we truly care about the world our children will inherit, we must work now, with all our strength, trusting in a gracious God for total victory. Our cause is just, and the need has never been greater. But we must get involved now if we want to see changes. We can't leave it to others to do the job for us. Imagine what might have happened on that fateful day in the Valley of Elah if young David had refused to come forward and accept the challenge of the Philistines.

Yes, the giant we are facing today is large and powerful, but a determined nation can curb its power. We have to believe that. There is a Judge over all the earth who hears and answers the prayers of His people. As that little shepherd boy said long ago, "I come against you in the name of the LORD Almighty, the God of the armies of Israel, whom you have defied. This day the LORD will hand you over to me, and I'll strike you down" (1 Samuel 17:45–46 NIV).

With God, all things are possible!

TABLE OF CASES

Bowers v. Hardwick, 478 U.S. 186 (1986).
Cantwell v. Connecticut, 310 U.S. 296 (1940).
Duncan v. Louisiana, 391 U.S. 145 (1968).
Everson v. Bd. of Educ., 330 U.S. 1 (1947).
Lawrence v. Texas, 539 U.S. 558 (2003).
Lee v. Weisman, 505 U.S. 577 (1992).
Roe v. Wade, 410 U.S. 113 (1973).

---

*To learn more about how to impact your
religious freedom on a local, state, and national level, visit*

www.courtingdisasterACTION.com

NOTES

Chapter 1: The End of American Democracy

1. Thomas Jefferson, "Letter to William Jarvis," ed. Wilson Whitman (Eau Claire, WI:E. M. Cole & Co., 1900), letter dated September 28, 1820.
2. For a related discussion of the topics in this chapter, see Texans for Life Coalition, "Judicial Activism," http://www.texlife.org/
3. *Everson v. Bd. of Educ.*, 330 U.S. 1 (1947).
4. Daniel Dreisbach, *Thomas Jefferson and the Wall of Separation Between Church and State* (New York, NY: University Press, 2002).
5. Joseph Story, *Life and Letters of Joseph Story*, vol. 2, ed. William W. Story (Boston, MA:Little, Brown, 1851).
6. John A. Garraty and Peter Gay, *The Columbia History of the World* (New York, NY:Harper & Row, 1981), 1163.
7. Bob Woodward and Scott Armstrong, *The Brethren: Inside the Supreme Court* (New York, NY:Simon & Schuster, 1979), 174–75.
8. Robert Bork, "Our Judicial Oligarchy," *First Things*, November 1996.
9. *Stone v. Graham*, 449 U.S. 39, 41 (1980).
10. Garraty and Gay, *The Columbia History of the World*, 1146.
11. Ibid.
12. *American Communications Ass'n v. Douds*, 339 U.S. 382 (1950).

Chapter 2: The Original Intent of the Founders

1. Alexis de Tocqueville, *Democracy in America*, trans. George Lawrence, ed. J. P. Mayer (New York, NY:Doubleday and Co., 1971), 293.
2. Ibid., 291.
3. Jonathan Mayhew, D.D., *Discourse Concerning Unlimited Submission and Non-Resistance to the Higher Powers* (Boston, MA:D. Fowle and D. Gookin, 1750). A copy of this original pamphlet is on display in the Rare Books Collection of the Library of Congress.

4. Ibid. "The God of Israel said, The Rock of Israel spoke to me: 'He who rules over men must be just, ruling in the fear of God,'" (2 Samuel 23:3 NKJV).

5. This story is compellingly told in Benjamin Hart's *Faith & Freedom: The Christian Roots of American Liberty* (San Bernadino, CA:Here's Life Publishers, 1988).

6. See Mason's declaration and related history at http://www.history.org/Almanack/life/politics/varights.cfm

7. Thomas Sowell, "No Stinkin' Badges?" *Washington Times,* December 12, 2000.

8. The attitude is perfectly described in the book of Genesis, where Satan tempts Eve with this bold claim: "Ye shall not surely die: For God doth know that in the day ye eat thereof, then your eyes shall be opened, and ye shall be as gods, knowing good and evil" (Genesis 3:4–5 KJV).

Chapter 3: Defying the Will of the People

1. Martin L. Gross, *The End of Sanity: Social and Cultural Madness in America* (New York, NY:Avon Books, 1997), 107.

2. Michael J. Glennon, "The Case That Made the Court," *Wilson Quarterly* (Summer 2003).

3. Charles J. Ogletree Jr., *All Deliberate Speed: Reflections on the First Half-Century of Brown v. Board of Education* (New York, NY:W. W. Norton & Company, 2004).

4. Thomas Sowell, Half a Century After Brown, part I, http://www.townhall.com/ (accessed May 12, 2004).

5. Ibid.

6. Paul G. Cassell, "Brief of Court-Appointed Amicus Curiae," 4-28 at 2, *Dickerson v. United States,* 530 U.S. 428 (2000) (No. 99-5255).

7. Thomas Sowell, "Courts Without Law," available at http://www.townhall.com/ (accessed December 16, 2003).

8. Rev. Edward J. Melvin, C.M. *The Legal Principles of the Founding Fathers and the Supreme Court* (Jenkintown, PA: Pro Life Coalition of Pennsylvania, 1977).

9. Clinton Rossiter, *Seedtime of the Republic* (New York, NY:Harcourt Brace, 1953), 449.

Chapter 4: The Court's Liberal Agenda

1. Hadley Arkes, "Liberalism and the Law," *The Betrayal of Liberalism: How the Disciples of Freedom and Equality Helped Foster the Illiberal Politics of Coercion and Control* (Chicago, IL:Ivan R. Dee, Inc., 1999), 96.

2. For an excellent discussion of these and related issues, see J. Budziszewski's *Written on the Heart: The Case for Natural Law* (Downer's Grove, IL:Intervarsity Press, 1997).

3. Oliver Wendell Holmes, Jr., *The Path of the Law* (Bedford, MA:Applewood Books, 1996), 1897.

4. Louis D. Brandeis, *The Papers of Justice Louis D. Brandeis* (Cambridge, MA:Harvard Law School). Associated with *United States v. Moreland,* 258 U.S. 433 (1922).

5. Russell Kirk, "The Meaning of 'Justice'," http://www.heritage.org/ (accessed March 4, 1993).

6. Edwin Meese III, *Perspective on the Authoritativeness of Supreme Court Decisions: The Law of the Constitution,* 61 Tul L. Rev. 979 (1987).

7. For a related discussion of this and other issues addressed in this chapter, see Edward J. Erler, "The Constitution of Principle," http://www.constitution.org/

8. Edwin Meese, address before the District of Columbia chapter of the Federalist Society, November 15, 1985.

9. Harold J. Rothwax, *Guilty: The Collapse of Criminal Justice* (New York, NY:Random House, Inc., 1996).

10. William J. Brennan Jr., "The Constitution of the United States: Contemporary Ratification," Conference Address given at Georgetown University, October 12, 1985.

11. William J. Brennan Jr., "What the Constitution Requires," *New York Times,* April 28, 1996.

12. Case citations and certain Latin references have been omitted from Justice Scalia's published remarks.

13. Hadley Arkes, "Liberalism and the Law," III.

14. Stephen Dinan, "Nation Rallies Around Pledge," *Washington Times,* June 28, 2002.

Chapter 5: Prayer and Bible Reading

1. 36 U.S.C.S. § 119 (2004).

2. Robert Bork, *Slouching Towards Gomorrah: Modern Liberalism and American Decline* (New York, NY:Harper Collins, 1996), 289–90.

3. "The Debate About a School Prayer Amendment Is Not About School Prayer," *First Things,* February 1995, 8.

Chapter 6: Free Speech and Equal Rights

1. Don M. Jackson, "Advocacy at the Crossroads" (1980), in dean's address to the International Academy of Trial Lawyers, http://www.iatl.net/

2. *Liebeck v. McDonald's Restaurants,* P.T.S., Inc., No. CV-93-02419, 1995 WL 360309 (N.M. Dist. August 18, 1994).

3. Richard Neely, *The Product Liability Mess: How Business Can Be Rescued from the Politics of State Courts* (New York, NY: Simon & Schuster, Inc., 1998), 4, 62.

4. "$8.1 Million Jury Verdict Tops 2001 List: Medical Malpractice Cases Dominate NC Legal Scene," *North Carolina Lawyers Weekly,* http://www.lawyer-sweeklyusa.com/ (accessed January 15, 2002).

5. Sen. Bill Frist, "Restoring Balance to the Scales of Tort Justice," speech to the Association for a Better New York, http://www.abny.org/ (accessed March 22, 2004).

6. Ibid.

7. Ibid.

8. Bruce Bartlett, "The Tort Tax: Greedy Trial Lawyers Are Slowing Economic Growth and Investment," *National Review,* March 3, 2003.

9. Deborah Tannen, "For Argument's Sake; Why Do We Feel Compelled to Fight About Everything?" *Washington Post,* March 15, 1998, C1.

10. John Leo, "Watch What You Say: The Left Can No Longer Be Counted On to Defend Free Speech," http://www.townhall.com/ (accessed March 14, 2000).

11. *Reno v. ACLU,* 521 U.S. 844 (1997).

12. H.R. Rep. No. 71-2290 (1931).

13. Roger Baldwin, *Liberty Under the Soviets* (New York, NY: Vanguard Press, 1928).

14. *Curley v. North American Man/Boy Love Association.*

15. *National Socialist Party v. Skokie,* 432 U.S. 43 (1977).

16. *County of Allegheny v. ACLU,* 492 U.S. 573 (1989).

17. Deroy Murdock, "No Boy Scouts: The ACLU Defends NAMBLA," *National Review* Online, http://www.nationalreview.com/ (accessed February 27, 2004).

18. Everson v. Bd. of Educ., 330 U.S. 1 (1947).

19. Charles Beard, *The Republic: Conversations on Fundamentals* (Oxford, England:Greenwood Press, 1980).

20. For more on this controversial decision, see Roger K. Newman, *Hugo Black: A Biography* (Bronx, NY:Fordham University Press, 1997), 361-64.

21. Thomas R. Eddlem, "Defender of the Decalogue: Interview with Chief Justice Roy Moore," vol. 18, no. 25, *New American* (December 16, 2002).

Chapter 7: The Dignity of Human Life

1. Edward J. Erler, "The Constitution of Principle," Still the Law of the Land? *Essays on Changing Interpretations of the Constitution* (Hillsdale, MI:Hillsdale College Press, 1987).

2. Stephen Goldsmith, "Who Owns the Sidewalks?" *Policy Review* (September–October 1996), 79.

3. Charles Fairman et al., *The Fourteenth Amendment and the Bill of Rights: The Incorporation Theory* (Boulder, CO:Perseus Book Group, 1970).

4. Edwin Meese III, "The Moral Foundations of Republican Government," *Still the Law of the Land? Essays on Changing Interpretations of the Constitution* (Hillsdale, MI:Hillsdale College Press, 1987).

5. Robert H. Bork, *Slouching Towards Gomorrah: Modern Liberalism and American Decline* (New York, NY:Harper Collins, 1996), 119.

6. Edwin Meese III, "The Moral Foundations of Republican Government," *Still the Law of the Land? Essays on Changing Interpretations of the Constitution* (Hillsdale, MI:Hillsdale College Press, 1987).

7. University of Maryland Medicine, "Fetal Development," Medical Encyclopedia, http://www.umm.edu/ (accessed 2002).

8. Justice Harry Blackmun delivered the Supreme Court's opinion, which was joined by Chief Justice Burger and Justices Douglas, Brennan, Stewart, Marshall, and Powell. Only Justices Rehnquist and White dissented.

9. Robert H. Bork, Max Boot, *Out of Order: Arrogance, Incompetence, and Corruption on the Bench* (Bolder, CO:Perseus Book Group, 1998), foreword, vi.

10. "Bush Signs Bill to Ban a Type of Abortion," *Los Angeles Times*, November 6, 2003, A1.

11. For related information, see "Priests for Life," Supreme Court Documents on the Life Issues, http://www.priestsforlife.org/ (accessed 2004).

12. Faith2Action, "Poll Results," http://www.f2a.org/ (accessed 2002).

13. Frederica Mathewes-Green, "The Abortion Debate Is Over," *Christianity Today*, December 6, 1999.

14. The National Pro-Life Religious Council, "Statement on Human Cloning," http://www.nprcouncil.org/ (accessed May 7, 2002).

15. Ibid.

16. From the earliest times, Christianity was strongly opposed to abortion, infanticide, suicide, and euthanasia, and there are hundreds of statements in the literature of the early church that contrast the views of Christians on these issues with the practices of the surrounding pagan culture. In the sixteenth century, John Calvin, the most prolific voice of the Reformation, said of the practice of abortion, "For the fetus, though enclosed in the womb of its mother, is already a human being, and it is a monstrous crime to rob it of the life which it has not yet begun to enjoy. If it seems more horrible to kill a man in his own house than in a field, because a man's house is his place of most secure refuge, it ought surely to be deemed more atrocious to destroy a fetus in the womb before it has come to light."

Chapter 8: Honoring Our Heritage

1. The Halakah is based on the commandments in the five books of Moses, the Torah, amplified by rabbinic literature such as the Mishnah and the Talmud.

2. Craige MacMillan, "The Other Ten Commandments Judges," WorldNetDaily, http://www.worldnetdaily.com/ (accessed August 28, 2003).

3. Manuel Roig-Franzia, "Ten Commandments Display Ordered out of Courthouse," *Washington Post*, November 19, 2002, A3.

4. Michael Novak, "Deeply Held Feelings: The Pryor Controversy," *National Review* Online, http://www.nationalreview.com/ (accessed August 4, 2003).

5. As reported by WorldNetDaily: "The House version, HR 3799, and Senate version, S 2082, are identical companion bills. Touted by some supporters as one of the most important pieces of legislation in U.S. history, the bill states: 'The Supreme Court shall not have jurisdiction to review, by appeal, writ of certiorari, or otherwise, any matter to the extent that relief is sought against an element of Federal, State, or local government, or against an officer of Federal, State, or local government (whether or not acting in official personal

capacity), by reason of that element's or officer's acknowledgment of God as the sovereign source of law, liberty, or government.'

"The legislation also addresses what many high-court watchers consider a dangerous trend: Supreme Court justices looking to foreign law and rulings for guidance when deciding cases. States the bill: 'In interpreting and applying the Constitution of the United States, a court of the United States may not rely upon any constitution, law, administrative rule, Executive order, directive, policy, judicial decision, or any other action of any foreign state or international organization or agency, other than the constitutional law and English common law.'

"Under the bill, any judge who violates the proposed rule by making extra-jurisdictional decisions will have committed an offense that is grounds for impeachment.'" ("Roy Moore-Inspired Bill Limits Federal Courts," WorldNetDaily, http://www.worldnetdaily.com/ [accessed March 30, 2004]).

6. George Washington, The Writings of George Washington, vol. V, ed. John C. Fitzpatrick (Washington, DC:Government Printing Office, 1944), 301.

7. Christine Tognetti, "Local Schools React to Patriotic Controversy," Hollister FreeLance, http://www.freelancenews.com/ (accessed March 26, 2004).

8. Elk Grove Unified School District v. Newdow, No. 02-1624 (2004), quoting Allen v. Wright, 468 U.S. 737, 750 (1984), quoting Vander Jagt v. O'Neill, 699 F.2d 1166, 1178–79 (CADC 1983) (Bork, J., concurring).

9. Elk Grove Unified School District v. Newdow, 542 U.S. ___ (2004) (O'Connor, J., concurring), 13.

10. Jeff Jacoby, "Quizzing the Democratic Candidates," Boston Globe, January 18, 2004.

11. Nicholas D. Kristof, "Overdosing on Islam," New York Times, May 12, 2004.

Chapter 9: Our Black-Robed Masters

1. Richard Lessner, "Judicial Tyranny," Washington Times, August 10, 2003.

2. The exceptions clause holds that "the Supreme Court shall have appellate jurisdiction, both as to law and fact, with such exceptions, and under such regulations as the Congress shall make" (U.S. Const. Art. II, Sec. 2).

3. The resemblance of partial-birth abortion (D&X) to infanticide means Nebraska could conclude the procedure presents a greater risk of disrespect for life and a consequent greater risk to the profession and society, which depend for their sustenance upon reciprocal recognition of dignity and respect. Stenberg v. Carhart, 530 U.S. 914, 963 (2000) (Scalia, J., dissenting).

Today, the Court inexplicably holds that the states cannot constitutionally prohibit a method of abortion that millions find hard to distinguish from infanticide and that the Court hesitates even to describe. Stenberg v. Carhart, 530 U.S. 914, 982 (2000) (Thomas, J., dissenting).

And the particular procedure at issue in this case, partial-birth abortion, so closely borders on infanticide that thirty states have attempted to ban it. Stenberg v. Carhart, 530 U.S. 914, 983 (U.S., 2000) (Thomas, J., dissenting).

4. George Will, "Brown v. Board, 50 Years Later," *Washington Post Writers Group,* May 16, 2004.

5. *Stenberg v. Carhart,* 530 U.S. 914 (2000), quoting *Planned Parenthood v. Casey,* 505 U.S. 833, 877 (1992) (O'Connor, J., plurality).

6. William J. Quirk and R. Randall Birdwell, *Judicial Dictatorship* (Somerset, NJ:Transaction Publishers, 1996).

7. Max Boot, *Out of Order: Arrogance, Corruption, and Incompetence on the Bench* (Boulder, CO:Perseus Book Group, 1998).

8. Robert H. Bork, foreword to Max Boot, *Out of Order,* xiii.

9. Ibid.

10. Robert H. Bork, *Coercing Virtue: The Worldwide Rule of Judges* (Washington, DC:American Enterprise Institute Press, 2003).

Chapter 10: A Nation at War

1. George W. Bush, "Remarks by the President During Federal Judicial Appointees Announcement," http://www.whitehouse.gov/ (accessed May 9, 2001).

2. 149 Cong. Rec. S 5440 (April 29, 2003) (statement by Sen. Durbin).

3. Edward Lazarus, "Picking Judges: Democrats Should Stand Their Ground," *Washington Post,* June 19, 2001.

4. Roger Pilon, "Picking Judges: The Senate Should Stand on Principle," *Cato Institute Daily Commentaries,* July 20, 2001.

5. *Boy Scouts of America v. Dale,* 530 U.S. 640 (2000).

6. *Ashcroft v. Free Speech Coalition,* 535 U.S. 234 (2002).

7. *Lambert v. Wicklund,* 520 U.S. 292 (1997).

8. *Good News Clubs v. Milford Central Schools,* 533 U.S. 98 (2001).

9. Ibid., 533 U.S. 98 at 138–39.

10. *Atkins v. Virginia,* 536 U.S. 304 (2002).

11. *Grutter v. Bollinger,* 539 U.S. 306 (2003)

12. Charles Krauthammer, "Courting a Crisis in Legitimacy," *Washington Post,* July 4, 2003, A23.

13. *Bowers v. Hardwick,* 478 U.S. 186 (1986).

14. *Romer v. Evans,* 517 U.S. 620 (1996).

15. *United States v. American Library Association,* 539 U.S. 194 (2003).

16. *United States v. Drayton,* 536 U.S. 194 (2002).

17. *Bd. of Ed. of Kiryas Joel v. Grumet,* 512 U.S. 687 (1994).

18. *Ratchford v. Gay Lib,* 434 U.S. 1080 (1978).

19. Joyce Murdoch and Deb Price, *Courting Justice: Gay Men and Lesbians v. The Supreme Court* (New York, NY:Basic Books, 2001).

20. Ibid.

21. Deb Price, "U.S. Supreme Court Evolution Stirs Hope," *Detroit News,* June 4, 2001, 11A.
22. Ibid.
23. Thomas Sowell, "Cheap Shot Justice," *Washington Times,* February 15, 2001, B3.

Chapter 11: To Restore Justice

1. David Limbaugh, *Persecution: How Liberals Are Waging War Against Christianity* (New York, NY:Perennial, 2004).
2. Pat Robertson, *The Turning Tide* (Nashville, TN:Thomas Nelson Publishers, 1995).
3. *Rasul v. Bush,* (03-334) 321 F.3d 1134.
4. *Sosa v. Alvarez-Machain,* (03-339) 331 F.3d 604, reversed.
5. *Ashcroft v. American Civil Liberties Union,* (00-1293) 217 F.3d 162, vacated and remanded.
6. "Letter from Fob James, Jr., Governor of the State of Alabama, to the Honorable Ira DeMent, United States District Judge for the Middle District of Alabama," http://www.alabamastuff.com/ (accessed June 23, 1997).
7. Ibid., 18–19, quoting William Brennan speech of November 21, 1982.
8. *Chandler v. James,* 180 F.3d 1254, 1266 (11th Cir., 1999).
9. *McCulloch v. Maryland,* 17 U.S. 316, 406 (1819).
10. *Stone v. Graham,* 449 U.S. 39, 41 (1980).
11. Gertrude Himmelfarb, *One Nation, Two Cultures* (New York, NY:Alfred A. Knopf, 1999), 67–68, cited in Bork, *Coercing Virtue* (Washington, DC:American Enterprise Institute Press, 2003).

Chapter 12: The Path to Victory

1. Rex A. Wade, "The Russian Revolution: 1917" http://assets.cambridge.org/ (accessed 2000).
2. Felix Frankfurter, "Memorandum on 'Incorporation' of the Bill of Rights into the Due Process Clause of the Fourteenth Amendment," 78 *Harvard Law Review* (1965), 764.
3. The Supreme Court Historical Society, *"History of the Court, The Chase Court: 1864–1873,"* http://www.supremecourthistory.org/
4. Oral Argument Transcript of *Elk Grove Indep. Sch. Dist. v. Newdow,* 542 U.S. ___ (2004), http://www.supremecourtus.gov
5. *Hill v. Colorado,* 530 U.S. 703 (2000).
6. "Cloture is the only procedure by which the Senate can vote to place a time limit on consideration of a bill or other matter, and thereby overcome a filibuster. Under the cloture rule (Rule XXII), the Senate may limit consideration of a pending matter to 30 additional hours, but only by vote of three-fifths of the full Senate, normally 60 votes." Senate Glossary, http://www.senate.gov/

INDEX